F.U.B.A.R

From Infl

F.U.B.A.R. From Inflation to Hyperinflation

Pawlo Lawriw

Published by Pawlo Lawriw, 2024.

F.U.B.A.R. FROM INFLATION TO HYPERINFLATION

First edition. February 4, 2024.

ISBN: 979-8215171226

Written by Pawlo Lawriw.

CONTENTS

INTRODUCTION

"The causes of events are even more interesting than the events themselves"

Cicero Roman statesman, lawyer, scholar, philosopher and academic skeptic 106 BC-43 BC

The first part of the book which explains what money is, what hyperinflation is, the different types of inflation and how it occurs, is written in a simple and easy-to-understand explanation to give the reader who has no background in economics but a real interest to understand what is happening in the real world and to try and make sense of what may appear a very complex and difficult issue to deal with, so apologies to those whom I am teaching their 'mother to suck eggs' if you are one of these people you may feel it worthwhile just to skip onto Chapter 3 and the Roman empire where I am sure from there on in you will find new and interesting facts about the subject.

Throughout this book we will see how hyperinflation does not occur in isolation and how world events can shape the destinies of countries decades and sometimes centuries later, hyperinflation can be a slow-burning fuse, but when it blows the bang and damage can be devastating. I use the analogy of the economy being a car owned by you but being driven by a government, when a car dash light comes on to tell you there is a problem, the government doesn't want to tell you there is a problem as they think you will blame them for the fault and you will take the car away from them as it will cost you money to fix it, so they continue to drive the car and ignore the problem, letting you know there is a light on the dash but don't worry it's nothing to worry about, everything is under control. The inflation is the light letting you know there is a problem, the problem is not the light itself. If the government continues to ignore the problem and eventually blows up the engine, they will blame the light say it was unexpected and not their recklessness in not solving the problem, but you are then left with a much bigger bill to fix the car.

Before discussing anything on hyperinflation and its causes, it is pertinent to clarify what the word F.U.B.A.R stands for, it is a military term and was first cited in 'Yank, the Army Weekly' and although it would not be appropriate to say what the F really stands for in polite society the rest means,

F****D
UP
BEYOND
ALL
RECOGNITION

It refers to decisions being made that are certain to end in defeat, failure or destruction, and that's what essentially has happened throughout history when currency debasement occurred as in the Roman Empire or overprinting of currency as seen in modern history, and that money printing without a stable backing of a commodity (predominantly gold and silver) has led to the increase of the Money Supply and eventually leading to the ruin of the nation. Although it could be argued that the most famous case of hyperinflation in history was that of Weimar Germany (but by no means the worst or lasting the longest) and that Germany was ruined before Weimar after losing World War I, throughout the book we will find that the hyperinflationary events that occurred were not the cause of the downfall of the empires or nations but that it takes hold after bad decisions being made, in essence hyperinflationary periods do not occur as isolated incidents but are the final nail in the coffin for societies that borrow way beyond their means to fund expansionary policies, and involving themselves in wars which lead to a reduced supply of goods and services as manpower and resources which should be used to promote the wellbeing of its society are being diverted to more dangerous and destructive purposes.

We will also discover this wasn't the first case in history where this happened and trace it back to as far as the Tang Dynasty in China (618-907 AD) and go on with an investigation of the Middle Ages and discover that the Money Supply does need to be expanded as the period of the Bullion famine shows that without it over a period of over 200 years very little progress was made in Europe. The history of banking which through the process of fractional reserve banking, has had a huge impact on the expansion of the money supply and increasingly so in the 21st century with modern technology now not being constrained by the need to have paper currency which at least needs paper, ink and printers to create it and so by default can at least minimise the impact, banks can create literally trillions in seconds at the press of a button.

In the conclusion I will try and piece together all the episodes discussed and determine if there is any relevance to what may be happening now and see if any dash lights are flashing up on the car, what I find may be a bit of an eye opener and may give you pause for thought.

1. WHAT IS MONEY?

"Money is a commodity" Karl Marx

"A commodity that comes into several uses as a medium of exchange is defined as being money" Murray Rothbard

Well, well, well, who would have thought it, Karl Marx, and a prominent member of the pro-free market Austrian school of economics agreeing, how is this possible? Read on and all will be revealed.

Before any attempt is made to start looking at any aspects of inflation, we need to initially get an understanding of what money is and what systems were being used to trade before the need for a concept of money to come into being. It is generally accepted that the barter system was used before the principles and use of money were established. Barter is quite simply allowing for the exchange of goods and services between two parties without the need for money. It is believed to date back to around 6,000 BC with the various tribes of ancient Mesopotamia which was then adopted by the Phoenicians who used it to trade with other cities. The obvious problem with barter is what economists call the 'double coincidence of wants' which simply states that both parties need to agree to the trade and secondly, both goods have equal value to the respective parties involved, what this means is should I make a chair to sell and someone else has a pound of pork sausages to sell? Firstly the seller of the pork sausages has to want to buy a chair, secondly, they then have to hope that I am not a vegetarian and that I actually want to buy pork sausages and not beef sausages instead, then finally we have to agree on a value for the trade to take place, I might view my chair as being worth five kilos of sausages and the seller of sausages may think it only worth 1 kilo, again we have to decide a rate of exchange for the two different items for sale. An example (a strange one!) is from the 1970's there was a children's TV show in the United Kingdom called the multi-coloured swap shop; it was presented by Noel Edmunds and amongst the various guests and topical conversations, there was a part of the show which included a reporter called Keith Chegwin going to a different town every week and the kids brought along a toy they no longer wanted or played with and they would then try and hook up with another kid who didn't want theirs, should they both agree a trade, toys swapped, everyone happy, barter heaven!! Money solves these problems, however as we shall see it can also create the problem of inflation leading to ruined individuals, families, communities, nations and even empires, where the need to resort to bartering has and is continuing to happen but before we get to the nuts and bolts of historical, present and potential future problems we need to take a deep dive look at the functions of money. The definition of money is quite simply defined as something that is generally accepted as a payment for goods and services and also to pay debts such as taxes. (Mishkin, 2007) Now that the simple part IS sorted, we must start thinking a little bit deeper and we need to ask ourselves what are the main functions of money? This part was broken down into broken down into four sections by the economist William Stanley Jevons in his 1875 book 'Money and the Mechanism of Exchange' they are as follows a medium of exchange, a unit of account, a store of value and a standard of deferred payment.

a/ Acts as a medium of exchange- A medium of exchange is quite simply an item which is accepted in return for a good or service, this item is termed as money, which takes all the problems and limitations that are associated with barter.

We can break money down into different categories, there is commodity money (or absolute money), representative money and a term which is starting to become increasingly used is fiat money. Commodity money consists of an object which can have an intrinsic value, (that is something that has a value or uses in itself) as well as the value they hold in which goods and services can be purchased (O'Sullivan et al, 2003) examples of this would include gold, silver, tea, copper, silk, corn and more commonly in recent times, cigarettes. Traditionally over the last 5,000 years gold and silver have become the de-facto standard of acceptable currency, the reason for this is money has to have certain properties which both gold and silver have; it needs to be fungible; this is where one unit is viewed as interchangeable with another, it needs to be durable, whereby the item must be able to being used repeatedly, it has to be portable where individuals can carry the money with them and then transfer it to other people when purchasing a good or service, it needs to be acceptable so everyone involved must be able to use the money for transactions to take place, it has to be divisible, this is the ability to divide it into smaller units, think of buying something worth £3.47 and using a £20 note to purchase to product, you would need smaller denominations to receive the change, in this example £16.47. (The properties of durability, portable and divisibility are starting to become redundant now due to digital payments) The two most important properties of money are that it must have uniformity whereby all versions of the same denomination must have the same purchasing power and finally, there must be a limit in the supply of money in circulation which ensures the value remains relatively constant. (As we will see later with the advent of fiat currency ignoring these two factors has caused individuals and nations alike an immense amount of problems damage and pain) However, as you can see all these items in themselves have a use, you can drink tea, and make food out of corn, but equally can be used as a form of money to buy other goods as the good has been subscribed to a value in the commodity money, for example five cigarettes could buy a kilo of sausages or one hundred cigarettes for a chair. This form of currency is not so unusual, and we will see an example in a little while.

Representative money, is any medium of exchange (usually printed on paper) that actually represents something of value but in itself has little or usually no value in its own right; To be more specific representative money has been used to mean a claim on an actual commodity again usually gold or silver but by no means limited to just those two commodities, it could be used to make a claim on grains, oil, etc. (Mundell, 2002) The face value of the representative money is greater than the value of the material of the substance that it is made of, we can see this with for example a £20.00 note where the cost of the ink and polymer that makes the note is not worth £20.00. As we shall see in a later chapter regarding the Song dynasty in China (around 960-1279 AD) representative money in the form of paper money arose partly because of the 'clipping' and therefore the debasement of the coin. Clipping the currency was practiced from the Roman Empire through to the Middle Ages and is a practice where you shave or clip part of the gold or silver coin, meaning it has less worth to it, for instance, if you had a 100-gram coin and shaved off 20 grams you have done two things, firstly reduced the value of the coin by 20% and secondly if you continued to shave other coins you would increase the money supply in the economy we can see this in the above example that if you 'clipped' 5 coins, in the end, you would have 6 coins. (5 x 20% gives you an additional coin) It's a great way to very quickly and with minimum effort improve your profit margin, however not entirely risk-free as being caught 'clipping' coins could result in punishments ranging from getting your hand chopped off to execution, I suppose they are the historical equivalent of working in the drugs trade, huge profit margins if you get away with but prison sentences, being murdered by other gang members (and sometimes by people from your gang) being the real downside of the business. Another major problem as we will come to see is that by doing this you inadvertently increase the money supply and without any other factors being changed (for instance increase the supply of goods, something we will look at later) it becomes a serious problem where inflation is concerned. Debasement effectively means the lowering of the value of a currency, clipping debases the value, so reducing the content of gold in the coin by either making it smaller or adding another metal in it. This was usually done to con the general public that the coin still has the same value; it tends to not be a very shrewd move as people catch on to this trick and we end up with a situation known as Gresham's Law.

Gresham's Law is an economic principle named after Sir Thomas Gresham (1519-1579) which states 'bad money chases out the good' The principle of this is if you moved from using gold coins and then started to try and impose bronze coins and insist, they have the same value as the gold coins people will hoard the 'good' coins (money) as they will use the 'bad' coins made of bronze instead. It is interesting to note that Gresham who was an English financier and advisor to Queen Elizabeth I never actually said the phrase, it was coined by an economist Sir Henry Dunning Macleod in 1860 after reading Gresham's works, however, the concept actually dates back even further and is noted in Aristophanes' play from around 5BC in his play 'The Frogs', guess it goes to show our ancient relatives were a lot smarter and shrewder than we tend to give them credit for.

Fiat currency, what is it? What does it mean? The word fiat is Latin which translates as 'Let it be done'. It first emerged in the English language in the 1630's to represent 'authoritative sanction", 1750 it also began to mean a decree, an order or a command, however it appears it was around the 1870s that the term 'fiat money' was beginning to be used with its modern meaning as money which has no backing of any commodity such as gold or silver behind it and is used as money purely because the government says it is money, it has no intrinsic value in itself whatsoever. The term fiat money is disingenuous as it is not actually money but currency as we shall see in C/ below. The most common form of fiat currency has been printed bank notes and although still widely used today is starting to be overtaken by the popularity of digital transactions, do not make the mistake but this is still fiat money. Digital fiat money is actually more dangerous by far than printed money, the main reason being at least there is a modicum of constraint with paper (or polymer as it is now) currency in that you need to have ink and paper to print on as well as the logistics of distributing it, as opposed to digital currency where eyewatering numbers can be added to an economy in a blink of an eye and distributed worldwide in the same blink.

The distribution of fiat currency is essential to the velocity of money which is a key factor in the creation of inflation and the equation MV=PT which was formulated by economist Irving Fisher is an integral part of understanding inflation, but for now, I'm going to leave you with bated breath for the explanation in a later chapter.

b/ A unit of account- Sometimes known as a measure of value, this ascribes values to each and every given good or service on offer. By developing a unit of account, it allows for a meaningful interpretation of the price of each good and service, it eliminates all the inefficiencies encountered with the barter system and the double coincidence of wants, meaning trade can become freer and easier to transact. Because the buyer can obtain the goods and services they require whilst the seller can use the acquired money to purchase what they wish. For this to happen, something vital must happen between not only the two parties involved in the transaction but the whole of the particular society involved. Two words can be used for the essential functions of buying and selling, but before we reveal the answer, have you ever wondered why is it when you give a £20 note or do a digital bank transfer to pay for something whether it be a good you have purchased or a service that is provided, it is accepted? Equally, why do you accept that note for something you are selling or for a service you are providing? What is it that creates the environment for these transactions to take place? Because we spend our whole lives involved in financial transactions and for the most part in economies that are run reasonably well, it is not an issue that anyone either asks or thinks about but asks the same question to anyone who has undergone periods of hyperinflation and there are only two words on their lips, the two words are CONFIDENCE and TRUST!!!! Without confidence or trust in the currency the seller would not take your money, because if they believe when it comes to buying items and it wasn't accepted, they have effectively given their product away for free.

This is also what happens in periods of hyperinflation when the value of the currency (NOT money, there is a difference as we will see shortly) is being devalued at such rapid rates people spend their money as quickly as possible (related to Irving Fisher's MV=PT formula, which will be explained shortly) because they don't want to be left holding pieces of paper that can buy less 'stuff' with the money they are holding in several weeks (in really extreme cases prices were changing by the minute as we shall see in examples later!!)

For an economy to have a unit of account, it also allows for a standard accounting system to develop where profits and losses are not only made but have a way of being recorded, this is essential to any modern functioning economy as it not only allows the individual in setting up businesses to record how efficient they are but also for potential investors to fund future growth as they would need to understand in numerical terms firstly the businesses past performance thus enabling a decision to be made on potential future earnings and projections of profits. However, it has to be appreciated that this only works in an ideal honest world where the books presented for analysis of company reports are honest and haven't been 'cooked' to distort or even deliberately lie about past performance earnings. Enron was an American energy firm which collapsed at the end of 2001 which saw not only investors suffer huge losses but many thousands of people lose their jobs probably the saddest part of it was many pensioners who had been previous employees lost everything and had to come out of retirement, some in their 70's and 80's and start working again to financially survive, however, most companies are generally quite honest in their dealings. The Enron scandal could have been spotted much earlier if investors and analysts hadn't been blindsided by short-term greed, thus sparing many ordinary working people the pain and misery they ultimately endured.

c/ A store of value- We have to make a crucial difference between money and currency, most people tend to use the word interchangeably however there is a fundamental difference. If we look back to why you would accept a £20 note in payment for a good or service, we see that confidence and trust are required, the next stage that has to be analysed is the two terms value and buying power. Value comes in two forms absolute (or intrinsic value) and relative. (That is the perceived value) So what do we mean by this, suppose you went to buy a kilo of sugar, that is absolute whichever shop you visited a kilo weight is a kilo weight, it does not change, a kilo is a kilo and it ends there, however, the relative cost of that kilo of sugar varies, you could go into ten different shops and buy that kilo of sugar for ten different prices. Another factor to take into account is the time period involved; you will all be aware that a kilo of sugar in 2022 is much more expensive than in 1922, this relative value is usually referred to as buying or purchasing power. Here we have the fundamental difference between money and currency and that is money is a store of value which relates to any commodity which retains its purchasing power into the future, it is an asset that can be saved, retrieved, and exchanged at a later period of time, and have the same value to be able to purchase an equivalent good. To see this in practice we can see an example of a commodity product (in this case gold) holding its purchasing power not over several years or decades but several millennia yes that's right around 2,000 years, don't believe me well here are the figures, an ancient Roman toga would cost around 1 ounce of gold, an equivalent quality fine suit today would cost around £2,000, what is an oz of gold worth today well its fluctuating around £1,800 per ounce (early 2022) so if the ancient Roman hid an ounce of gold 2,000 years ago and came to dig it up now they could attire themselves in the style they are accustomed to. Now imagine if you hid £2,000 in paper currency today what do you think that would be worth in 20 years let alone 2,000?

d/ A standard of deferred payments- To understand what a standard of deferred payment is we need to understand what debt is. A simple explanation would be to regard debt as an amount of money (or currency) owed by an individual, business or government, they are known as debtors, to a lender who is known as the creditor. Debt repayment requires the total sum borrowed to be paid off in full, with an interest charge added on for the duration of the loan. It is this function which allows for individuals to purchase big ticket items such as houses and new cars, it gives businesses the means of expansion and enables governments to borrow, which in theory is meant to be spent for the benefit of its citizens on projects for example to develop and expand infrastructure spending. This doesn't always go to plan as money can be spent recklessly due to 'moral hazard.' Moral hazard is where someone who is given money to spend but doesn't suffer the consequences personally, if it is squandered, that responsibility is passed onto someone else, so if the government borrows money to spend on a particular project and the project fails, the individual government minister responsible for spending the cash doesn't suffer personally in any financial capacity, it is you and I as taxpayers who are on the hook, and that debt unlike individual debt which is the sole responsibility of the borrower, government debt is passed onto future generations of children and grandchildren, an example of this is that the British government finally paid off its loan from the First World War with bonds issued in 1917 on the 9th March 2015, seems bad enough but it is actually much worse than that as that debt was rolled over debt going back to the Napoleonic Wars which ended in 1815 and can be traced even further back to the governments issuing bonds issued in 1720 to fund its liabilities for its disastrous involvement in the South Sea Bubble, that is many generations paying for the moral hazard of our forefathers and also goes to show that when we look back in history believing our forefathers were financially responsible, goes to show that this isn't necessarily so. Money by allowing the deferring of a payment means a person can pay for a product and service at a future date, a simpler way to look at it is the sales slogan of 'buy now pay later'. Deferring payments along with interest charges has led to the modern society we have today, however, irresponsible borrowing and lending have led to many problems for individuals, businesses and governments, and the usual solutions governments have found to get out of these problems have been to debase the currency, come off from the restraining effects of money and use a fiat currency, leading to the inevitable collapse of the economy causing financial devastation for many.

Now if we can rewind all the way back to the barter system that needs to be mentioned, firstly it never actually went away and with the advent of the internet barter sites are appearing where people can trade directly with one another but unlike the multi-coloured swap shop where you had to be in that town when the show was on to secure the potential numbers of people to trade with, the internet means you can barter with people from around the world and secondly it periodically makes a guest appearance when markets collapse due to war, mismanagement or global catastrophes. Think bartering is limited to individuals and small groups? nope, with the world financial system payment settlements for goods and services dealt with by the Bank of International Settlements (BIS- which will be explained in greater detail in Chapter 5) and world trade centred around the US dollar being the world currency, it has given the United States a vast amount of power to 'turn off the taps' and impose sanctions on any country it doesn't like or agree with, not by imposing sanctions as in the past by having the navy blockade the ports, but by simply flicking a switch to stop anyone purchasing goods from the sanctioned country, so what does a country have to do? You guessed it they begin forming trading alliances and start bartering with one another (multi-coloured swap shop alert again). Iran which had been an international pariah since the fall of the Shah in 1979 but really fell out of favour with the US under the Donald Trump administration, began bartering with different nations for various things (the more eagle-eyed economists amongst you will notice this is David Ricardo's Theory of Comparative advantage coming into play here where nations do what they do best and trade with others for things they can't produce as well as other nations can) So what happened with Iran a barter system set up around the world and they traded with India and 70 sacks of 2lb rice (140lb) cost 1 barrel of crude oil(42gallons) whilst, with the EU, 1 washing machine cost 10 barrels of crude oil (420 gallons) (Fouriezos, 2019).

No matter how desperate the situation a system develops which uses 'money' and groups can even develop their own micro-trading platform. There is an excellent article by R.A. Radford who was a Prisoner of War in World War Two and he describes beautifully how the US prisoners started to initially barter with goods that were sent by the Red Cross. When the parcels arrived, everyone got equal shares of the rations, but as life always dictates the human species has different needs and wants so for example non-smokers could trade their cigarettes for biscuits, jam, margarine, etc. Pretty quickly exchange rates were set up in individual huts but with different rates being set up in different huts it allowed for arbitrage to take place (someone who deals in arbitrage can spot the differences in two different trading huts, so if hut 1 biscuits traded at 5 cigarettes and hut 2, they traded at 10, what they would do is enter hut 1 and buy a packet of biscuits for 5 cigarettes, then go to hut 2 and sell them for 10 thus pocketing the 5-cigarette difference. They also moved onto future trading as well where if the deals went wrong, they could be wiped out of all the cigarettes they had accumulated and go out of business. He writes about a trader who not only used to advance credit but would purchase cocoa at a certain price, one time an unexpected delivery meant the price of cocoa that people were prepared to pay had fallen lower than the price he had agreed to pay (a futures contact), this meant his 50 carefully saved 'trading cigarettes money' was wiped out and he went out of business. Even Gresham's Law was in play as all cigarettes had an equal value which meant the good quality cigarettes were smoked leaving the inferior quality cigarettes for trading, they even attempted price fixing as the Medical Officer became worried that some men were not getting the required calorific intake as they were selling their rations. This led to periods of inflation and deflation as the supply of the parcels and cigarettes was inconsistent, so trying to fix and constantly adjust the prices were always behind the curve, wages have this problem when trying to deal with inflation, in economic terms this is known as wages being 'sticky'. (Radford 1945)

What makes things like tinned fish and ramen noodles money? Well, they are non-perishable, come in standard units, trade easily and have an intrinsic value, they are a commodity. After the US Federal jails banned smoking in 2004, cigarettes were less reliable as a currency, so there entered on to the stage tinned fish such as tuna and mackerel as well as ramen noodles. The cost cuts that were being incurred in US jails gave ramen a super valuable status due to its high calorific content, with inmates reporting how well a man was doing in prison with the packets of ramen they owned. Another complex trading place was emerging with everything from inmates racking up debts, earning high credit limits and even refinancing fish debts with different reserve holders. There were payday loan shops, bookies and even bankers, however unlike outside of prison (unless you go to loan sharks) violence against the debtors for non-payment of debts is normal and being moved onto another wing and placed in isolation are all risks to the creditor, family details are required as part of the agreement, an insurance policy to ensure eventual payment, in effect it almost makes it a secured as opposed to an unsecured loan.

There has recently been attempts to redefine money and it has become known as Modern Monetary Theory or MMT. The origin is in the theory of a German economist Knapp termed chartalism which argues that money historically originated from the states' desire to control economic activity, rather than as a solution to the problem of barter and that the fiat currency has value because the sovereign power has the ability to levy taxes in the currency it has decided to issue, in essence money is not a commodity but a function of the law. Supporters of MMT argue that because of this governments can never run out of money and that therefore debt doesn't matter meaning governments can use deficit spending to help economies reach full employment. From this it is argued by its main proponents such as L Randall Wray and Stephanie Kelton that inflation won't kick in until full employment has been reached, in fact this is exactly what Keynes argued, which really doesn't make the theory very modern!! It could also be argued that some amount of unemployment is required in society as a pool of workers are always required to keep society progressing, if we had full employment since the Middle Ages for example, then nobody would be free to do the new jobs that leads to innovations meaning we would be permanently stuck with the jobs and technologies of earlier times. Another problem with the definition of full employment is if people become used to full productive capacity, if a doctor was having to work as a waiter, we may achieve full employment but are skills and resources being used efficiently and effectively. It does seem a stretch to argue for the validity of MMT theory, this can be seen in Keynes similar arguments on inflation and unemployment, he was proved wrong by stagflation in the 1970's after OPEC tripled the price of oil. (It appears the members of OPEC at the time didn't get Keynes' memo) The final argument supporters of MMT make is that once full employment has been reached and price inflation does take hold, they can always increase taxes to take money out of the economy. (maybe someone should have told Zimbabwe or Venezuela about this) Another problem here is that the way the government would look at spending the newly printed fiat currency would be on public spending such as education or health care, the problem with this is that although they are essential components of society, they do not actually produce any additional goods for people to buy anything, in addition it takes people away from working in the private sector as there is more security working for the state, resulting in less goods. (Hutt 1977) MMT followers point to the fact that QE (Quantitative Easing) has been used in Japan since the 1980's which has record amount of debt to GDP (264% as of 2022) and has been used in the Western World since the Global Financial Crisis of 2008 and no inflation has occurred, this shows the lack of understanding of QE which is a monetary policy used by governments via the central banks to purchase securities such as government bonds and mortgage backed securities from the open market to reduce interest rates and increase the money supply. It creates these new bank reserves to provide banks with more liquidity to encourage lending and investing, in reality this extra money has sat on the banks asset balance sheets, in effect increasing the M3 money supply, whereas the money via MMT will be directed straight into the mainstream economy as M1 money supply, an effect has already been seen with the fiscal response to the Covid lockdowns where supply chains were snarled, economies stopped producing and money was placed directly into the hands of citizens. There is always a time delay, but this is one of several factors as to why inflation has hit many nations, especially in the West. The most important problem that would face a sovereign country and in particular America whose dollars are the world's reserve currency is that the reserve not by an act of law but by the consent by the rest of the world, this consent was given because the US economy and by default the dollar was seen as stable, if other countries start doubting the currency's stability (which is already happening) that consent can be withdrawn. It may take time and may be painful, but they will withdraw that consent.

To understand another important aspect of MMT it is necessary to look at how governments actually raise money to spend on public services, it can either tax it's citizens or alternatively can borrow from either other countries or large financial institutions/investors. To do this the government treasury department of the government instructs the central bank to enter into the marketplace and sell its bonds, (effectively an IOU) which has interest payments attached to it. The amount of interest charged depends on firstly the supply of bonds already in the marketplace but more importantly the demand for these bonds. If the government is seen as prudent and managing its economy efficiently then the interest rate will be lower due it to been seen as less of a risk for the investor if they seek their money back. The variation in interest rates is effectively a braking mechanism on government profligacy. Advocates of MMT would skip the process of bond issuing and go directly to 'printing money' to pay for their ambitious social welfare programmes without the burden of having to pay interest on it, and should price inflation actually kick in then all they would have to do is raise taxes to remove this excess money out of the economy. In theory this is perfectly reasonable, in practice however as many countries have found to their cost, theory and reality don't always work hand in hand.

2. INFLATION: WHAT IS IT?

"Inflation is the process of making addition to currencies not based on the commensurate increase in the production of goods" Federal Reserve Bulletin (1919)

"Most prominent amongst these inflationary forces were a drop in the exchange rate of the dollar, a considerable increase in labour costs and severe weather" Federal Reserve Bulletin (1978)

"Either the rise in prices might be due to the scarcity of goods, or it might be due to the superabundance of money, but as a matter of historical fact.... That it is the change in the money that makes the changes in the value of money and not, changes in the goods" Irving Fisher (1923)

Working it out is relatively easy to explain, inflation is measured each month by the Office for National Statistics, (ONS) which collects about 180,000 prices from approximately 700 items and within that there are broken into three components, Consumer Price Index, (CPI) Consumer Price Index plus Owner-Occupier Housing Costs (CPIH) and Retail Price Index. (RPI) What they effectively do is use a 'shopping basket' of these 700 goods, this basket of goods changes over time with new goods added and some taken out to reflect consumers' changes in shopping habits as well as technological advances. Additions in 2021 include electric and hybrid cars, hand sanitisers, and smart watches whilst out went the rather strange staff restaurant sandwiches and gold chains. This basket of goods is then 'weighted' as to the importance that they have, for example, if salt went up from £1 to £1.50, although it is a 50% rise the impact will be minimal, whereas if fuel went up from £5.00 a gallon to £5.50, there is a similar 50 pence rise and although it is only a 10% rise, its impact would be much greater thus would have a higher 'weighting' in the basket of goods to reflect its importance and impact it will have. We can start with CPI which out of the 700 items mentioned, does not take into account housing costs but factors in all other goods and services, CPIH (which is rarely used but needs to be mentioned if you ever come across it) does not include mortgage payments but how much rent the householder would pay for an equivalent property (pretty useless as a lot of guesswork involved hence not used very often) and the RPI which does include mortgage interest payments, this is obviously heavily influenced by house prices and interest rates. OK, so which measurement does the UK use? Well, it depends, for instance, items linked to RPI are train tickets, mobile phone tariffs, car tax, air passenger duty, tobacco and alcohol duty and interest on student loans. Items linked to the CPI are state pensions, public sector pensions, universal credit, Personal Independence Payments (PIP) and statutory Sick Pay. Why do they use these different methods I hear you asking yourselves, well just look at these two simple statistics and all will begin to reveal itself in its full splendour.

In October 2021

RPI= 7.5%

CPI= 5.4%

Do you see the pattern? it's simple, if the Government is taxing you for something because it uses the higher price inflation figure and if it must pay out, it uses the lowest price inflation figure!!

They also deceive you in several other ways to help keep the inflation figures down, firstly there is shrinkflation, which is where you pay the same price for a particular good as in the past but get less of it now, for example a company could charge £5 for a 20 pack of toilet rolls one week, then the following week the price is still £5 but now you only get 15 rolls, technically no price inflation as prices haven't risen but you are getting 25% fewer toilet rolls for the same price, so it is actually a 25% price rise but not recorded as thus on official statistics, this is a tactic I believe companies are increasingly going to use across a whole range of goods from 2022 onwards. The second really sneaky way is hedonic regression and this is how it works; you buy a laptop in 2020 for £1,000, and in 2022 you go to replace it and the same model of laptop costs £1,500 so a 50% increase right, well no not according to hedonic regression it's a reduction of 25%, how can it be that you pay £500 MORE and it is 25% LESS, what form of sorcery is this? what alchemy does the government weave? What they do is say ah yes you have paid £500 more but the computer is a better model and if you had purchased the same computer in 2020 it would have cost you £2,000 so you've saved £500, doesn't matter that you don't want the extra features, your now obliged to purchase it and pay more. The quality of the product can also be reduced by manufacturers using cheaper products so it may seem the price rise is not so great, but the inferior product may need to be replaced more often. Substitution in the basket occurs more rapidly than it used to so if the price of beef is going up, they can take it out of the basket of goods and replace it with something that is a cheaper foodstuff at the time of calculating say chicken, and automatically you have lower prices and if chicken goes up in price and beef falls, simply reverse the procedure. Another tactic is the government simply has the statistics manipulated so comparisons from previous eras cannot be made, governments are always manipulating the way the data is collated citing the need to improve accuracy, but can we be truly surprised if the data is manipulated to make the price rise figures seem lower, after all arguing in an election that inflation is only 3% and not 13% is an easier sell.

We can now move on to the actual definition of inflation and the most common understanding of it is that it is a rise in the prices of goods and services, this seems a simple and easy-to-understand explanation of the meaning, unfortunately, it is not the full or truthful picture as anything to do with economics it is rarely that simple, the first quote from the federal reserve Bulletin and the quote by Irving Fisher states that it is the increase in the money supply, without an increase in the production of goods and services, this theory posits that you will have much more money chasing the same amount of goods thus causing the price to rise, alternatively known as price inflation, what they are effectively saying is that inflation is not a statement about price rises but a condition that was specifically about the increase in paper money or the money supply. (It actually was classed as money then as it was backed by the gold standard) In other words, it was monetary policy to increase the supply of money onto the market, the money supply is essentially all the money (in reality at the moment currency) and other liquid instruments such as short-term deposits in banks where it may take 30 days 'notice' to release this money as opposed to the instant access available on a regular bank account. (there are various classifications of the money supply such as MO, M1, M2 and M3 but these are technical issues and not relevant to the understanding of inflation but do play a part in how the figure of inflation is arrived at) A monetary policy is a tool used by where the government uses either interest rates and or increasing the total supply of money circulating in the economy, this is opposed to a fiscal policy which is used to collectively describe the usage of taxation and the spending of a government to either stimulate or cool down an economy.

It is said of economics that it is a mile wide and six inches deep meaning there is a lot of different subject matter but not that much detail to it, this is simply untrue, the disciple buries down and each subject matter can intertwine and travel to the core of the earth and you still wouldn't get an answer, with this analogy we can try and untangle this understanding of inflation, starting with looking at the origin of the word and how the term has evolved and changed its meaning and more importantly why?

The original word inflation was from around the mid-14th Century and used to define a swelling caused by a gathering of 'wind' in the body. (In other words, flatulence) Around the 1600's it changed to mean the action of inflating something with air or gas and eventually in the same century used in the financial sense to mean the increasing the amount of money in circulation.

It can be observed from the quotes above by the Federal Reserve Bulletin that the definition of inflation has changed in the span of a mere 59 years, the first defines inflation purely as a result of the increase in the money supply and the second blames absolutely everything and anything they feel they could get away with except the money supply, so why do you think this is? Before we answer that we need to look at how the Federal reserve came about and the chequered career before its formation in 1913.

The First Bank of the United States (1791-1811) and the Second Bank of the United States (1817-1836) had a twenty-year charter with a charter to issue currency, make commercial loans and accept deposits; There were also multiple branches and they acted as fiscal agents for the US Treasury. (The US Treasury manages the federal government's finances by collecting taxes, paying bills, and managing the currency, government accounts and public debt. The department also enforces finance and tax laws. The approach taken was that the federal government was required to purchase 20% of the banks' capital stock shares along with the appointment of 20% of its directors. This left the remaining 80% of the stock in the hands of wealthy corporate and private investors (Johnson, 1977). The good people of America had the wisdom and foresight to see through this rouse and realised they would be on the hook to maintain and support the reserve if anything went wrong with higher taxes, their wisdom and foresight were impressive, it's as if they could foresee what would happen to their great-grandchildren in the banking crisis of 2008. In other words, the federal reserve was not liked by the average citizen, it was seen as too much state interference in the lives of ordinary citizens, and they had a healthy mistrust of government.

What changed? Well, fear happened with the panic of 1907, also known as the 1907 banker's crisis or even more affectionately as the Knickerbocker crisis, it was so named after the Knickerbocker Trust Company of New York which was one of the largest trusts in the United States at the time and was central to the 1907 crisis. There had been many banks go bust before 1907, in fact in what is regarded as the Gilded Age of America, which was a period between the 1860s and 1900 which saw an era of rapid growth, especially in the Northern and Western parts of the United States. The rapid expansion of industrialisation saw the United States overtake, the United Kingdom as the world's leading economy. Money poured in from the United Kingdom and Europe, yet despite this there were bank panics in 1837, 1857 and 1873, however the first serious panic which took place before 1907 was the Panic of 1893-1897; this was an economic depression that took place in America which saw around 500 banks close, 15,000 businesses fail and numerous firms ceasing operations; unemployment rates were as high if not higher than the Great Depression of 1929 with rates hitting as high as 43% in Michigan. (Parshall, 1992) There were many reasons for the failure including crop failures, Australian and South African property collapse, and a bubble in the railroad industry. (a bubble is essentially too much rapid investing and exuberance in certain stocks and shares, which means the product is trading at much higher than it is worth, once this bubble 'pops' people tend to lose of a lot if not all their wealth) However the final nail in the coffin for the American economy leading to a perfect storm through the 1860's until the 1890's the US economy grew due to the high prices of commodities, however when the price of wheat crashed in 1893 a 'run on the banks' started. A 'run on the bank' is where people who try and get their money out of the banks find the banks don't have enough money to pay everyone out, once the public finds out there is a problem, panic ensues, and people 'run' to the banks to try and get their money out. The run on the banks led to a credit crunch, (this is a sudden reduction of the availability of loans, something most people will remember this being a consequence of the 2008 housing bubble) as European investors feared the problem might spread (there's that confidence and fear thing again) started to sell American stocks and obtained their gold reserves instead, leading to the gold reserves being dangerously low, this was a real problem for the government as the dollar at the time was backed by gold and any dollar presented needed to be paid out otherwise the government would have defaulted on payments, leading to a loss of credibility, and forcing the cost of borrowing up. (Would you want to lend money to someone you know has previously reneged on a deal, you might but you would definitely charge a higher interest rate for the risk) The solution came in the form of John Pierpont (JP) Morgan who put together a consortium of several prominent investors who lent President Grover Cleveland $60 million in gold. This $60 million of gold did come at a price for President Cleveland and the American people with Morgan extracting favourable rates on the government's 30-year bonds. It was discovered that JP Morgan made millions but wouldn't disclose how much (Rowan), thus enraging the American public even more, making them even more distrustful of private enterprise involvement in the creation of a Federal Reserve Bank.

The 1907 crisis was really the first real crisis to hit America that spread throughout the nation with many local and national banks entering into bankruptcy and causing real panic amongst the American people. The crisis started by mid-October 1907 as a cornering scheme (a cornering scheme is one which attempted to take control) for the stocks of the United Copper Company; the failure of the bid led to the banks which had lent money to the scheme seeing 'a run on the banks' taking place. Once the bizarrely named Knickerbocker Trust, which was the third largest Trust in New York failed, confidence was lost, and fear took over. An excellent example of this is in the film Mary Poppins where the little boy tries to get his pocket money back from his father who is a banker and wants him to put his money in the bank where it is explained it will be ultimately along with other people's money invested all over the world, the little boy wanting the money for more pleasurable purposes (to feed the pigeons in Trafalgar Square) starts shouting that he wants his money back, the people in the bank misunderstand what is going on and think there is no money left in the bank and start demanding their money, now there is a genuine shortage of money (as banks practice fractional reserve banking, see Chapter 6) and are forced to put down the shutters causing more panic, word gets out, creating more panic which then ultimately spreads to other banks, in Mary Poppins things worked out ok in the end, in reality when this happens it becomes a disaster for most people as livelihoods are destroyed.

The reality of what happened to end the 1907 crisis could almost be another Hollywood film script, and here we see the intervention of that giant in the banking industry again, yes you figured it out and take a bow Mr JP Morgan, who strode once again onto the stage as a larger-than-life figure, pledging huge sums of his own money and convincing other New York bankers to do the same to prop up and support the banking system. In 1907 J.P. Morgan along with other Wall Street Bankers rescued the banks, the stock market and even Ney York City from financial ruin, this is what ultimately led to congress finally passing the Federal Reserve Act in 1913, which put the Government in charge of managing any future financial crises' that may occur and not be on the hook to any private individual. Confidence began to grow after the 1893-97 crisis, where by 1900 there were more than 20,000 banks operating in the United States, with people depositing their money into these banks, who promptly lent this money out to businesses and individuals at an agreed rate of interest. Banking regulations, at the time, required the banks to maintain a percentage of the corporate bonds deposits that people make, either in ready cash or at least have the money easily available. The small banks rather than holding the percentage themselves would deposit some of their reserves in larger city banks as this fitted into the criteria of 'easily available' with the added benefit of earning interest. These banks in turn deposited part of their required reserves in the biggest city banks, which in turn saw a large percentage of those deposits flowing up to the financial institutions on Wall Street. Wall Street made loans not to small investors and individuals but to large corporations, the ever-increasingly money-hungry railway companies, stocks and even buying US Government bonds. While things appear to be running smoothly and confidence is high, inefficiencies and any flaws in the system tend to get overlooked, however unease began to grow after the San Francisco earthquake in April 1906 saw massive losses for British insurers, forcing the Bank of England to raise interest rates to stem the flow of gold from the United Kingdom to the United States, America in turn raised its own interest rates thus creating a liquidity crunch. Between September 1906 and March 1907, there was an 8% drop in the stock market in America leading the US economy into a recession by May 1907.

Trouble continued throughout 1906 when Charles M Morse along with another private investor Augustus Heinze suffered huge losses due to taking substantial positions in the copper market and in particular the United Copper company. Dozens of institutions, including banks and trusts, in particular the Knickerbocker Trust Company whose President Charles T Barney had invested in the copper stock company and was an associate of Morse, investors feared the worst and the memories of the losses people could make from the 1893-97 crash resurfaced, they realised if the banks failed, they could lose all their money, depositors fearing the worst rushed out and caused another 'bank run.' As it turned out Knickerbocker had not in itself as a company invested in the scheme and was a stable company, still never let the truth get in the way of a good panic. Wall Street turned to the man they felt had the honour and integrity to help them out Mr J P Morgan, he initially along with two other banker friends raised $13 million, but still, the run continued, New York city mayor said it needed a loan to pay the contractors, with the fear that the city of New York might collapse. Morgan and his banker friends now purchased $30 million in city bonds, however brokerage firms were now paying exorbitant interest rates and also began to fail, Morgan put together another $25 million to try and lower the interest rates, however this money pails into insignificance compared to the problem of just one brokerage firm Moore and Schley, who on their own were in hock to the tune of a cool $25 million, so if that company failed it would almost certainly trigger a crash of biblical proportions on the stock market, think of the 2008 crash but probably worse. (what a brokerage firm does is essentially act as an intermediary between an investor and a securities exchange such as the London stock exchange, or the New York stock exchange, this is because these exchanges only accept orders from individuals or firms who are members of that exchange, individual traders need the services of a stock broker if they wish to participate in share buying and selling) The problem with the company was that its assets, in which a percentage of its working capital was secured was against a common stock in the Tennessee Coal and Iron company which had questionable valuations against it, nobody knew if Moore and Schley were underwater or not, which in a climate of fear and panic is definitely not a good look. On the weekend of November 3-4, 1907, it was felt by Monday 5th that the company would fail, triggering a huge collapse in the stock market. Morgan called a meeting of the city's commercial and trust company managers, put them in a room, locked the door and wouldn't let them out until a deal was done in which they would help their fellow bankers 'Brothers' who were struggling with bank runs, whilst he for his part would sell a steel company, he owned to the US Steel company. (a company he also conveniently had stocks in, as well as being a member of its board of directors, this would thus make the US Steel company a virtual monopoly in the steel industry, so no conflict of interest there from Mr Morgan!) The deal-making worked and even though much economic damage was done around the country, the resulting depression was much less severe than it could have been and lasted approximately 18 months. The unfortunate effect for Morgan and the other bankers was that it looked bad, and people were starting to question whether the various crises were being deliberately caused by this small cable of powerful bankers who profited financially from the chaos that ensued from each panic. The Pujo hearings were set up and attacked these vested interests for having too much power and for collusion in controlling these large corporations. The Federal government finally enacted the Federal Reserve act in 1913, which is still in operation to this day and is probably the most powerful government body in the world. (Strouse, 2014)

What has all this got to do with definitions of inflation? With the regular crisis that was happening with increasing rapidity throughout the Gilded Age, it was felt that capitalism couldn't be trusted to regulate itself and too much corruption, power and self-interest was being concentrated into the hands of a few individuals, the formation of the Federal Reserve was seen as a clean break from this past and they had a sense of responsibility to maintain both integrity and fiscal disciple, they probably naively thought they could prevent any future panics so were being honest with their first definition, once they had several crisis to go at and were found to make things actually worse, they had to pass the buck and blame someone else, "nothing to do with me Guv, honest" so now the fault of price inflation, is greedy businessmen, speculators, profiteers, banks for lending too much, you and I for being reckless in our borrowing and spending, anything or anyone but the Federal Reserve or the Federal Government, this is something you can apply that logic to any government or central bank in the world.

What we can see from the Irving Fisher quote is that he is essentially arguing that there are two aspects to price rises, with it either being the fault of supply or demand, the theory goes if either less goods are supplied onto the market prices will rise and equally if there is too much demand for a certain good, (backed by the ability to pay for it due to excess supply of money in the economy) prices will also rise. You can actually increase the supply of money and not get price inflation as long as you can produce the extra goods, in other words, if there is an increase in productivity so there is more supply of the goods, prices won't rise or rise by very little, you may even get deflation where prices can fall because you can have a situation where there are more goods on the market and not enough money to chase those goods so producers need to lower the prices to attract sales. What Fisher is arguing is that throughout history it is always excess money supply that causes price inflation and not the supply of goods. Irving Fisher was the first celebrity economist of the modern era and is generally regarded as one of the greatest economists the United States have ever produced, so we must take what he says quite seriously although his reputation was completely and irreparably damaged when just nine days before the wall street crash in 1929, he commented that the stock market had reached "a permanently high plateau." Fisher is part of a long and distinguished line of economists, investors, fund managers and anyone who tries to predict the market, eventually no matter how smart you are you will be found out to be what you are, a mere mortal, you are no Sybil who has the power of vision, just lucky when you predict correctly and unlucky when you're wrong.

We have discussed in detail what inflation actually is and with all things in life that seem quite simple on the surface, in reality when you start digging there is many a rabbit hole to go down, but it seems quite clear that Inflation is an increase in the money supply, think of it as a balloon being blown up whilst price rises are an effect of the increase in the money supply, prices actually do not inflate, they are linear, they go up and down and nothing else, unlike the balloon blowing analogy where the air expands everywhere.

Now we need to look at different types of price inflation and the first we can look at is what we alluded to earlier which is deflation, prices of goods and services can go down as well as up, deflation is the price of goods falling, so what can cause this and is it all a good thing? To look at the causes of deflation is quite simple, one of two things can cause it, firstly a contraction in the money supply which means there are more goods on the market with much less money chasing those goods, thus producers need to lower the prices to attract customers who have enough money to purchase whatever they are selling. Another thing that can cause a fall in prices is either increased productivity where the employees work either harder or smarter or the more likely technological innovation which makes the production of goods either cheaper, faster or both. We can see now that depending on what makes the prices fall, deflation can either be a good or a bad thing, falling prices due to innovation and improved technology is good, whilst falling due to lack of demand can be very bad, the key to this is what the consumer is anticipating happening if they think prices are going to fall further, they will put off purchasing goods as they feel they will be cheaper later on, if this goes on for too long we can enter into a circular domino doom loop where goods that aren't sold because of people holding off purchases means lower profits, which leads to more bankruptcies, followed by further layoffs and higher unemployment, higher unemployment leads to overall lower income in the economy, thus lower demand and back to the circular doom loop of lower profits, more bankruptcies, etc.

One example of how deflation really can damage an economy was in 1924 when Winston Churchill became the Chancellor of the Exchequer. After initially dismissing the idea, he was convinced into placing the UK back onto the gold standard. When he did put the UK back on the gold standard, he made the unfortunate mistake of overvaluing sterling at $4.87, (its pre-war value) when in reality it was only worth $4.40, this meant the pound was overvalued by approximately 10%, on the flip side this meant that gold and the dollar were undervalued. America with its powerful economy and as the owner of the majority of the world's gold reserves had ensured that the dollar and not sterling had now become the global reserve currency. The US had fixed the price of gold at $20.64 an ounce, this meant that a pound at its overvalued rate of £1=$4.86 would buy 0.235 oz of gold when in reality in the market it could have only purchased 0.2115 oz of gold, an arbitrage position had been created. Arbitrage is simply making a profit by trading the difference between two sell and buy positions, to give a simple example, suppose you walk down the street and see someone is selling a bike for £50 and you know of someone on the next street who is looking for the exact same bike and is willing to pay £100, all you have to do is buy the bike for £50, sell it for a £100 and the profit of £50 is the arbitrage.

The reason for the devaluation of the pound was the British government's suspension of the gold standard at the start of World War 1. The suspension of the gold standard had led to huge volumes of paper money being printed to finance the fighting. When the war had finished Britain couldn't possibly redeem all the newly printed currency against its gold reserves. After Britain returned to the gold standard in April 1925 at the old rate it meant a 10% overvaluation of its currency, its exports (and the UK was largely one giant factory which imported raw materials and exported finished goods so this 10% was a really significant factor) which should have cost Americans $4,40 to purchase a pound worth of British goods meant they were now having to pay $4.86. Churchill and the British government hadn't worked out that the cost of fighting the war had led to Britain losing its world power status, as they had won the war on the battlefield, they believed it was going to be business as usual, this was not going to be the case as the British people were going to find out to their cost. The overpricing of the pound not only meant exports had become more expensive making British firms uncompetitive abroad, it additionally meant foreign imports had now become cheaper, these combined effects created not only a high rate of unemployment but also contributed to a deflationary economy. This almost led to national bankruptcy at a time when millions of Britons had to endure appalling living conditions. (Reed, 2023)

In an interesting quirk, it could be argued that without this decision to go back on the gold standard the Great Depression in America and by default its disastrous consequences might never have occurred. If the difference in the price of both currencies were allowed to continue then

Britain would have eventually lost all its gold reserves due to its undervaluation in the UK and thus both exporters and traders could take advantage of the arbitrage position that had been created. Exporters could buy gold in the UK and then purchase goods overseas with more gold than they actually should have had due to the arbitrage position, leading to an outflow of gold and then eventual bankruptcy. The recently formed Federal Reserve Bank deliberately depressed the value of the dollar at the request of the British government to keep up the fantasy of the strong British pound. This artificially cheap interest rates led to the roaring 20's boom which set it up for the Wall Street Crash and the Great Depression which will be looked at in greater depth in Chapter 10. Britain eventually left the gold standard on the 20th September 1931 and almost immediately saw a revival in the economy.

Price inflation has four different stages, creeping, walking, galloping and hyperinflation; and although the first three are destructive in the medium to long term, hyperinflation is what we are predominantly looking at, is generally regarded as a relatively modern phenomenon, now this is not quite accurate but has predominately taken place since the 20th Century. It was defined in 1956 by economist Phillip Cagen, who stated that a hyperinflationary period is within one month of an inflation rate that exceeds 50% and that the hyperinflation ends when the monthly inflation rate falls below 50% and must stay below 50% for at least one year. (Cagen, 1956) This seems quite an arbitrary number, are we saying that if inflation is only 49.9% per month, then all is well in the economy? To do this we need to look at some simple maths so if we have hyperinflation as defined by Phillip Cagen, we can work out how much a loaf of bread would cost after 1 year assuming it costs £1 at the start, so if on January 1st 2022, a loaf of bread cost £1, let's see how much it would cost on January 1st 2023. To start with we need to understand working out to the power of which is quite simple, for example, if you have 10^2 that simply means 10x10 (100) 10^4 is 10x10x10x10=10,000. Next, we need to use the base number of 1 to represent 100%, and finally an inflation number, so if inflation is 50.1% that means after one-month inflation would be 1.51 (1x50.1 = 1.51), if this rate of inflation continued for a whole year, we can calculate how much the loaf would cost by using a simple calculator that can calculate to the power of, close your eyes if your squeamish now as things are about to get ugly so we have an inflation rate of 1.51 in 1 month and this continues for 1 year (12 months) it leaves us with the figure 1.51^{12} This works out your £1 loaf a year later would cost £140.51, if inflation was below Phillip Cagen's definition and inflation is 49.9% those figures plugged in would be 1.499^{12} and the price would be £128.72. As you can see you would technically not be in hyperinflation territory, but you may as well be, however, despite the technical difficulties of the definition it does provide a guideline so in that sense, it has a generally useful purpose. As we shall see most countries when they achieve hyperinflation go much higher than just the 50% mark and this can have devastating consequences. Brazil in the late 1980s and early 1990s suffered from an inflation rate of approximately 80% per month, so let's plug those figures in bearing in mind it is only 30% more than the 50% threshold to be classed as hyperinflation, we get 1.8^{12} = which means a £1 loaf would cost £1,156.83 after 1 year, if we work out that Brazil went through this price increase for at least 3 years the new numbers would be 1.8^{36} (36 is 36 months in 3 years, 12x3) and the price of that £1 loaf would be £1,548,139,828.43, to make it easier for you that is £1billion 548million 139 thousand 828 pounds and 43 pence. The major psychological problem you have to overcome when these numbers get so large is for the people to grasp such large numbers, if a loaf of bread can cost several hundred million pounds, how do you evaluate the cost of a car or the cost of a house, the numbers are just too large for the human brain to compute.

How Brazil got out of this is a fascinating story which starts back in the 195O when the government built a new capital city in Brasilia, and printed vast quantities of money to fund it, by the 198Os hyperinflation was setting in and a pattern of a new president being elected with promises of a new plan which included price freezes and or bank accounts, the president then fails, then either gets ousted, voted out or impeached, this pattern is then rinsed and repeated and the only thing it succeeded in was to convince the general public that the government had no clue on how to solve the problem.

In 1992 by sheer chance four gentlemen from the Catholic University of Rio, the main person being Edmar Bacha. He was contacted by the new finance minister who knew nothing about economics and asked for his help to solve the problem, their plan was unique and what they did was to create a new currency that was stable, dependable and trustworthy, the only problem, this currency did not actually exist, there were no notes printed, no coins produced, it was fake, a made-up fictitious currency, and it was called a Unit of real value. (URV) The people still had to use the existing currency, the Cruzeiro to purchase anything but everything would be listed in URV's, taxes, wages, and goods purchased in the shop were all listed in URV's, but its genius was that it was kept stable, what changed was how many Cruzeiros each URV was worth, for example if a loaf of bread cost 1URV on a given day and that loaf was 1,000 cruzeiros, the next day the loaf may cost 10,000 Cruzeiros but it was still listed as 1 URV. The principle was to get people to start thinking in terms of URV's and to stop assuming prices would always go up. It was confusing for the population at first but after a few months, they got used to it and saw prices in terms of URV's as stable. Once they saw that the population accepted the URV's they declared that the virtual currency would become actual currency and be called the Real, it replaced the Cruzeiro, people received their wages in the new real and purchased goods and services in the real. Inflation disappeared almost overnight, and Brazil became a major exporter in the following years. (Joffe-Walt, 2010) This should have been an amazing ending to the story of inflation in Brazil, but unfortunately, their successive governments have slipped into old bad habits and turned to the printing press to fund large-scale projects such as the Olympic games and the World Cup as well as extravagant public spending, which has seen high inflation start to rear its head again in the 2020s.

To summarise the causes of price inflation in economic speak, we have what economists call.

1/ Demand- Pull inflation, where the demand for goods and services Pull up the cost of these goods, this happens when too much money (usually fiat money but not always as Spain in the Middle Ages section will show) is chasing too few goods.

2/ Cost- Push inflation, where the cost of the raw materials or labour increase and thus push the cost of goods and services higher, sometimes this is a self-fulfilling prophecy where the cost of goods rise due to a variety of factors such as war, bad harvests, geopolitics and then workers demand higher wages to compensate for the rise in the cost of living, leading to more price rises, this then can become a vicious circle which leads to potentially the worst scenario where there is an anticipation of price rises; fear and panic sets in, confidence is lost (just like the bank runs) and the economy can enter into freefall with inflation destroying the fabric of society.

3. THE ROMAN EMPIRE: WAR, POWER AND THE DEBASEMENT OF CURRENCIES

"Gold is the money of kings, silver is the money of gentleman, barter is the money of peasants-but debt is the money of slaves" Norm Franz, Money and Wealth in the New Millenium".

Now that we have a bit of background information regarding what money is, what the different definitions of inflation are, etc, we need to apply these economic concepts (there is more to come but I am just trying to give you all a breather) within a historical context; our first port of call on our deep dive into history is the Roman empire, which has the most enduring of legacies for what it not only left behind in both its splendour and ingenuity but its cruelty and callousness. It has been argued that hyperinflation is a modern phenomenon, however as we are about to discover, it's not but before we start let's take a brief look at how coins came about.

Ancient Greece is usually dated between 800-300 BC, but with the golden age being around the 5th and 6th century BC, it was a period which led to the birth of democracy and city-states such as Athens leading the way in philosophy and the arts. Greece was a fragmented society and was divided and sub-divided with literally hundreds of independent cities due to its geography of many hills, mountains and rivers, some of the most famous being the city of Athens and Sparta, however, they did share many common traits such as their culture, language and religion. The first known coins discovered was in the city of Ephesus at the temple of Artemis, it was made of electron which is a naturally occurring alloy of gold and silver. This coinage principle eventually spread to the rest of Greece, where in Athens the name Drachma was given to it, this name was retained by the Greeks until they eventually joined the European Union in 1981 which eventually adopted the Euro as its currency in 2001. Each city-state had private minters of the coin and very early on the state saw the benefit of monopolising the minting of the coin. With all these different states and cities now minting their coins, it led to the development of money changers who exchanged foreign coins into local coins, with a fee added on, in essence, it is the ancient world equivalent of a modern-day Forex trader. The next stage was the development in the 3rd and 2nd Century AD of what we would today essentially see as private banking, where money would be lent out at approximately 12% interest. This whole concept eventually spread to the first Persian Empire (550-330 BC) and unlike the Greeks minting individual coins, meaning each one would have differences, the Persians were the first to introduce mass production of coins, in addition, they were of made of gold as they had plenty of the metal from all its conquests. We can move swiftly onto 334 BC where Alexander the Great, conquered large territories including the whole of Persia, thus allowing the further spread of the coinage even further, eventually reaching the ancient Indian and Chinese empires.

Rome began life as a Kingdom with a monarch as its head from around 753-509 BC, it was a small entity based primarily on a rural economy, constantly feuding with other nearby states. It's quite interesting to note that they actually had 7 Kings all of whom were elected and never took the position by force, unless you count Titus Tatius of Sabine as the 8th King who shared power with Romulus after he attacked and defeated Rome because the first King Romulus kidnapped Sabine women to try and populate Rome, strange times indeed!!! The last Roman king was Tarquinius Superbus, overthrown due to his son Sextus Tarquinius' rape of a noblewoman, Lucretia. Now we enter into the period of the Republic dating around 509-27 BC, where the Romans began to dominate the Italian peninsula, they had very little silver or gold, and some outside trade did bring a small amount in but not enough to support the population as a whole, what they did have was a lot of bronze. Unlike the Kingdom where bronze was used but had no uniformity, the Republic's bronze was actual standardized bars with impressions and symbols imprinted upon it. Rome's main rival was Carthage, predominantly a maritime empire, but its main advantage was its access to gold from the African continent and the silver mines in the Iberian Peninsula, areas part of its empire. It would not be long before Rome flexed its military might and the first of the three Punic wars would begin, but before those wars began Rome would strengthen its standing with the conflict known as the Pyrrhic Wars. (280-275 BC)

These were fought between the Roman Republic and Pyrrhus, the king of Espirus who had been asked by the Greek city of Tarentum in Southern Italy for help in their war against Rome. As a skilled commander with a strong army, he had several victories, but each time suffered heavy losses, Pyrrus said after the second battle "If we are victorious in one more battle with the Romans, we shall be utterly ruined." Eventually, the Romans defeated Pyrrus, captured Tarentum and with this drew attention that it was on its way to becoming a power in its own right." It was this dogged determination of the Roman Republic and then the Empire, which led to the continual expansion with this expansion eventually contributing to its downfall. For now, the downfall was centuries away and to prove the resolve and determination of the Republic the inevitable showdown with Carthage had to happen and it did in the three Punic wars between 264-146 BC. The first war was fought over the island of Sicily as Rome was now beginning to flex the military muscle it undoubtedly had, with this flexing the message went to Carthage that Rome had imperial ambitions, and this could not go unchallenged, Carthage with a strong navy and Rome the strong army. Rome eventually won the first war and under the peace treaty Carthage was forced to pay large war reparations, the first war officially ended in 241 BC. The second Punic War was led by Hannibal who was annoyed about Carthage losing the first war, his father was a leading Carthaginian general during that war and he had a lot of angst, and anger and talked a lot about honour. Hannibal has been regarded as one of the greatest generals in history, unfortunately for him, Rome had an efficient war machine and probably more important than this military machine was the state of mind concerning how it saw itself, it just would never be beaten, it would lose battles but always keep coming back, just as Pyrrus discovered how resolute the Romans could be, Hannibal was also about to find this out to his cost. In 218 BC he attacked Saguntum (now Sagunto in Spain) which was an ally of Rome and sparked the second Punic war, I'm quite sure on reflection he probably wished he had let sleeping dogs lie, but initially things were looking quite good, after Saguntum he invaded Italy by crossing the Alps with his North African war elephants, he won a succession of victories at the battles of Trebia, Lake Trasimere and Cannae, inflicting heavy casualties on the Romans, yet they still they continued, adopted new battle tactics and eventually defeated Hannibal at the battle of Zama and ending the war, ending Hannibal and finally ending his country Carthage in the third and final Punic war, which was destroyed and never recovered. This dogged determination led to many victories throughout the centuries which in turn produced not only a vast amount of treasure from the spoils of war but many silver and gold mines as well.

As mentioned earlier, the Roman Republic was a melting pot of instability and the period 60-53 BC was a particularly chaotic time with the republic fragmenting, political order was in chaos, street violence and rioting were now becoming commonplace and the Roman leadership was corrupt, leading many to conclude it was only a matter of time before the Republic fell. Cue the three toughest guys of the time Gaius Julius Caesar, Marcus Lincinius Crassus and Gnaius Pompeius Magnus, (also affectionately known as Pompey) these three set aside their differences to form a 'gang of three' otherwise known as 'the triumvirate.' Although they seized the opportunity to form this political alliance for personal gain, they eventually dominated both the consulship and military commands, but true to form and with everything Roman, it ended with mistrust, violence and war. Crassus although regarded as the richest man in Rome for his time (think of Elon Musk, Bill Gates and Jeff Bezos all rolled into one but with a huge private army) went seeking both power and more riches, was defeated and killed at the battle of Carrhae by the long-time enemy of Rome, the Parthians. This death led to a civil war between Caesar and Pompey, with Caesar eventually defeating Pompey in 48 BC at the battle of Pharsalus in Greece. Pompey fled to Egypt hoping for sanctuary and to try and raise another army, but unfortunately ended up being beheaded on the orders of Ptolemy XIII, who was trying to court favour with Caesar in his struggles for the throne with his sister Cleopatra VII, bad judgement call as firstly Caesar felt this act was an insult to the Roman Empire (strange as he was trying to defeat him anyway) and secondly, he was known as a real hot blooded male with a string of affairs to his name, so given the choice of a young teenage boy (although the Romans, in reality, had no moral dilemma with young boys being used for sex) or an attractive temptress there was going to be only one winner. Ptolemy was ordered to disband his army, which rather foolishly he didn't do, so you guessed it another war breaks out where this time Ptolemy is killed in the final stages of the Alexandrian War. Caesar's fate was not to be a happy one either as he was assassinated on the Ides of March in 44 BC, still, he did reach his lifetime ambition of becoming dictator, be it for a brief 4 years.

The second triumvirate consisted of Octavian Caesar (Augustus) Marcus Aemilius Lepidus and Mark Anthony. It was officially created in 43 BC and differed from the first triumvirate in that it was a legal entity, endorsed by the state and not a private backroom deal agreed between, like the first triumvirate it constituted of the three most powerful men in the republic of that period. If you thought this triumvirate was going to fare any better, you're going to be sadly disappointed, internal bickering and jealousy led it to becoming weak and finally collapsing. First to fall was Lepidus, he had the lack of foresight to understand how shrewd an operator Octavian was, so after a power play, in which he tried to claim victory over Sextus Pompey (Pompey's son who never forgave Caesar for the death of his father) and claim Sicily for himself after the battle of Naulochus in 36 BC, when in reality it was Octavian's brilliant general Marcus Vipsanius Agrippa who was the real reason for the victory. Octavian firstly stripped him of all his titles except that of Pontifax Maximus, (chief high priest, which was the most prestigious position in ancient Rome's religion) and then banished him to Africa where he had been governing. This left Mark Anthony and Octavian and as the previous triumvirate broke down when there were only two left, so did this one with tensions that had been simmering between Mark Anthony and Octavian for the previous year's finally erupting into conflict and leading to a naval battle in the Ionian Sea called the Battle of Actium (Gill, 2020). This was probably the most complex and difficult of battles that were fought involving both triumvirates as the power politics and strong personalities that were involved meant both had large armies, with both splitting Caesar's army into two factions, those that supported Octavian as he was the adopted son and his anointed heir, whilst Mark Anthony was one of Caesars most popular and successful generals. The situation was made even more complex as Anthony had become Cleopatra's lover, who also claimed that her son Caesarion was the rightful heir to the Roman empire as Caeser was his father, this naturally spooked Octavian who felt he was the rightful heir to the empire, the stage is set for the seemingly ever popular and ever costly Roman pastime of war, which with the help of his superb general Agrippa, Octavian won, resulting in both Mark Anthony and Cleopatra committing suicide, whilst Caesarian was quietly executed. (Mark, 2020)

We now enter the period known as the *Pax Romana*, (Roman Peace) which was a period of supposed peace lasting approximately 200 years, it started under Augustus (27 BC-14 AD) with the objective after all the turmoil of both triumvirates being the guarantee of law, order, and security within the empire. It has to be mentioned that it is supposed peace as it was peaceful for all the conquered nations if they fell into line with Roman rule by swearing an oath to the emperor and to Rome (which included paying taxes) then all was well, however, the 'Pax' part wasn't quite so much 'Pax' for you if you didn't as Pax Romana would include military intervention and conquest if so required. Calgacus a leader of the Britons shortly after the conquest of Britain said in a speech "The liars call it Empire: they create desolation and call it peace." What Augustus started and wouldn't have known was the seeding of the destruction of the Roman empire, as all this additional expansion and protection became expensive and despite the additional taxes and gold and silver mines that were acquired, the coffers of the treasury weren't limitless. As we shall see Rome was an economy based on gold and silver, and the various provinces were increasingly unstable; as the empire grew with each conquest and tried to incorporate new people, customs, traditions and values, it, therefore, could and often did quite easily crumble, most of the problems occurred due to increasing threats of the Germanic tribes, expenditure of the military and the debasement of the coins to support this spending, it started around the 1st AD and was recognised as collapsing and finishing as an empire about 400 years later. Before we start getting into the detail a brief look at the coinage the Romans used and how the amount of silver used in the coins became less and less thus ultimately debasing the coin to becoming worthless. (debasement simply means lowering the value of the currency) Silver was more popular metal for transactions than gold for the simple reason that there is a more abundant supply of silver than gold on the planet there is a ratio of approximately 15:1 which makes it cheaper, less valuable and thus easier to make transactions for day to day purchases and smaller goods, whilst gold is more revered and was used to either show how ostentatious you were or deal in large transactions like paying for large purchases such as a villa. The most famous coin used by the Romans was the silver denarius, it had 95% silver content and was trusted and respected which gave the people confidence to trade with it. The Romans were clever in giving it two values, it had a face value which was always slightly above the silver value, this was first to increase profit and secondly to prevent the silver from flowing out of Rome, to plug some simple numbers in if the face value was £10 and the silver value was £9, you would have to give £10 worth of goods to get a silver value of £9, so easy profit or more goods for your money, either way you're a winner if your Rome and you manage to keep more of your silver in the city. Rome's economy was stable for many centuries, and although it remained mainly an agricultural society where the vast majority of its population was very poor, the peoples of both China and India were much wealthier. Despite the massive inequalities within Roman society, it remained quite stable for many centuries, although there was always the potential for inbuilt volatility. It had a sophisticated economy with what were the makings of modern banking we would recognise today along with a semi-state bank such as the Federal Reserve or the Bank of England. many silver and gold mines as well.

Ancient Rome's government deficits in the first three centuries AD was believed to have been due to the increase in the money supply, which was created by the debasement of the silver coinage. Diocletian attempted to restore confidence in the coinage by issuing good quality gold and silver, however, he made the mistake of introducing a significant number of bronze coins as currency, which in turn increased the money supply with the resultant inflation estimated in the region of 4-5% per annum. (Prodromidis,2009) In a modern context inflation of 4-5% per annum may be seen as slightly high but certainly manageable, however in the context of antiquity historians such as Parkin (1987) describe this type of inflation as massive, Starr (1987) saw it as severe, Duncan-Jones (1982) describes this type of rise as staggering. Instead of taking these historians' word for it let's do the maths to see the impact of this inflation by taking the lower amount of 4% and by using the previous formula of finding how this affected the prices over that period. So back to the equation of working to the power of numbers and using 1 as the base for 100% as before (see explanation under hyperinflation) a 4% inflation rate would be 1.04 and we multiply that number by the power of 300 (the persistent inflation period) and we get 128,825, this effectively means that a loaf of bread that cost £1, 300 years later it would cost £128,825. Ahh, I hear you say but surely their wages would have gone up as well, well yes but nowhere near the same rate, you'll see what happened to Roman soldiers' pay over that period and it was nowhere near enough to compensate for the rise in inflation and they were the section of the populace that were looked after, the rest fared much, much worse!!! At the time the Roman empire stretched over the Mediterranean including large parts of South-Eastern and Western Europe, however unlike the 1st and 2nd century AD, the States of the Eastern and Northern frontier faced serious external threats which were compounded by political and internal instability, as a result, other matters such as economic stability gave way to securing loyal armies and the defence of these frontiers. There were successive changes of government and foreign invasions which disrupted economic life, affecting both productivity and trade. To add to the problem policymakers in an attempt to either replenish or raise new armies began to debase the coinage and it has been argued by Callu (1975) that the volume of coinage increased seven times between 238 and 274 AD. If this is anywhere near true, then that is huge for the time period. It is here we can also see that Fisher's theory starting to create potential inflation as we are getting imbalance in the equation with the money supply increasing on the one side due to debasement and reduction in GDP due to instability in the empire. With all these factors, in conjunction with several attempts to change the type of currency, (they went from using coinage such as the Denarii, the Sesterce and the Antoninianus), confidence in the currency as a store of value declined and led to the return to the much more inefficient barter system. The total effect of this led to a decline in government taxes as they were paid in the debased currency and the good currency (real gold and silver) was hoarded. (Again, we see here Gresham's Law which states that bad money drives out the good).

The debasement of the currency can be seen in the following, the denarius at the beginning of the first century by Augustus (27BC to 14AD) having 95% silver, falling to 85% in Trajan's rule in 117AD, to 75% in 180AD (Marcus Aurelius) to eventually by 268AD to having 0.5% silver, so in less than 300 years the value effectively fell until it became worthless. Due to all this debasement, to pay for both the civil servants and the military, the government wouldn't accept its coinage, it was with the emperor Caracalla in the early 3rd century that the debasement of gold began. Under Augustus it was 45 coins per pound of gold, Caracalla made it 50 and within 20 years of his assassination (217AD) it was 72. This many-fold debasement meant that the government wouldn't accept its own gold coins and required taxes to be paid in bullion, meaning the owners of the coins had to smelt the coins and create bullion to be sure it was pure gold, the irony is that it would be then further debased creating even greater money supply. The cause of inflation was firstly war which saw an increase in the soldiers' pay rising from 225 denarii to 300 in the first 100 years of the first century, 100 years later it went from 300 to 500 and 10 years later to 750. To add to this the size of the army increased from 250,000 to 600,000 in 200 years, (Peden 2017) even in terms of the population size of the world being infinitely greater than the Roman period this is a huge army, for this period it is almost incomprehensible. If we try and relate the scale to the size of the Roman Empire to present day, according to Scheidel (2007) in Augustus' era there were 6 million people, an army of 250,000 would equate to approximately 4.5% of the population, this would mean a country the population size of the UK of approximately 70 million would have an army size of 3 million (UK's military size is approx. 70,000), China with approximately 1 billion people would have 45 million soldiers (China's military size approx. 2.8 million) and the USA the most powerful economic and military power in the with 350 million people would have 15.5 million troops (the size of the US military is approximately including National Guard is approximately 1.4 million) this not only shows the power and size of the Roman empire wealth but also how the resources of labour were being under used and the drain on the budget this must have caused, by the time the army reached 600,000, the population is estimated to have been 61.4 million thus making it only approximately 1% of the population, it is still an extraordinary number. The Roman army was such a strain on the economy because of its huge wage bill. Soldiers were paid the equivalent of a skilled craftsman, and officers' salaries accounted for a quarter of the whole army payroll, in addition, the cost of provisions (food, etc) would also rise in times of war which was quite frequent. By the mid-2nd Century, the whole expenditure of Rome was 1 billion Sestertii out of that a staggering 700 million was spent on the army, 70% is still an enormous amount to stump up, add on extra for welfare provisions for pensioned soldiers, 'Bread and circuses', free water provision, public hospitals, (all of which will be discussed later) and pretty soon you could be running into financial trouble. Eventually, the budget deficit grew so large that there were only several options left; first, you could defer the payments, this was not a good generally regarded as being a good idea as unpaid soldiers tended to mutiny, there is a story when one Roman emperor refused to pay a donative on his accession (a bonus paid to soldiers when a new emperor was proclaimed) he was simply murdered by his troops, it seems sometimes people, even emperors have to learn the hard way. This puts strain both on the fiscal policy as the continuing debasement of the currency and hence an ever-expanding monetary supply and secondly the supply side of the economy is heavily reduced, firstly by having so many soldiers but also taxation had to be paid for with goods and services to support the military and government state officials as the government no longer even trusted its own coinage, to the extent that taxes that needed to be paid, were not accepted in coins and bullion only, thus leading to the absurd situation where the coins had to be smelted into bullion to pay taxes, the next effect led to even greater money supply as the bullion was again cast into coins but debased yet again.

The second is to increase taxation, again never a popular move in any time period of history. The effect on the Roman citizens was nothing short of a disaster across all classes, taxes went unpaid leaving large shortfalls in the government's budget. Under Emperor Diocletian things moved in a seriously bad way for all classes; The *Decurions* who were prosperous landowners and were the dominant elements of the cities of the Roman empire can be seen as today's upper middle class who also had a sense of moral and virtuous duty to the state. By the middle of the 3rd Century, it was this class that was chosen to collect taxes as the central government were inefficient, however, they turned out to be equally as bad at collecting the money, leading to a law being passed where any deficiency in the money collected had to be made up by them directly, eventually, they left everything including their land and fled in huge numbers, going into hiding around the empire, unfortunately, this was not the end of their problems as if and when they were discovered, they were taken back to Rome shackled as slaves, until they were restored to their former positions. Merchants and Artisans also struggled as they were forced to donate goods to and then eventually work for the government, they were not allowed to leave their jobs and laws were eventually passed that children had to follow in the same occupation, Rome had effectively moved into a feudal form of serfdom when the peasantry known as the *Coloni,* who were leaseholders on both the imperial and private estates yet an essentially free class fell under the same pressures as there social betters, because once they began drifting away to look for better opportunities, they became 'tied to the soil' meaning they were forced to work the land from one generation to the next. (Peden, 2017) All these pressures led to a flight from the land, massive tax evasion, people leaving their jobs, and homes, and losing their social status. Diocletian now did what all dictators, tyrants and bad governments do under increasing pressures of inflation, they made a bad situation worse, instead of facing the reality of the situation and trying and restore confidence and trust in money, which can be painful in the short run and also take time to restore that trust, they go down the route of price controls, and this is exactly what Diocletian did by issuing his now infamous Edict on Maximum Prices in 310 AD. The problem with the edict was that the Roman Empire was vast and incorporated both sophisticated and primitive economies each having a varied cost of living from province to province. (it is one of the main problems the European Union faces today) Egypt had a low cost of living, Palestine cost twice as much and Rome was twice as much as that, sadly Diocletian ignored this problem and created a standard price throughout the empire, the result of this was that in Egypt the Edict had little to no effect as the Prices set by the edict was very rarely reached, it was the Roman people who found the maximum price lower than the market place, this resulted in rioting, the disappearance of goods and a flourishing black market. The penalty for violation of the edict was death. The edict eventually was no longer implemented and then phased out after a couple of years as it wasn't working. (And funnily enough never has)

Yet despite all this Rome's top 1% controlled 16% of the wealth compared to modern-day America where the top 1% control 40%, a figure which continues to grow. Looking deeper we can see the Gini co-efficient (the Gini coefficient is a measure of inequality where 0=perfect equality and 1=perfect inequality) Rome measured between 0.42 and 0.44, whilst modern America scores 0.45, (Lubin, 2011) the United Kingdom does fare better but stands at 35.1. (World Bank, 2021) The worrying thing regarding this statistic is that despite the empire failing and eventually collapsing, this didn't seem to bother the elites of society, they continued in their lifestyle without regard to the suffering of their citizens, could we see history beginning to repeat itself?

Did inflation eventually destroy the empire? The simple answer to that is no, it played an important role, but the Roman empire did not fall purely because of inflation, there were three other crucial factors that were intertwined with inflation and when all these four things combined, eventually led to the death blow of the empire. The first was the plague and although the Empire had had many epidemics in its history the first true pandemic in history (a pandemic is defined as an endemic that impacts a large geographical area and a large number of people) had a terrible effect on the empire was between 165-180 AD and became known as Antonine's plague, which was believed to have been contracted and then spread by soldiers returning after a campaign in the Near East. Scholars generally believe it was smallpox although measles has been suggested as the culprit. Strangely enough, it wasn't named after the emperor of the time, where there were two, Lucius Verus and Marcus Aurelius, but by his father who had adopted them Antonius Plus. It is estimated that the pandemic killed between 2% and 33% of the population but most historians tend to agree that it was around 10%. (Duncan-Jones R.P, 2021) With a total population of 75 million (a quarter of the world), that's 7.5 million people, today's equivalent would see the deaths of about 800 million people but if you think that's bad, hold onto your hats folks it's going to get a lot rougher!! Another plague followed approximately 75 years later called the Plague of Cyprian (249- 262 AD) but the real monster of them all was the Justinian plague.

The plague of Justinian so named after emperor Justinian, who ruled the Byzantine empire between 527-565 AD. The empire had essentially split into two, the western empire, which was governed by Rome and the eastern empire, which was ruled by Constantinople. (Present day Istanbul in Turkey) The plague arrived in Constantinople around 542 A.D. about a year after the disease initially appeared in the empire's outer provinces. It occurred in waves for approximately 225 years, finally disappearing in 755 AD. It was the first bubonic plague and is sometimes called the first pandemic as opposed to the Antonine's plague. The origins are believed to be in China, but the proximate point of entry to the empire was thought to be in Pelusium, on the river Nile's northern and eastern shores. From there it quickly spread along both the trade and military routes, moving between both the Roman Eastern and Western Empires, afflicting the entire Roman world. The belief is that between 25% - 50% of the population died of the pandemic, totalling around 50-100 million people during the two centuries, which translates to approximately 2.5 to 5 million people every year for 200 years. (Goldweik et al, 2011) To put that into modern-day context with approximately 8 billion people, which would equate to 10-20 million people every year from now for the next 200 years, now that is a real serious pandemic!! The only period that was worse in human history for this scale of death rates was when the bubonic plague hit in the 14th Century (Black Death). The knock-on effects of this loss of population were, firstly productivity in the economy was lost, secondly it was harder to replace the loss of military personnel who were not only dying from the plague but in wars as well and thirdly the weakened defences, which led to increasing barbarian attacks on the empire, finally sacking Rome. It's interesting to note that the barbarians were not as susceptible to the virus then the Romans, which helped contribute to the fall of the Western Empire, however this was not true of the Eastern Empire's foes, with the Sasanian Empire every bit as susceptible to the pandemic. This resulted in both the Eastern and Sasanian empires fighting each other to a stalemate. (Latham, 2021) This ensured that the Byzantine (Eastern) Empire survived in one form or another until 1453, unlike the Western empire which fell in 476 AD.

The second cause was the invasion by the Barbarians, where it is generally assumed that the 31st of December 406 AD, (we assume 406 AD as it is sometimes argued that the crossing is in 405AD but to quibble over 1 year in a thousand-year history seems a bit pointless) due to the writings of Prosper of Aquitaine, a contemporary Christian writer of the time. According to Prosper, there was a large-scale crossing of the barbarians into the Roman empire which although Proper wasn't to know would eventually reach Rome itself. The first thing we need to clarify is that the Barbarians were not an actual tribe but a collection of groups. The Romans called all tribes that were none Roman barbarians, so tribes like the Huns, Vandals, Quadi, Sarmatians, Gepids, Burgundians, Herules, and Saxons, with plenty of others all fell into this category. The crossing was seen as a seminal moment for the start of the collapse of Roman order in the provinces, with widespread raids which would eventually lead to Rome itself. The crossing or 'Barbarian Invasion' lasted until the 560's. The arrival of the Huns in Europe in 375 is generally regarded as the beginning of the Migration Period, whilst the conquest of the Lombard tribe conquest of Italy in 568 marks its end, certainly for the Western part of the empire, as discussed, the Eastern part continued for nearly another thousand years. The question that needs to be asked is what caused this migration? Was it purely for the conquest of Rome, revenge for the centuries of domination, yes these may have played a part later when it could be seen how weak Rome was due to the inflation taking place, the debasement of the coins and the general unhappy conditions of the majority of Roman citizens, but the initial mass migration was for the reasons people migrate today, fear and looking for a better standard of living. The fear was the tribes crossing into Italy were not warriors but refugees fleeing from more powerful groups in the East such as the Huns, even the construction of the Great Wall of China has been cited as a reason for the cause of the migration as it forced tribes westward. Another factor as to the cause of the migration is climate change, (what, climate change happening without fossil fuels and the human race not being to blame, surely not!!!) which caused the rise of sea levels, leading to the failure of harvests, with even population pressures being argued as the reasons for the mass migration, seems like little has changed in the last 1500 years.

The third reason which may come as a bit of a surprise is welfare provision and this didn't just include the free provision of food assistance to the poor, but also free water, healthcare, and a pension plan for the veterans. The phrase 'Bread and Circuses' was attributed to the poet and satirist

Juvenal. The most famous games took place under the Colosseum, which was built under the emperors Vespasian and Titus, at its peak accounted for approximately half of the working days a year being declared a public holiday, the real problem here then became a lack of productivity. Juvenal argued that the distribution of free food and entertainment may have been a noble cause, but this was done at the cost of moral decay with people no longer caring about their civic duties, just free stuff, this being enough to keep the public passive and when they are passive, they can be easily manipulated or controlled. Under a 'Bread and Circuses' regime, the public grows more dependent on its leaders for everything thus leading to increased political polarization. In the end, politics mattered more to the Romans than the country and empire did. In conjunction with all this, we start to see the demise of democratic norms and the rise of authoritarianism. (Hazlitt, 1971) At the peak of the welfare programme under Caesar, approximately 320,000 people benefitted from free grain, where all you had to do was show up to the distribution points and you would get your grain. This was becoming increasingly expensive, so a means test was introduced with the effect of reducing the numbers to 150,000 of the poorest citizens who were eligible. Augustus expanded it to 200,000 and it remained at that figure for several centuries until Emperor Aurelian re-organised the relief programme where in addition to grain, pork, olive oil and salt were included for free distribution. (Hazlitt 1971).

As the city of Rome expanded and the water supply of the Tiber and local rivers became increasingly polluted, aqueducts were built to bring distant water sources to Rome; the first was built in approximately 312 BC and by the 1st century BC there were a total of nine aqueducts. With a total of 591 major delivery points in the city, delivering an average to each point of 60 cubic metres of water per day, with an estimated 900 individuals served by each delivery point per day, consuming 67 litres. (Bruun, 1991) This was a large operation and had significant costs to the treasury however as water is essential to life, so were the viaducts to the city. In addition to clean water, it may be of great surprise to know that they had healthcare provisions for the poor; the Romans were acutely aware that infections could spread diseases and the health and wellbeing of not only the poor but also the slaves and foot soldiers were vital to the Roman economy, so public hospitals were made available and free, with funding received via pledges and donations from wealthy patrons, (Carcopino 1943) however as both taxes increased and inflation eroded the wealth of a large number of the upper echelons of society, so these hospitals fell into disrepair and eventually ceased to function.

The final drain on the purse strings of the treasury was the military pensions, these were seen as a must by Augustus who created the system as he identified the fact that any retired military men who fell on hard times and financial constraints were ripe for eventually supporting a coup or cause unrest, so a soldier earned a one-time payment or discharge benefit upon completion of his service. Funding came through a dedicated pension fund which was obtained via a 5% inheritance tax. The payment was made after 25 years of military service, with the legionnaires receiving 12,000 sesterces and the Praetorian guard receiving 20,000, this was the equivalent of 12 year's salary in the army, again a necessary financial evil but no small change to find, especially as the army grew in size what happened as the funds ran low was to increase the length of service required before payment was made, I guess the older a soldier got, the slower he would be, also the more campaigns a soldier was involved in both would, in turn, increase his chances of dying in battle thus sparing the payment of the payment and if you thought that the soldiers would be disgruntled that their families would need some payment, the system had that covered too, soldiers weren't allowed to be married (this was largely ignored but again this law of non-marriage saved on pay-outs).

We can conclude that inflation didn't ultimately cause the downfall of Rome, several factors combined to cause this and inflation and debasement of the coins played their part when you cannot pay your army, you cannot defend your borders and once the initial migration took place with the more peaceful migrants looking to escape the more violent, warlike tribes, the likes of the Huns were able to see and then exploit the weakness of the Roman Empire, the weakness of the borders were further exacerbated by the plague until eventually the Roman citizens were so miserable they simply opened the gates and let the barbarians in. We can leave the last few words on this chapter of history to a Christian priest at the time, Salvian of Marseille, who wrote an account of why the Roman state was collapsing he said "Because it deserves to collapse; because it had denied the first premise of good government, which is justice to the people." What he meant by justice was a just taxation system and honest money and he argues that the mass of the population had just one wish after being captured by the Barbarians, which was to never again fall under the rule of the Roman bureaucracy, in essence he argues it was the state that had become the enemy of the people, the Barbarians were the liberators and the main reason for this was the start of debasement and inflation in the 3rd Century. The state was living in an ivory tower or a bubble with a blinkered vision, the state had solved the monetary problem for itself but failed to solve it for the masses, using ever-increasing oppressive taxation methods to fill the coffers of the ruling bureaucrats and soldiers at the expense of the masses. (Purden, 2017) If only the modern-day elites could learn the lessons of history, it really could save a lot of pain and misery in the future.

4. CHINA: PAPER MONEY AND THE FIRST FIAT CURRENCY

"Only gold is money, everything else is credit" J. P. Morgan.

China is regarded as the oldest civilization in the world, with a culture that stretches back over 4,000 years, people have lived in the Chinese area for around two million years, with the earliest human inhabitants of China being in Niewehan. Its early history can be broken into three periods; the Bronze Age dynasties which ran from Xia (2070-1600 BC) to the Zhou dynasty. (1046-256 BC) The second dynasty would be classed as the Imperial period where under Emperor Qin Huang-di centralised control over various regions and thus is regarded as the founding father of what can be now seen as modern China in 221-207 AD. This period finished with the Southern and Northern dynasties which only lasted three years (586-589 AD) and overlapped with the third and final period; the Imperial period, which started with the Sui dynasty (581-618 AD) and finally ended with the Qin dynasty which lasted from 1641-1911 AD. It will be this late Imperial period and in particular the Tang dynasty, (618-907 AD) the Song dynasty. (960-1279 AD) we will be looking at in greater detail, with the occasional reference to other dynasties.

We have a great understanding of ancient China as they have had written script for over two thousand years oracle bones have been found which are dated from the Shang dynasty Dating (16th – 11th Century BC) and have inscriptions on which can be still read to this day. (Clayre 1985) It is this remarkable longevity and continuity of history in the written language that has played a key role in the development of the Chinese monetary system from the ancient through the medieval period, right to the present day. The Chinese were the first to use paper money substitutes on a large scale and the first to circulate fiat money 'centuries' before the West, because of this China also felt the pain of inflation as well as depreciation of the value of its currency with the loss of purchasing power that ensued.

To start at the beginning Commodity money was a medium of exchange in ancient China and three thousand years before the birth of Jesus Christ,

China used copper as a medium of exchange, with gold and silver being used much later. (Einzig, 1951) despite the use of copper cowry shells being a far more common currency than precious or semi-precious metals, not just in ancient China but many civilizations around the same time, the reason for this is that they were scarce, beautiful and could also be used as ornaments, (Kemmerer 1935) In addition to cowry shells being used other commodities such as sheep, tea, silk, grain and rye were also being used as a medium of exchange. In the 11th century BC, the Chinese government started to take a larger role in regulating money. King Tcheng of the Zhu dynasty (11th Century – 221 BC) employed treasury offices to develop a rules-based system where copper rings began to serve as money. Fines for some crimes were legally fixed in relation to the fixed weight of the metal, we also see government lending institutions being set up to provide loans for both consumers and producers. These rules of government became much more developed and advanced than those developed by the Ancient Egyptians and Babylonians, with money playing a much more active role than either of these other two empires. (Einzig 1951)

The next development in Chinese money was a rather strange but unique currency known as 'Knife Money.' Around 1,000 BC small agricultural implements made of bronze became a popular medium of exchange, the shapes of these implements were mainly knives but also included hoes and sickles. Although this had a 'first-use' value by being used as the tools they were designed for, were effectively a commodity in two senses; First for the bronze content and secondly for the fact they had a use of being a tool, this use is as any commodity would have whether it be oil or grain; the implements became smaller over time until they became round coins from the ring of the bronze knives handle. Chinese knife money had almost exclusively been issued privately, especially via merchants whilst before this cowry shells had been used as a means of storing wealth, by 852 BC were starting to become in short supply and by the end of the 7th Century there were so few left they could no longer effectively serve as money.

Although the shape of the coin was mainly due to the shape of the ring at the end of the knife money, by the 4th century BC these small round coins had square holes in the centre, the square hole had both a symbolic and functional significance, The functional significance was that it made it easier to mint and to use less copper as well as allowing string to go through them which allowed for ease of transportation as well as counting. The symbolic square hole also represented earth with the circular circumference representing heaven, whilst the concept of 'yin and yan' was displayed by the two sides of the coin. These copper coins were known as 'Cash' and a thousand of them would normally be placed on one piece of string and tied off, prices later came to be measured by 1,000-coin strings of coins.

Unlike Western coinage, these cash coins never bore the image of its rulers, mainly because these coins were largely developed by private merchants until 221 BC. This is an important year for Chinese history as well as the development of money in China as this was the year Qin Huang-Di consolidated rule and founded the Qin dynasty (221-226 BC) which sought to not only centralise China as a nation but monetary system as well. Emperor Qin declared the 'Banliang' (half-ounce) bronze coins were to become the official money in China and although some coins continued to differ markedly from region to region, it was the beginning of the consolidation of state control over money, with the emperor passing China's first legal tender laws forbidding the use of cowry shells, tin, gems and pearls as money. (Williams, 1997) The keener-eyed amongst you may have noticed no mention of what was developed as commodity money in the other civilisations gold and silver, did the Chinese not want to use these metals, well yes, they did but they had so few gold and silver mines available, there wasn't enough to sustain the development of the economy, hence the use of the more abundant metal copper and thus the need for so many coins per string of cash.

Before getting into the nitty-gritty of the main dynasties involved in money printing and its final inflationary effects, we need to give a big shout-out to the Han dynasty, (206 BC- 220 AD) where urbanisation, entrepreneurship, economic prosperity, and the growth in the money economy really took off. The population grew under this dynasty to approximately 60 million people, which was noted under an official census in approximately 4 AD. Along with this population growth, we also see the expansion of the money supply with approximately 220 million cash coins produced every year. Cash coins (Zhiqian) were originally produced in China in the later part of the 1st millennium BC and created by a cast mould with a hole in the middle, the reason for the hole was that due to the relatively low value of the metals they used (they were mainly made of copper with some other metals mixed in) in comparison to silver and gold, they therefore needed a lot of coins to complete financial transactions so what they did is put string through them and carry them in string bundles of 1,000 cash coins. The scarcity of gold and silver mines (which rather ironically China is now the world's largest producer of gold) was the reason for the need to use these cash coins and should you be wondering if we get the name for cash from these coins, you'd be right to wonder and the answer is yes, we do get our word 'cash' from the ancient Chinese 'cash' coins with a hole in it. The most important thing that came out of the Han dynasty however was not these coins, as mentioned earlier the Greeks were the first to use coins, it was that most wonderful invention that has transformed our society and how we live, paper making takes place in this period, and although the Egyptians had papyrus, that was much thicker, courser and uneven so the invention of paper making was a huge advancement not just for the Chinese but mankind as a whole. We can now begin to explore the main dynasties where firstly paper money was introduced, eventually becoming a currency thus fiat currency, finally leading to China abandoning all forms of paper money leading to centuries of stagnation.

a) TANG DYNASTY (618-907 AD)

The Tang dynasty was another prosperous period for the Chinese where it began to increase westward toward inner Asia, it had grown its army until it numbered in the hundreds of thousands and culture flourished along with the Silk Road. It was probably comparable if not more prosperous than the Byzantine empire or the Middle Eastern golden age of Islam. It was a maritime power, sailing along the Indian Ocean going along the Persian Gulf and developing lots of contact and trade with other civilizations. There were several trade routes but the most important was the Silk Road which stretched between the Islamic world, the centre being in Baghdad and reached the outskirts of India on the Indus River, all the way through Saudi Arabia, into North Africa and also covering most of Spain as well as covering the Byzantine empire with routes to Constantinople. The Silk Road became an integral part of this trade with exports of silk and porcelain as both were highly desirable. In 621 AD they established a viable currency where the throne also took measures in the late 7th Century to end the counterfeiting of coins, which had taken place in the Sui dynasty, the death penalty was imposed on anyone caught privately minting coins and by 755 AD the government had established eleven mints, with ninety-nine furnaces, producing coins in various parts of China. These coins were all uniform in shape, weight, and metal content. (Benn 2002).

In this period the woodblock printing method was developed, initially for use in textiles to give the fabric patterns, but quite quickly it was used on paper, which was essential for the eventual printing money (moveable type was eventually developed much later, emerging around the 11th century in the Song Dynasty. The expansion of the money started to expand in this period with lots of cash coins being issued, approximately 327 million per annum, which was almost double what had previously been created. They were still predominately made of copper (approximately 85%) so they still had a relatively low value, it was estimated that 1,000 coins were needed for 1oz of silver, however as trade developed out of China, merchants required a more portable form of money, so they turned to the wooden block printers. At this stage, it was the merchants and not the state which developed the concept of 'Flying Cash' it was issued by private merchants with the state playing no role in its initial concept or development, however, it wouldn't be long before it did and as all state bodies are prone to do, they take a great idea and eventually ruin it.

According to the New Book of Tang, a work of official history about the Tang Dynasty compiled by teams of scholars in the Song Dynasty (it was customary for dynasties to compile the histories of their immediate predecessors) and they quote the use of 'Flying Cash' being used between the years 805-820 AD. Flying cash which is also called Bianhuan, (translated as easy money) was used as a bill of exchange (essentially an IOU) and became the precursor of real paper money or Jiaozi. During the reign of emperor Xianzong (805-820 AD), there wasn't enough copper coins on the market to ensure smooth transactions firstly there was a shortage of copper coins, this was due to Buddhism finding its way into China via India and people melted the copper coins and made Buddhist idols (Einzig 1951) and secondly the reform of the taxation system. The creation of flying cash coincided with the reform of the 'twice taxation' method, which beforehand the taxation was based on three types of taxes (the Zuyongdiao system) which had to be delivered by every male adult. The first consisted of grain where 2-3% would be taken, the second of silk fabric or linen, where 20 feet of silk or 25 foot of linen was handed over and the third in a corvee, (unpaid labour for the construction of roads, etc) where two months of the peasants time was given up, however, to compensate for the taxes' peasant families were allowed a free fixed piece of land, this was known as the 'equal fields' system, which was an ingenious way for the state to ensure the filling of its coffers through increased grain and cash. The land was given to all peasants from the age of 17-59, (although the emperor still actually owned all the land) then every three years a census would be taken when 80% of the land would be taken from anyone 60 or over and handed to anyone who had reached the age of 17. This would ensure an efficient workforce as someone of the age of 17 would be fitter and stronger than someone aged 60 or above, however by retaining 20% they could be self-sufficient and thus not a drain on the system. (Benn, 2002)

Another change was that part of the tax could be now paid for in cash, this further exacerbated the increase in demand for money; in response, the central government intervened by strictly forbidding the merchants from 'depriving' the capital city of its coins, it did this by 'scattering' the coins to the various circuits. (Circuits were a territorial administrative unit, directly responsible to the central and not provisional governments. Special officials called transport commissioners or prefects were appointed to collect the correct taxes from their respective circuits and send the money to the capital, where it would again be redistributed) An additional change that was made that instead of trading with coins, local markets were forced into a form of barter system where items such as silk were used for market transactions all this was to ensure that the coins circulating in one region did not leave for another region, this may seem a bit strange as it did harm long-distance trade and were an impediment to the development of the economy that the flying cash rectified. In fact, we can see that it was quite an astute observation to keep money circulating in an area, a modern-day example of where it is a huge problem which hasn't been fully recognised yet but within the European Union, money is leaving regions, in particular the southern regions such as Italy where the economy is in almost permanent recession and being deposited in the Northern member countries such as Germany and Holland where it is seen as being safer. This is debatable in the long run as the European Union uses a system known as TARGET 2 to deal with these imbalances, it is not the remit of this book to debate the hows and whys of this system, but essentially it turns the weaker economies into debtors but a debt that is interest-free and essentially never has to be paid, and stronger economic countries into perpetual creditors who are essentially never going to be paid. (Hubble 2018)

The purpose of mentioning the comparison is the Chinese seemed well aware of the dangers of money flowing from one area to another, it is the ancient Chinese way of solving the problem of 'capital flight' but instead of money leaving from one country to another, it stopped the movement of capital from one state to another. The use of flying cash overcame this obstacle where in exchange for cash, merchants were handed bills on paper, issued with the respective sum of money, once the merchant arrived at their destination, they then exchanged their bills for cash. The exchange of bills for cash took place in the circuit's capital Chang'an (modern-day Xi'an) liaison offices along with the houses of specialised merchants in the circuits, these were the Chinese equivalent of the Miges goldsmiths. It was mainly the tea merchants who profited from the introduction of bills of exchange as they helped traders in Chang'an to buy tea from Sichuan and to the south-west, whilst reciprocally helping traders from these regions to buy merchandise in the capital. In essence, what we are seeing is that Chinese tea merchants are the first to start what we can see as modern-day banking.

The central government weren't initially too impressed with the bills of exchange and repeatedly banned their use, it was only in 812 A.D., did they declared these bills as a valid means of payment, and soon they started to issue their bills of exchange. (Theobold 2000)

We now begin to start seeing the direct involvement of government in the financial system, so was inflation a contributory factor to the downfall of the Tang dynasty, well actually no it wasn't, however, financial instability did eventually play a part in the demise of the dynasty, it actually for four reasons, with the first reason being unusual, it was down to Eunuchs, yes you read that correctly Eunuchs. Eunuchs had been in both Imperial service as well as the administrative departments of the state (known as mandarins) for centuries, originally used as guards and servants in the women's quarters, (for the two obvious reasons that firstly they wouldn't get romantically involved and secondly they were never going to have children who could potentially pose a threat to the emperor) but eventually they started to gain power and control once they became advisors to the emperors, being a eunuch became so popular that both rich and poor families wanted to have their sons castrated for the chance of having a better life in the Imperial court. (Schulz, 2001) This growth in power leads into and overlaps with reason number two, which entails the conflicts and struggles of different cliques within the court of not only the eunuchs, but the two different groups made up of the noble class and the civilian class. All these internal disputes chipped away at the power of the central regime.

The next two reasons are interlinked and were regarded as the main catalyst for the failure of the Tang: The separatist regions of Fanzhen. These separatist regions of Fanzhen can trace their origins from the organisation of Jiedushi (regional military governors) which was set up to safeguard the border areas, yet by the late Tang periods, these Jiedushi gradually became separatist regions known as Fanzhen. The competition between the Fanzhen and central court over farmland and labour led to battles which effectively threatened the unification of China as these Fanzhen regions effectively became small kingdoms where these military forces were only responsible for themselves. The final and probably the most influential reason for the decline of the Tangs was the peasant revolution which occurred in the later period of the dynasty; all the land grabs in the Fanzhen regions led to both oppression and exploitation by not only the landowners but the eunuchs forcibly occupying the peasant's farmland that they were given under the 'equal fields' system and then extorting the peasants for their cash as well. (Kind of ruthless these eunuchs) The subsequent wars that were fought over the years meant that even more tax was imposed upon them. To add to their woes, during the rule of Emperor Xizongs reign (805-820 AD) there was a devastating drought which lasted several years, this had the effect of drastically reducing food production, this, in turn, did lead to inflationary food prices, however, this inflation is not the man-made kind of increasing the money supply which would have been quite easy to do and so often has been done by simply printing lots of paper currency so big kudos to the Tang dynasty for showing self-restraint, made all the more remarkable by the fact they had no precedence to follow, an excuse we don't have in the twenty-first century. To try and end on a more positive and balanced note to the eunuchs who have been portrayed in quite an unfavourable light so far, the invention of paper was by a eunuch called Cai Lun, around 105 AD. Some sources state that paper had been invented earlier in the Han dynasty, but Cai Lun's undisputed achievement was the development of a technique that made mass production of paper possible, (Prasad, 2017) so let's hear it for Cai pulling one back for the eunuchs.

b) SONG DYNASTY (960-1278 AD)

Under the Song dynasty, China became even more prosperous and advanced, they were the first dynasty to establish a standing navy and explore the South China Seas, the Indian Ocean and the Persian Gulf, slowly but steadily they started to dominate these areas, it was becoming a very commercialized civilization and the population increased to 200 million. In the economy a real free market was being established with joint stock companies and private investment being advanced, with relatively little to no interference from the government in the market, this dynasty was a prosperous economy in the early period.

The Song dynasty is remarkable for three things, first, it is one of history's wealthiest periods, with the 'Golden Age inventions that can be credited to it including gunpowder, the compass, water-powered mechanical clocks, industrial textiles, movable print, windmills, and the use of coal as a source of fuel. These innovations were spurred on by mass production and then the commercialization of rice. This powerful economic empire eventually succumbed to the Mongol empire, many of their resources and practices were taken over by the Mongols who subsequently used them to conquer most of Eurasia. The most significant invention, which has subsequently affected the rest of human history was the use of paper money and sadly along with it, the inflationary and hyperinflationary consequences due to the ease of its overuse.

The Song is also an intriguing period as it collapsed not only once but twice, with both collapses occurring similarly. (They never learnt the lessons from the first time) It is a pattern of failure which has eerily similar hallmarks throughout history; firstly, by the use of populist policies and laws by the central government to retain power which ultimately burdens the private sector, followed by inflationary deficit spending, leading to hyperinflation, secondly wars are fought in alliance with what appears to seem like inferior neighbours and finally conquest by the seemingly less powerful allies. That this pattern happened not just once but twice in a very similar timeline, makes it an intriguing period to try not only to make some sense of it but to gain an understanding of what is happening in the 20th century and why, can look at one of the most significant events of human history, which has affected mankind ever since, welcome to the world of 'The Fiat Currency'.

Emperor Taizu of Song is the founder of the Song dynasty, with the dynasty being divided into two periods, Northern Song and Southern Song. During the Northern period (970-1127 AD) it controlled what is now known as Eastern China, the Southern Song period (1127-1279) refers to the period after the Song lost control of the Northern half of the dynasty to the Jurchen led Jīn dynasty in the Jīn-Song wars. (Jurchen is a term which collectively describes several East Asian Tungusic-speaking people, descended from the Danghu people. They lived in the Northeast of China, which later became known as Manchuria and the Jurchens were later renamed Manchus).

In 1115 the Jurchen tribes rebelled against their overlords of the Liao dynasty, they allied with the Song against their common enemy the Liao. The Jīn promised to cede to the Song the sixteen prefectures (sixteen areas in Northern China which now include areas such as Beijing and Tianjin) which the Liao had conquered and controlled since 938 A.D. Once the Jīn's saw how quickly they defeated the Liao, but observed the Song's military failure, they took the opportunity and refused to cede the territory, loss of empire number one. With more wars and both sides invading the territory of the other eventually leading to a stalemate, the Song became allies with the Mongols who again were a weaker ally (I'm guessing you've worked out what happens next, but here goes) in 1233, leading to the Jīn being defeated and that dynasty collapsing in 1234, however, the second alliance the Song had with the Mongols was more fateful than the Jīn alliance, it led to the collapse of the Song dynasty in 1279 and the start of one of the most powerful empires in history the Mongol empire.

As claims go the Song dynasty can be regarded as the first truly industrialised society in history with a modern, legal regulatory framework, tax, and financial institutions. In the first century of the dynasty, there was huge economic growth, output rose fivefold, in particular, the output of bronze, tin and lead rose by twenty to twenty-five times; these are growth rates which are unrivalled until the Industrial Revolution in the United Kingdom. (The Industrial Revolution started around 1760 and continued until around 1840). To show the scale of the Chinese accomplishment the transition in this period in the Industrial Revolution went from hand production methods to the use of machines, chemical manufacturing, the use of steam power, the development of machine tools and the mechanized factory system. The Song achievement is quite remarkable in terms of output in that what they were doing took almost a thousand years before it was matched. Along with arts and culture, the standard of living improved dramatically seeing the population doubling in a century, with a thriving consumer society, so much so that in an eerie comparison to the present day, contemporary observers complained that young people had lost the ability to cook for themselves because everyone was always buying take-outs. (Gernet 1962) The first hundred years of the dynasty saw a rise in living standards due to the economic output and development of what can be considered a large, urbanised middle class with an increasingly complex economy, (Miyakuwa 1955) and military expenditure tripled between 979 and 1041. (Ebrey 1996) By the late 1080's we start to observe prosperity on the decline never to recover until the eventual fall of the dynasty.

With all the innovation, unprecedented economic growth and military spending, the question that begs to be asked are why the dynasty conquered not once but twice in a relatively short period of time by what was effectively at the time a bunch of nomads, with the Song dynasty not only having all this economic might but a having superior military advantage in terms of numbers in some cases as large as 50:1 (St Onge 2017) Most historians tend to argue that it was predominantly military factors that led to the Song collapse, however this is a lazy and simplistic view to take and a perfect analogy from St Onge (2017) "If the United States had been seized and ruled by, say, the Sioux, we might look less to Sitting Bull's horseback skills or to General Custer's order of battle and more to institutional reasons why the governing regime had become so brittle that it was easily broken." If not the military, where do we look? Well, unlike the Tang which had several factors for its downfall, we can trace the Song collapse to a particular individual and his effect on Chinese society to this day, enter the stage a Mr Wang Anshi. Wang was a socialist reformer (he was way ahead of Karl Marx) and as Chancellor between 1069-1976, seized the means of production, issued widespread price-and-wage controls as well as established state pensions. (Nourse 1942) His policies followed a strategy of the state being responsible for the entire management of commerce, industry and agriculture, to assist the poor in economic hardship and prevent them from "being ground into the dust by the rich." (Goetzmann and Koll 2005) Wang's intervention reached well beyond his economic policy, with extensive reforms and purges of opposition figures within the bureaucracy. If that wasn't enough the two main pillars of his policy were to have an inflationary monetary policy and permanent war. One policy which was to led to his downfall was the provision of credit to the peasant farmers known as the Green Sprouts Law (qinqmiaofa) which was a loan to the peasants where they could buy seeds at an interest rate of 2% to escape the cycle of dependence that kept them in debt to landlords and also improving productivity and thus filling up the state coffers (presumably to fund the wars), state planning what on earth could go wrong!!! Well wrong it went, firstly public officials abused the system by forcing loans on peasants regardless if they didn't want it or not and then extracting higher interest than the official 2%; poor families were unable to pay the money back so instead of filling the treasury with more loot, the programme began to lose money and actually cost the state, (what no money for wars) leaving the people even more indebted to the landlords and even greater inequality strikes again.

Wang's military escapades during his brief but eventful tenure as Chancellor was to wage several wars simultaneously against various regional powers, one of which included the Ly dynasty in what is now modern Vietnam. As economic and population decline took hold the increasingly stretched military resources suffered its first major military loss, eventually having to cede the northern half of the empire to the Jurchen, who had initially been invited into the alliance against a third kingdom, the Liao. Encouraged by the Song's military incompetence in a battle against the Liao, the Jurchen quickly turned on their allies, took the capital and forced the Song court to escape to the South. (St Onge 2017)

Before Wangs election as Chancellor, the early Song economy was not matched in China or anywhere else on the planet until well into the 20th Century, it exceeded the Ming Dynasty by 50% and the Qing Dynasty by 90%. (Bannister 1987) It has been estimated that GDP per capita (total GDP divided by the population, which gives the average output per individual in the society) in 1990-dollar terms at $1,328 in 980, seeing it fall to $1,244 in 1086, after which it fell to $962 by 1120, a massive decline of 23% in 34 years (Broadberry 2013). To add a further perspective and a modern context the World GDP per capita average only surpassed China's 980 AD average in 1976, with a GDP per capita of $1,277, only four years short of a thousand years, the European Union took until 1977 to achieve $1.225, whilst the OECD (Organisation for Economic Co-operation and Development) took until 1961 at $1,349. (Macro Trends 2022) Other indicators of a rising economy can be seen with the rise of agricultural productivity which had risen dramatically in early Song; and the introduction of new seed varieties including the Champa variety (the Champa area is now Vietnam) of rice. (Golas 1980) This additional productivity led to a shift in the population moving from North to South and rising yields of crops being seen across the empire. (Deng 2013) This growth in agricultural productivity and GDP can be correlated with the increase in population estimates. The population is estimated to have doubled in the Song era between 742-1100. (Ebrey and Waltham, 2013) To put some figures to this explosion in the population it was estimated that it rose from 54 million in 1014 to 108 million in 1086. (Bannister 1987) For comparison, it is estimated that Europe between 1,000 and 1340 grew from 38.5 million to 73.5 million. Once Wang's policies started to take hold, we can see the population growth initially slowing down until it went into reverse so that by 1193 it was 122 million, whilst in 1103 it had been 123 million. (Bannister 1987)

Further evidence of Wang's folly and the effect his policies had can be seen in the output figures of the economies' raw resources, such as iron which before Wang had grown approximately 600% since 800 AD (Wright 2007) finally starting to decline between 1064-1078. (Wagner 2001) Another indicator of productivity comes from evidence of coal output, which along with the iron output data, gives us an insight into the wealth of a nation. The peak of pre-modern China's use of coal was just before 1125, (Hartwell 1962) which is just before the Jurchen conquest. It could be argued that they had been exploited fully for their resources and productivity would have come to a halt anyway, but there is evidence via eminent authority on the subject Robert Hartwell regarding the production of iron in the main Song region declining after the mines were abandoned by 1100 despite their being so much reserves that they were exploited by the Qing dynasty (1636-1912) and even after World War Two. It is also clear that Wang's policy influence was now starting to take hold with a definite and drastic decline taking place before and after the conquest (Hartwell 1967). It is expected to see the economic decline and disruption after the invasion and conquest by the Jurchens, but the decline starting around 1100 which was preceded by three hundred years of rising economic prosperity and only several decades after Wang, leads him to be the main culprit of the economic decline of not only the Song dynasty but the difficulties that have plagued China ever since to the present day.

How is it we can come to blame Wang for China's misfortunes even though he was only in power for a short time? The answer is quite simple and something that is potentially infecting modern Western societies today, it was his influence and thinking that he left behind that was so disastrous. In the early Song period, the economics in the government was essential based on Confucianism (living life based on moral principles, the importance of education and learning from ancient wisdom) where the state and the economy were viewed as symbiotic and officials were encouraged to practice wu-wei ('no action' or to use a modern economic term 'laissez-faire') along with pacifism. (St Onge 2017) When Wang became the de-facto ruler, he criticised the Confucian philosophy which he saw as being tolerant of both injustice and the potential of invasion. To solve these problems Wang increased taxes on large landowners, used credit in particular to peasants, (green shoot law) nationalised the main industries of the economy namely tea, salt, and wine and finally debasement the currency by both promoting and continually printing paper money.

Wang also changed the strategy of pacifism and started to spend huge sums of money on foreign policy which included spending on the military and invading the Champa region to the South and the Jurchen to the North. His main legacy was to completely rewrite the canon of the imperial examinations; eliminating classic texts which had been used for centuries demonstrating the importance of allowing the natural market prices to happen, light taxation and regulation (these guys were way ahead of Adam Smith!!!) and objective analysis as to the nature and causes of inflation, this part was really important as inflation tended more often than not to cause peasant revolts, it is something that the Chinese Communist Party probably worries about more than anything else to this day. Wang steered the system to be more interventionist between the regulators and the markets, creating a strong bureaucratic role of constantly interfering in the markets and even though the policies were quickly abandoned as the economic consequences became apparent, Wang's legacy was to pack the bureaucracy with ideological allies in conjunction with this he led a campaign of imprisoning and exiling his critics. (St Onge 2017) Wang's tenure was short and by 1075 he was temporarily imprisoned as his policies were blamed for the famine of 1074 which took place in Northern China, driving many farmers off the land, this disaster was made even worse by the debts incurred from the green shoots programme where along with the corruption the government started to charge 20-30% interest (Twitchett and Smith 2009) leaving many farmers to go bankrupt, this inevitably led to other peasants revolt in Northern China.

It is interesting to compare Wang with the Italian Communist Antonio Gramsci, who in the 1930s realised that Marxist ideology wasn't being adopted by the working class (arguing patriotism and nationalism was too ingrained) which was believed to be needed to overthrow the system, so he adopted the strategy of 'The Long March Through the Institutions' thus bypassing the need for a violent revolution but achieving Marxist goals by taking over the established institutions such as the civil service, judiciary, media, etc. His movement, although short-lived has had extended influence a century later, not through its policies directly but by the intellectual legacy these policies had. (St Onge 2017)

What inflationary effects were inflicted on the Song dynasty? This period is probably the most significant period of human history as it was the first nation to ever have the widespread use of paper money. In 970 the Song credit bureau started to issue paper commodity certificates, these certificates were redeemable for commodities such as tea and salt, these commodities were controlled by government monopolies thus making the certificates effectively quasi-money and not fiat currencies (Gernet 1962). By 991 the first edict was issued to forbid the smelting of coins for household goods, (Hirzel and Kim 2008) this is now suggesting that the certificates were now taking the role of quasi-money and was being over-issued as the melting of the coins would only occur if their value was declining relative to the value of the copper once it was melted. The deterioration in the purchasing power of the coins done in conjunction with a rising economy which had been occurring for 300 years previously only occurs in two circumstances; one, is if the new coins were being debased compared to the old coins by having less copper in them and two, the certificates were increasingly drawing monetary demand away from coins, either way signs of inflation are starting to been seen.

By 1024 local governments had begun printing their certificates, and these often traded at a premium for more than sixty years, this was until Wang's reform took place. (Von Glahn 2005) A premium effectively means the certificate's current value is trading above the value issued on the note, for example, a certificate with a redeemable value of £1,000 would trade at £1,100. This premium suggests the market believes the redemption of the certificate is virtually guaranteed in the backing of the commodity of tea and salt. Another reason which has resonance in modern society is the acceptance of the certificate in tax payment thus losing its quasi-money status and becoming fiat currency instead. The effect that using certificates as payments for taxes later became rooted in chartalism and the Modern Monetary Theory (MMT) which was discussed in Chapter 2.

It was at this point when the decision to accept payments of taxes and therefore need no backing by any commodities effectively created the first fiat paper currency. This distinction was a crucial one as it was realised in practice there was no constraint on how much could be printed. The Songs didn't use this possibility for decades until Prime Minister Wang Anshi worked out that the printing of unbacked notes could be used for budgetary purposes and he did need this financial alchemy as his programmes were expensive, to say the least; he had a shrinking private sector to pay for it as his key source of revenue had been nationalised, interventions in the agricultural markets and taxes were replacing labour conscription. (Wang 1997) If this didn't cause enough problems the targeting of large landlords under Wang became outright seizure and wholesale redistribution to government lackeys and supporters under the Jia Sidao period (1260-1273) of the Song dynasty. (Adshead 2004) It is interesting to note that in Zimbabwe the policy of redistribution of land to government supporters coupled with mass money printing has led to not only hyperinflation but a drastic reduction in food production from an area that had previously been recognised as the breadbasket of Africa.

In the meantime Wang's costs were escalating in a seriously dramatic fashion; there was the increased expenditure with fighting wars on several fronts, (not cheap at all) in addition spending on public assistance and subsidies for the poor added to the draining of the coffers, so as his fiscal situation became dire, new copper coins that were being issued began to rise from 1.7 billion in 1064 to nearly 6 billion in 1081, this is in comparison to just 100 million during the Tang dynasty in 834 AD, as price inflation inevitably started to take off, the government response was between 1079-1085 was to order private copper mines to be closed down. (Ch'en 1965) This did have a limited amount of success in controlling inflation in the short run, but it was a total waste of time in the long run as the coins were replaced by the ever-increasing issuing of certificates. This continuous inflation and excessive printing of the certificates led the previously trustworthy government certificates, which were backed by commodities, to move from having a 10% premium in 1076, to a certificate that was now fiat having a 10% discount in just nine years. (Von Glahn 2005) A discount is essentially the opposite of a premium where people were paying 10% less than the face value of the certificate issued as confidence in it had weakened.

New technology in the form of woodblock printing exacerbated this problem as the certificates could now be printed more rapidly and thus in greater quantities, leading to the first recorded monetary crisis, which was attributed to the overprinting of paper currency. (Goetzmann and Koll 2005) an example of how bad it had become was to see the jiazzi certificate falling to just 10% of its face value; because of this a new imperial currency the qianyin was introduced, yet within one year this too had fallen to 10% of its face value, (Von Glahn 2005) showing real evidence of lack of faith in the currency and by any definition proper hyperinflation territory. Hyperinflation continued on its upward trajectory and continued as both military requirements, social spending and economic disruptions took its toll.

After the war was lost to the Jurchen and the Song court retreated to the South, the copper coins were devalued once again with the copper content being reduced from 65% to 54%, (Ch'en 1965) whilst the relentless printing of the currency continued from both the central and local governments. The central government seemed, at least temporarily to have learnt its lesson and maintained a conservative, stable issuance; the local authorities unfortunately had no such reservations and aggressively continued to print paper currency. (Von Glahn 2005) It may seem counterintuitive for the local authorities to keep printing but was actually quite logical as what was happening was the printing of the currency was being spent in other regions, thus exporting the inflation, whilst in the meantime keeping the seigniorage. (this is the difference of the face value of the currency; for example, the printing of a £10 note may cost £1 to produce once the cost of paper, ink, etc is taken into account, which means the seigniorage is £9) The problem with this is if a region A was exporting its inflation to another region B, that is all well and good for region A, the problem that will arise for region A is that region B will eventually try do the same thing and export its inflation to region A; this leaves both regions having inflationary pressures placed upon it.

With the rise of emperor Xiaozong in the early 1160s, the Southern Song returned to Wang's policy of money printing and war; it ramped up the annual note issue and finally ended the convertibility to commodities in 1168. From a base of 10 million Guan, (a guan was the equivalent of 1,000 cash coins) rising to 18 million in 1183, then 30 million in 1195, by 1207 it had reached 55 million, peaking at 140 million by 1234, (Von Glahn 2005) which was the last issuance before the Mongols seized the palace along with the money printing blocks. It also seems the Jurchen hadn't learnt the lessons of the currency printing folly as the Jīn dynasty imitated the Songs paper fiat currency and introduced their currency the 'Jiaochao'. These notes at first did not cause any inflation as they were being gradually expanded into the new regions of the empire, as always, this continued unchecked expansion of the money supply led to inflationary pressures and governments simply did not know when to stop. The point of saturation was reached in 1190 as the rising issuances led to bouts of inflation. By 1209 the price of rice had doubled against the price of 1200. (Goetzmann and Koll 2005) The serious inflation continued until the Mongol wars, which saw even greater currency printing due to the additional burden on the state's finances, which always accompanies any war. This led to a terminal and widespread discontent with peasant riots and defections to the invading Mongols by the rich and landowners, who by now had enough of being ripped off by the Wang-style policies and having their land and wealth arbitrarily seized by the government. (Adshead 2004) The Southern Song dynasty was only spared the ignominy of complete and utter collapse, with the occupation of the dynasty, followed by dissolution at the hands of the invading Mongols. (Schlichter 2011)

There we have it, the same dynasty collapsing twice, the first one under Wang Anshi to the Jurchen and the second under emperor Xiaozong to the Mongols. The question that needs to be asked is, was inflation to blame? We can compare the same question posed about the Roman empire and the same conclusion can be reached the answer is no not in itself, but it was certainly the catalyst for the collapse of both the Song empires; without inflation, it would be quite certain that either of the two collapses would have taken place the way it did. The timings of the conflicts with both the Jurchen and the Mongols were too close to each other to be seen as a coincidence. The Jurchen and Mongols had lived in peace side by side with the Songs for several centuries, yet despite having infinitely inferior resources and a massive disparity in the size of the armies, both conquered the Song within decades of each other. It can only be concluded that Wang-style policies that were implemented caused the Song's downfall. The wars that subsequently took place appeared to have been started as a knee-jerk reaction to conquer other lands to fill up the coffers of the treasury which had become emptied after the folly of spending more than it received in taxes, all be it for in part altruistic reasons to improve the welfare of the peasants. Once the free bonus of printing money was discovered, it became like a runaway train which has brake failure, it's impossible to stop until it crashes. The recklessness led to the neglect of tax revenues and the patching up of the deficits it was incurring by constantly increasing its currency printing. This 'print and spend' policy then finds it has two problems; Firstly, it allows the government to increase unchecked thus leading to constant finding of new ways of spending on welfare and secondly, it reduces the government's reliance on taxation as a method of putting checks and balances on excessive government spending. In essence, it insulates the government from the effects of its policies, allowing it to become entrenched in the 'bubble' thinking it creates for itself. It was this 'print and spend' policy that led to the loss of value of everything due to inflationary pressures which led to a weak army, peasants' revolts and the defection of the rich and landowners to the opposition which led to the decline and ultimately the demise of the Song. (St Onge 2017)

5. THE MIDDLE AGES

"There is a great deal of ruin in a nation" Adam Smith, who is generally regarded as the father of modern economics.

The Middle Ages are generally broken into three periods: The Early Middle Ages, The High Middle Ages and the Late Middle Ages. The Early Middle Ages is sometimes referred to as the Dark Ages, the period is generally thought to have begun with the fall of Rome in 476 AD and ended around the 11th Century. It encompasses the reigns of Charlemagne, (he is regarded as succeeding in reunifying the majority of Western Europe in 800 AD since the fall of the Roman Empire and became Emperor of what was later called The Holy Roman Empire) Alfred the Great, the Danish kings of England and the birth and rapid expansion of Islam in Northern Africa and Spain. Over these centuries Christianity also spread over Europe and the papacy evolved into a powerful political force.

The High Middle Ages is generally regarded as the period which typifies the Middle Ages the best. It is generally believed to have begun around the 11th Century and ended around the 14th Century. The period saw events such as the Norman Conquest of England in 1066, (around the same time the Chinese Song dynasty was ordering takeaways!!) the earlier Crusades and the Magna Carta. By the end of the 11th Century, nearly every corner of Europe had been Christianized, except for most of Spain, which was under Islamic rule. (It had been conquered in 711 and lasted until 1492) We also start to see what is sometimes referred to as the 'flowering' of medieval society, in main due to the rise of an intellectual renaissance in the 12th Century, with philosophers such as Peter Abelard and Thomas Aquinas, along with the establishment of great universities in Oxford, Cambridge, Paris and Bologna. This period also saw the meteoric rise of stone castle-building and the construction of some of the most magnificent cathedrals in Europe. Trade in luxury items as well as staples, flourished; a well-fed population was beginning to grow which saw Europe at the end of the 13th Century being at its economic and cultural height.

The Late Middle Ages is generally associated with the period which sees the transformation from the medieval world to the early modern one. It is considered to have started at the beginning of the 14th Century and ended around the 16th to 17th Century. This was a period of great upheaval with cataclysmic events in the 14th Century including the One Hundred Years' War, and the Black Death, but also great moves forward with the Italian Renaissance. The 15th Century saw the fall of Constantinople to the Ottoman Empire in 1453, the Moors being driven out of Spain, the Jews expelled and finding itself now a devout Catholic country, the invention of the Guttenberg printing press by goldsmith Johannes Gutenberg. The 16th Century saw the reformation of the Catholic church grow and although had many early advocates, it is regarded to have been caused by Martin Luther's publication of the ninety-five theses in 1517, leading to his eventual excommunication by Pope Leo X in 1521. The Italian Renaissance which had started in the 15th Century went into overdrive in the 16th Century and saw some of the greatest works of art ever created from artists such as Leonardo Di Vinci whose works dated late 15th to early 16th Century, Michelangelo, and Raphael. (Snell, 2021)

If we leave the Dark Ages period for the moment as effectively nothing was happening on the economic front except the start of one important event the Bullion Famine, we need to explore both the High and Late Middle Ages where we see the real development and birth of banking, the development of usuary, trade from the far east mainly China but India as well, leading to the explosion of renaissance Italy as a hub for trade between the far east and Europe, along with inflation taking hold in the whole of Europe after what became known as the Spanish Price Revolution.

With all the changes and advances happening in this period, what kickstarted the period which led to the banking revolution, the Renaissance and ultimately to the period of enlightenment which can be seen as the true birth of modern science and democracy? For this, we have to have a brief foray back to the Chinese empire again where the Mongol empire took over from the Song dynasty. They ruled over not only China but the Middle East, and all of Central Asia and began to dominate the Silk Road to the borders of Europe. The empire was also subdivided having Mongol rulers over areas such as Persia and China, with the Chinese division being known as the Yuan dynasty and lasted less than 100 years, (1271-1368) but the effect it had on Europe was immense. It was still interested in money printing despite seeing the flaws and the fate of the past two dynasties that went before it; they created a government-sponsored printing office and established centres for printing across China; in the late 13th/ early 14th Century, private printing businesses started to develop, printing everything from educational, literary, medical and calendars. The problem for the Yuan dynasty in their money printing endeavours, unlike the Jaazi which was backed by bronze coins, the Yuan issued a fiat currency called the Jiaochao, unbacked by any form of commodity, it was irredeemable, totally unconvertable. It was legal tender in all public payments for things such as taxes and fines which gave the currency a value in the marketplace.

If the printing of fiat currency wasn't enough to secure the fate of the Mongol empire, it added to the lethal mix of endless infighting amongst their leaders, (sound familiar!) an inept, incompetent, and corrupt government (sound familiar!) which overspent and overtaxed (sound familiar!) along with the customary floods and famines. (They cannot blame them for that, but not preparing for this eventuality does sound familiar!!) The last strategy which accelerated the dynasties' downfall was a relatively new phenomenon and affected Europe then and still does to this day. The Mongol rulers made superficial attempts to integrate into the Chinese population, in reality, they were seen as second-class citizens and they continued to maintain their separateness from the native population and utilised foreigners to staff government policy (Cartwright, 2019). Now this is the point where the connection with Europe gets interesting, one of these people used by Kublai Khan (grandson of Genghis Khan and third Mongol ruler) to do this work is Marco Polo. Mr Polo was an interesting character who, in 1300 published his book about his travels throughout China called quite aptly 'The Travels of Marco Polo.' Although many of the accounts of the book are disputed what does hold was a chapter in the book which caused shockwaves throughout Europe and was entitled 'How the Great Kaan, Causeth the Bark of Trees, Made into Something Like Paper, to Pass for Money All Over His Country.'

(In case you were wondering it was made from the bark of the Mulberry tree) The passage that caused people to scratch their heads in wonderment was: "All these pieces of paper are issued with as much solemnity and authority as if they were pure gold or silver... he shall find these pieces of paper current and shall be able to transact all sales and purchases of goods by means of them just as well as if they were coins of pure gold." With this innovation we can now usher in the era of banking, fractional reserve banking, central banking lending on a vast scale, the growth of Northern Italy as a major trading hub, the Medici's, the Fuggers, Renaissance Italy, the development of the arts and sciences, the formative beginnings of modern society as we see it today and yes along with all this the eventual and inevitable price inflation, culminating in the Spanish Price Revolution.

What is it that the development and use of paper money enabled these events to take place? The answer was the development of and the demand for credit, there was a boom in commercial property which was funded by this monetary expansion, wars between city-states led to a huge demand for government borrowing and an increase in the volume of coin, largely driven by the Spanish Price Revolution where we see the demand for deposit banking. There were three main developments within the financial institutions during the High and the Late Middle Ages which supported these three individual types of borrowing, and it is where we begin to see all the credit agents starting to become distinguishable before each was perceived very differently by society: the pawn brokers, money changers and deposit banks, with the last development being the Merchant banks. The pawnbroker had been in existence since Biblical times and were the equivalent of the medieval usurers. Usurers in this period were used to describe the charging interest on loans, no matter how low the interest was, in contrast to the modern-day definition, which suggests the excessive charging of interest, usually associated with payday lenders. The pawnbrokers as the usurers were seen as sinners because in the eyes of all the main religions being practised in Europe; Catholicism, Islam and Judaism because earning an income from simply charging interest and not physically having to work for it was seen as immoral, they were viewed as parasitical by conjuring wealth out of thin air somehow being able to rearrange wealth which already existed but distributing it a way that allows an unfair portion of it to themselves. Dante in his epic poem 'Inferno' puts Usurers in the seventh circle of hell. The seventh circle was made up of three rings of sinners, the first ring was for people who committed violence against their neighbour, the punishment being that the souls were forced to swim in a boiling steam of blood, the second ring was reserved for people who committed violence against themselves, people who committed suicide were transformed into thorny trees and ripped apart by Harpies- a creature that had the head of a woman and the body of a bird, perched on a suicide tree ready to tear and pick at the limbs and leaves of the tree, the third ring was for blasphemers, sodomites and usurers, who were condemned to a desert of blazing sand with a constant rain of fire; so as you can see being a usurer wasn't seen as a very noble profession.

We have one very important and crucial amendment in one of these religions which has affected the perception, ultimately leading to discrimination and persecution for centuries all the way to the present day; the religion being Judaism, and this is due to a passage in Deuteronomy, which is the fifth book of the Torah stating "You shall not charge interest on loans to your brother... You may charge a foreigner interest, but you may not charge your brother interest" Deut 23 19-20. This effectively allows the Jews to lend to other faiths but not to other Jews, it also means Jews can borrow from people of other faiths, just not from other Jews. The combination of it being illegal to lend money for usuary as a Christian along with the Jews's limited capability to lend money, meant the Jews had a long history of not only being established as moneylenders but dealing with all the unsavoury elements of finance that is generally resented by the vast populace, one example would be that the Jews in the Middle Ages acted as intermediaries by the nobility to collect taxes or rents from the peasants; this has led to resentment towards Jews, who were protected by the nobility, however periodically this protection would be withdrawn which would led to persecution and even death.

An infamous example of this in England was the 1190 massacre in York where a wave of antisemitic riots led to the death of the entire Jewish community totalling approximately 150 people; although the Jews were officially protected by King Richard I, they found themselves barricaded in a wooden keep in the royal castle. Antisemitic feelings were running high, with Christian fervour being stoked by the crusades, which not only directed aggression against the Muslims in the Holy Land but also the Jews across England, France, and Germany. Riots which had previously taken place in Norwich, Stamford and Lincoln finally reached York. The Jews in the Keep who feared treachery, locked out the royal constable, who in turn ordered the castle to be captured by force. Seeing no way out most Jews committed suicide rather than renounce their faith and become baptised, or suffer death at the hands of the mob, those that didn't commit suicide were either burnt to death in the Keep after the rioters set it on fire or murdered as they tried to get out.

The rioters had been egged on by members of the local gentry, who saw the riots as a way of wiping out the extensive debts that they owed to the Jewish moneylenders in the city. These men had borrowed heavily on the potential of securing lucrative royal appointments, and when they failed to materialise, they were unable to pay off their debts; after the massacre they even burnt the records of their debts, meaning they were absolved from payment to the king who would acquire the property and debts owed to the murdered Jews. (Jones et al, 2103)

How is it that despite all this persecution the Jews became very influential in money lending in Renaissance Italy? Quite simply it was because of more persecution they ended up in Italy; the Jews were expelled from Spain in 1492 along with the Muslims who were finally with the capture of Granada, the last Muslim enclave in Spain. The Jews found refuge in the Ottoman Empire, then with contacts they had in Constantinople, migrated to Venice. Venice was a natural point for migration as it had been trading with the Ottoman Empire; the first recorded date of several thousand Jewish migrants moving to Venice was 1509, a mere eighteen years after fleeing from Spain, they found themselves in Spain via Constantinople. Once in Venice, they were only allowed to live in certain ghettos, they were withheld certain rights and couldn't enter certain professions, this meant that money lending was one of the few professions they could feasibly enter. Even when they entered this profession the discrimination continued, being forced to wear red hats to make sure they were easily identified, they were forced to pay the Venetian government a fee as well as forcing them to loan money to the state, in essence for protection, (all this is very reminiscent of what the Jews were forced to endure in Nazi Germany) and just to add to their unpopularity they were charging an interest rate of between 15% and 25%, although interest rates of this premium were not uncommon throughout most of this period, with even records from 3,000 years previous in around 1,800 BC, Hammurabi, a king of the first dynasty of ancient Babylonia, giving his people the earliest formal code of laws, with some of the chief provisions for this code regulating the relationship between creditor and debtor. It allowed for the maximum interest rate set at 33.5% per annum for loans of grain, repayable in kind and an interest rate of no more than 20% per annum for loans of silver by weight. Included in this all loans had to have a written contract which was witnessed by government officials, and should the debtor try and extract a higher interest rate by either subterfuge or force, then the principle of the debt was cancelled. Land and movables could be pledged as security for a debt along with a person of the creditor including his wife, concubine, children, or slaves, but just to make things a bit more palatable, this personal debt of slavery was limited to three years. (Homer et al, 1996) The money lenders were seen as the lowest of the low, however, the other two classes of effective money lenders were the deposit banks, which incorporated money changers; the modern-day equivalent would be foreign exchange traders and the Merchant banks.

A question that needs to be asked is why a boom in the development of both deposit banks and Merchant banks was there who found a way to develop credit. The answer can be found starting in the Dark Ages and continuing throughout the Middle Ages. The phenomena lasted until the Spanish Price Revolution with the discovery of vast quantities of gold and silver in the Americas; the shortage of bullion became known as the 'Great Bullion Famine' and propelled both these new forms of banks with one added ingredient, the bills of exchange.

The financial system really is just a part of the system that greases the wheels to allow for economic transactions and more specifically, the financial system facilitates the lending, and the payments and allows for the trade in risk-taking. Lending as previously discussed via the money lenders is often seen as the main act, yet the financial system in allowing for the facilitation of the payments of trade, as well as allowing for risk to play its part in the trade, is equally essential. (Kohn, 1999, 99-02)

Before 1600, because of the poor quality of the coinage due to debasement and clipping, along with the inadequate quantity of coins leading to the 'Great Bullion Famine', the payments function became particularly important. As commerce began to expand in the High to late Middle Ages, the need to develop an adequate means of payment saw a great deal of financial innovation, in particular the emergence of the deposit banks and the bills of exchange. The deterioration of the coinage began in the Dark Ages after the fall of the Roman Empire. By default, mining was taken over by private goldsmiths and silversmiths who had neither the incentive nor interest in maintaining the quality of the coinage, in conjunction with this monetary deterioration, invasion and raids by; amongst others the Vikings, Moslems and Magyars, brought long-distance trade to a halt, leading the economy to fragment into largely self-sufficient areas, with this leading to widespread demonetization. Money is an essential medium of exchange amongst strangers, there is much less necessity for it within a small, closed community. The collapse of long-distance trade also led to the ending of the mining for silver as the bullion had little direct use in this period. The inevitable increase in the scarcity of the bullion raised the value of the remaining coins, which in turn led to their hoarding, rather than being spent. (Gresham's law at play again) In the 10th Century, the invasions began to abate, leading to the revival of long-distance trade, which in turn led to a renewed need for money. This was met from new sources of silver, in particular from Goslar in Saxony. By the 12th Century, the re-use of money had spread from the towns and cities to the countryside as feudal landlords increasingly needed money to pay for trade and to pay for labour.

To add to the confusion, if the local coins were of a particularly poor quality, as it happened to be in Flanders, the better-quality foreign coins such as Sterlings, from England or Florins from Florence, would be imported and then circulated alongside the local coins. The problem in the early part of the Middle Ages was silver was so scarce and even the smallest individual coin was too valuable to be of much use for small payments, in England during the 12th Century the average daily wage of a domestic servant was about a penny, which could buy a quarter of a sheep, however, this coin would be of no use if you wanted to buy a pound of mutton as there were no coins that were small enough to give change. It started to become common practice to set the price of the loaf of bread at the value of the smallest coin 'The Penny Loaf' as there was no coin smaller than the penny it was impossible to adjust the price of the loaf, if and when the price of wheat fluctuated, what happened instead is they varied the size of the loaf, therefore a rise in the price of wheat meant a smaller loaf. An example of this was during the famine of 1329, the standard 'quattrino loaf' in Florence shrank from a pound in weight to a meagre 6 ounces and for those too young to remember imperial metric 1Ib was equal to 16oz, therefore the had shrunk by 62.5% in size. (Remember earlier we talked about shrinkflation, here it is in action in the 12th Century!!)

As silver production started to increase going into the 14th Century, we see record silver being transported to England to be struck as English sterling. In 1305 John de Everdon, England's warden of the exchange reported that "Merchants were bringing silver there in great quantities" to the extent that the mint was running six weeks behind. The money supply surged between 1305-1310 causing the humblest commodity price to rise at an alarming rate. Eggs in 1305 which cost 4 pence per hundred rose to above 6 pence in 1306, a 50% per cent rise in 1 year, whilst laying hens had doubled from 1 penny to more than 2 pence. (Mate, 2008) Despite the increase in silver production, the continuing currency chaos was a major impediment to any expansion in trade or commerce as throughout that period there was still a chronic shortage of money circulating within the European economy, which was leading to the paralysis of trade. At the height of the 'Bullion Famine of the 15th Century coins had become so scarce that "The economy of Europe ground to a halt at every level, from the humblest purchases of bundles of leeks, up to the great merchants, whose galleys had to row away with goods unsold." (Spufford, 1988) The problem we had in the Middle Ages was the limited variety of different denominations and values of money.

Europe had been a major producer of silver but had little gold of its own, so before the discovery of gold in the New World (the Americas) by the Spanish, most gold came from West Africa via, either the Sahara Desert or the Maghreb, which consisted of North-West Africa, North Africa and the Arab world including regions such as Algeria and Libya, Morocco, Tunisia as well as Egypt. With the disruption of trade in the Dark Ages, gold became increasingly scarce in Europe and as a result ceased to be used as money. In a parallel world, Byzantium along with the Muslim world was cut off from the supply of European silver, which had become their only source as the silver from Central Asia had been lost in the 10th Century to both the Turkish and Mongol invaders; this scarcity led to the minting and usage of gold coins only.

With the Crusades came the resumption of trade in the Mediterranean, silver once again flowed South, whilst gold flowed North. During the 14th Century, bar silver had largely been replaced in international trade and commerce by the usage of gold coins with the Italian merchants becoming increasingly active, not only in trade with the Mediterranean but with the Muslims and Byzantium, leading ultimately to the Italian Renaissance. In the 13th Century, due to the continued debasement of the Muslim Gold Dinar and the Byzantium Gold Hyperpyron, intra-Mediterranean trade was threatened, leading the Italians to respond by minting their gold coins, the 'Genovino' in 1252 and the Venetian 'Ducat' in 1284. These coins were initially used in the Mediterranean, but their use gradually but surely spread Northwards. Gold increasingly displaced bar silver for large payments as the increasing supply, leading to the inevitable fall in value in the 13th and 14th Century, meant increasingly large quantities were needed for payments; when Edward 1st paid a subsidy to his allies in the Low Countries, it took 17 ships to carry the 120 tonnes of silver. By the 1320's when the price of silver in ratio to gold reached its peak of 14:1, (which is an accurate ratio as it is estimated there is approximately 15 times more silver on the planet than gold) the discovery of gold in Hungary saw this increase in supply in Europe and Northern European countries begin to strike gold coins of their own, however even this caused problems as can be seen with the report of his management in 1362, the bookkeeper of the papal treasury noted he had received 15,654 Florins, 1,397 Leopards, 299 Ecus, 103 sheep, 5 Royals.... Of the Florins 4,223 were Chamber Florins, 3,869 Sentence Florins, 7,438 heavy Florins, 59 Florins of lesser weight, 6 Cambrai Florins and so it went on. (Favier, 1998) Despite the problems of having so many forms of coinage, by the end of the 14th Century, Europe had switched from a purely silver-based economy to a bi-metallic continent with gold being seen as the most valuable. (Kohn, 99-02).

The fundamental principles involved in the price or value of any good or service is the supply and demand of the good or service, this is also applicable to the value of gold and silver, this is most notable in the Middle Ages, with supply being increased by new production output, was counteracted as new sources of the metals were discovered, whilst old ones ran out. Output also depended on technology, with better technological advances made production and output increase, along with the ability to extract silver from both new sources and new types of ore. The wear and tear in circulation along with losses due to shipwrecks and lost hoards, coupled with the wastage in the processing of coining and recoining led to an estimated total loss of as much as 1% per annum. (Patterson, 1972).

It is important to note that the 'Bullion Famine' over the three periods of the Middle Ages was punctuated with peaks and troughs, which itself could be divided into three periods of high output along with two periods of decline. The first period of high output was from 960-1060 AD where Saxon silver, especially from the Golsar region, contributed to the recovery of European trade and its re-monetization. In the 11th Century, the money suddenly ran out, resulting in a subsequent shortage, which was made even worse with the outflow of silver due to the Crusades, leading to both the deterioration of the coinage and trade then slumping. The 12th and 13th centuries saw a series of silver discoveries across Europe, as well as gold in Serbia and Hungary; the consequent recovery of trade contributed to the resurgence and what became known as the 'Long Thirteenth Century.' The 'Long Thirteenth Century' was a period of not only growth in trade but a period in which, the monasteries in particular created networks of shared cultures, ranging from theology to new music and sermons, (Bisgaard, 2014) effectively trying to both spiritually and culturally create a more forward, progressive thinking society, it was essentially the forerunner to the period of 'Enlightenment' which took place in the 17th and 18th Century. Throughout this period great building projects were taking place and by 1224 the Cathedral of Chartres in France made the town the capital of Europe's richest province, with even Rome calling it the 'Greta Diocese'. In the 12th

and 13th centuries, France constructed more than 80 new cathedrals,500 Abbeys, and 10,000 Parish churches, with the building programme consuming more stone than the pyramids of Egypt and more labour than the roads of Rome. (Braudel, 1984)

The 'money famine' of peaks and troughs saw a long wave of price rises that appeared to be a flutter in the markets and fairs across Europe, with prices becoming slightly higher in goods such as firewood and food. (Essentially commodities) The money changers (Jews) were getting more for their services, thus setting themselves up for additional waves of persecution as resentment grew, whilst labourers seeking employment noticed wages were lagging behind the cost of living. In Sienna in 1298 following the collapse of its greatest bank The Gran Travola of the Bounsignori, which amongst its clients were great merchants, cities, nobles, kings and even the pope and was a modern-day equivalent of a world bank, with agents throughout Europe and the Mediterranean basin, led to an ensuing banking panic which saw many lesser enterprises follow a similar fate. The economy of Sienna didn't recover from this disaster and work on the great cathedral remains unfinished to this day, the workers downed tools in the 14th Century and the city's magnificent central square is frozen in time. (Bowsky, 1970) By modern standards the price rises grew slowly at first, which was primarily due to a lack of specie, thus not enabling any form of velocity to take place. With an estimated secular rise in the price of goods between 1225 and 1345, being no more than a rate of 0.5 per cent per annum. (Posta 1973) In 1224 price rises had barely begun yet once it started would develop into a catastrophe that scarcely anything survived from that era, except the stunning cathedral in Chartes.

We also begin to see an increase in demographic and urban growth along with markets, guilds and fairs in this period, along with the glaring intellectual achievements of St Thomas of Aquinas, where he has influenced modern Western thinking in areas including ethics, natural law (a system of law based on close observation of human nature, where all people have inherent rights conferred upon them not by acts of legislation but by God), metaphysics (a branch of philosophy that studies the fundamental nature of reality), epistemology, (the theory of knowledge itself) political theory, psychology and economics. This is all set against a backdrop of at least five crusades against the Muslim world throughout that Century, these being.

4th Crusade (1202-1204)

5TH Crusade (1217-1221)

6th Crusade (1228-1229)

7th Crusade (1248-1254)

8th Crusade (1270-1270)

In addition to these main crusades, smaller crusades were waged against dissident Christian sects within Europe, such as the Albigensian Crusade,

(1209-29) that saw the nobility of Catholic Northern France, pitted against the Southern part where the Cathar dualist religious movement was branded heretical by the Roman Catholic church. (The dualist believed that there were two separate entities; good and evil which were equally powerful; in Christian terms, God represented the good, Satan the evil, however the Roman Catholics believed that although Satan had some power, he was no equal to God) These disputes were to later become the forerunner of the Protestant movement in particular in Northern Europe, but it does leave the question as to how many people had to die over essentially the percentage of power God had over Satan.

The growth in the supply of silver led to the price of goods steadily rising, and the increase in the price of gold which mainly originated in Africa, along with the discoveries in Serbia and Hungary began to see the facilitation of minting gold coins in Europe in 1252. The lack of discoveries after the 1320s, coupled with the output of existing mines dwindling saw the scarcity of silver start to increase from the 1360s to the 1460s, gold did remain in reasonably plentiful supply until it too started to dwindle and become scarce by the 1450's, this combined scarcity of bullion resulted in the fall of the price of goods as trade suffered. (Kohn, 99-02) The consequence of the 'Bullion Famine' allowed for the promotion of widespread prospecting and major technological progress, which brought the famine to an abrupt end around the mid-1460s. The Bullion Famine also led to the voyages of discovery, from explorers such as Vasco De Gama and Christopher Columbus; dating from around the late 15th Century this period became known as the 'Age of Discovery'. The Portuguese navigators had a major impact in the long run, where the opening up of new routes to the East around the Southern tip of Africa, broke the Venetian monopoly of trade between Europe and the East. Vasco Da Gama, whose initial voyage to India via the Cape of Good Hope was the first maritime link of Europe to Asia. Christopher Columbus in 1492 was sponsored for four voyages by King Ferdinand and Queen Isabella after they had finally defeated the Moors in the same year. The Spanish encountered three major civilizations; the Incas in what is now modern-day Peru, along with the Mayans and Aztecs in present-day Mexico and Central America. They were amazed by the immense wealth of gold and silver, along with complex cities rivalling and even surpassing those of Europe, along with amazing artistic and scientific achievements. The Spanish were driven by the 3 G's- Gold, Glory, and the Gospel. This discovery of gold meant by the early 17th Century the prodigious output and low costs actually drove most European silver mints out of business. The vast increase of bullion did help the revival of trade, however along with an increase in the price of goods and services (Hamilton, 1952)

These discoveries led to the Spanish Price Revolution which initially made Spain a world-dominant empire and superpower, eventually ruined it and left it an impoverished state, with little industry and a very low standard of living for the majority of its population; in modern terms, it suffered what is known as the 'Paradox of Plenty', the 'Natural Resource Curse' or the 'Dutch Disease' something that modern economies will come to suffer in the 20th and 21st Centuries. All three phrases mean essentially the same thing and refer to the paradox that a country or region with an abundance of natural resources, especially commodities such as minerals or fuels, tends to have worse economic growth and development outcomes than countries with fewer natural resources. There are several different reasons for this but in essence, the pattern is an economy gets lazy and complacent, with resources shifting towards working in these industries whilst leaving other industries to stagnate, decline and eventually collapse altogether. The term 'Dutch Disease' was coined in 1977 by the magazine The Economist to describe the decline of the manufacturing sector in the Netherlands after the large discovery of the Groningen natural gas field in 1959. (Economist, 1977)

The discovery of gold and silver by Spanish explorers in the 16th Century has been the traditional explanation as to the reason inflation was abundant in Europe. We can see in the table below the rates of inflation throughout this period.

It was observed that inflation was occurring throughout Europe over this period with Bernholz and Kruger (2007) arguing that price increases in the 16th Century were 3 to 4 times higher than at the beginning. As seen in the table below the rates of inflation throughout this period, with Fisher (1989) shows some figures below.

COMPOUND ANNUAL GROWTH RATES

YEAR 1525-1618

ENGLAND 1.51%

FRANCE 1.64%

SPAIN 1.19%

GERMANY 1.20%

AUSTRIA 1.31%

Two things appear to jump out with these figures, firstly they may seem trivial amounts compared to modern-day rates of inflation, but for societies that had not seen any price rises for literally centuries due to the Black Death was enough to cause serious food shortages and riots. Other factors in the rise in inflation were the end of the plague and the significant rise in the European population between 1460-1620 meant there were now more people to feed, clothe and house; producers were unable to meet rising food demands as marginal costs were increasing as less fertile lands were being used, resulting in yields per capita falling, this led to shortages of staple foodstuffs not just in Spain but throughout Europe, meaning people were living in a perpetual state of hunger. (Wernham, 1968)

Secondly, an additional consequence for Spain was as trade developed in the 1600s, it maintained its feudal social structure remained unchanged with the landed aristocracy holding onto the balance of power and most Spaniards aligned themselves to the values of the aristocracy, believing that business was only fit of foreigners, Arabs, and Jews. It was predominantly these values that led to Spain using overseas workers for most jobs as the Spaniards both rich and poor felt any work other than that of the land was beneath them. To compound matters Spain's nobility was about 10% of the population, yet it was the poor that the government taxed the most heavily, firstly leading to greater inequality and secondly, the work done in collecting the harvest being essentially done by French workers, who ultimately took their pay back to France leaving Spain collecting even less taxes. (Smitha, 2015) Another effect of this was that it was now exporting its inflation around Europe as can be seen in the figures above.

Within this period, precious metals from the new world resulted in an increase in the supply of money and thus higher prices, leading us to the first analysis of the quantity theory of money which is attributed to Nicolas Copernicus. Copernicus was born in 1473 in Royal Prussia, which is now Poland and he became the first person to set forth clearly "The Quantity Theory of Money" which stated that prices vary directly with the supply of money in the society, doing all this before having the benefit of seeing the inflationary influx on Europe, of gold and silver from the New World, this theory was also adapted and used by many economists but most famously in recent times by Irving Fischer. Copernicus was primarily a scholar of Astronomy, Astrology and Mathematics; he was more famous for developing the theory that the planets have the sun as a fixed point and the earth is a planet orbits around the sun, this representation is known as helio-centric. (from the Greek Helios meaning sun) This theory had important consequences for the later thinkers of the Scientific Revolution, influencing major figures such as Galileo, Kepler, Descartes and Newton, ultimately leading to the period of Enlightenment, it also had a profound effect on the Roman Catholic church, as in the Bible it clearly stated that God made the earth at the centre of the Universe and everything else revolved around it; the problem for the Church was the Bible was everything and couldn't be challenged as it was the Word of God, yet if it was wrong about the earth being the centre of the Universe, then what else could be wrong in the book? Ultimately any edict from the Pope could be challenged, meaning the Papacy could lose the stranglehold on power that it had. The contribution Copernicus made to economics cannot be understated as it was too helped usher in the great economic thinkers in the period of the Enlightenment such as Adam Smith, David Hume, John Locke, and Jeremey Bentham who advocated the concept of utilitarianism (a theory that advocates for the maximum happiness and wellbeing for all individuals) but more profoundly realised the inefficiency of mercantilism, (the mercantilist system was a way of managing the economy of a country through regulation if necessary, of foreign trade to establish a positive balance of trade) and thus helping to champion the era of the classic gold standard and modern capitalism.

Spain was about to learn the lesson of when the 'Paradox of Plenty' and the 'Quantity Theory of Money' clash. By 1564 despite the discovery of this gold and silver, the Spanish debt was 23 million Ducats, in 1574 it rose to 35 million Ducats which meant that the interest alone consumed all payments of taxes, so in 1575 all payments were stopped where they tried to negotiate the lowering of interest rates. Since most of the great merchant banks in Europe were lending to the Spanish crown, many were pushed to the brink of bankruptcy and beyond, this led to the reorganisation of the debt with the interest rate being lowered. Phillip II appeared not to learn the lesson from his father and exacerbated the situation further with a war in the Netherlands and hostilities against England, leading to the destruction of the Spanish Armada; this led to the deterioration in the countries' financial woes with an estimated debt of 100 million Ducats by 1598. The final nail in the coffin for Spain was the creation of the Vellon in 1599 which was a coin made purely from copper, devoid of any silver whatsoever, the economy continued to collapse until finally in 1660, a new silver coin the Modena was minted, putting a halt to the sliding economy. (Gaettens 2010)

One problem of the Spanish Crown, government and people faced was although only 26% of the American treasure went directly to the Spanish Crown, the money that should have been going to private parties was effectively sequestered, borrowed and taxed, with much of the treasure they received from private individuals, funding the Crowns never-ending appetite for war. It is estimated that Spain spent approximately 70% of its public revenue on war (Weber 1927), an example Spain fought 135 wars, battles and sieges in the eighty-year war between 1568-1648, and this was by no means exhaustive. The impact of these wars can be seen in 1557 when the Spanish Crown declared the first of a series of bankruptcies. In 1599 yet more crushing debts forced King Phillip II to secure any income at all to order the production of the Vellon coin, this was pure copper and devoid of any silver content, replacing all gold and silver specie and accounting for approximately 92% of the money spent by the 1650's. (Hamilton, 1943)

The effect of the Vellon coinage led to civil unrest from numerous mutinies of the Spanish armies in the Netherlands who required payment in bullion which was not forthcoming, as well as riots due to food shortages and price rises. A vicious circle ensued where international financiers were called to loan vast sums of money, with the Crown needing to pay in bullion and eventually mortgaging up to seven years of revenues. Payments became impossible to make leading yet again to numerous rounds of bankruptcies and defaults. (Parker, 1970) An additional consequence would be Gresham's Law, in this example it seems to be reasonable to assume that once the Vellon was introduced people would hoard their gold and silver, thus reducing the amount in circulation.

Spain was kept afloat by money lent via the Republic of Genoa who risked the majority of its wealth in the Spanish monarchy. Genoa merchants settled and married Spanish nobility meaning Genoa flourished as long as the Americans were sending gold and silver to the *consulado de mercanderes*. (The merchant guild of Seville which had the monopoly rights on goods shipped to and from the Americas) As the gold and silver were eventually exhausted and Spain fell into decline in the 17th Century, the Genoa houses also suffered due to the continual defaults of Spain meaning the loans could no longer be provided to give the financial support Spain continually required.

The common theme of debasement and shortage of the coin, (until the Spanish discovery of gold and silver in the New World) war, Inflation, famine, and plagues, what was the thread that enabled trade to continue internally within a nation but internationally as well? Quite simply commerce adapted to these problems by relying on cash as little as possible, with commerce finding various means to economise on the actual use of coins for conducting business transactions. The overwhelming majority of trade at every level was conducted by using credit, to quote Lopez (1976) "Unstinting Credit was the Great Lubricant of the Commercial Revolution." The extension of credit and the assignments of debts (assignment of debt is debts being passed between various parties, for example, if a merchant owed 200 florins to a supplier and was owed 150 florins by a customer, they could assign the customer debt of 150 florins in part payment to the supplier) was only practical amongst people who know each other well, usually within a local community, whether a community of merchants or a small village, each knows the others credit, with continuing and repeated transactions giving each the incentive to honour their debts. When trade is extended to strangers, the creditor is usually unknown, reducing the incentive, if any at all to act in an honourable manner. The payment in coins which has previously been discussed, was difficult due to a range of problems but a major problem being the quantity needed to complete large transactions; the solution to this problem was the formation of deposit banks and the bills of exchange. (Kohn, 99-02, 99-03).

The term bank originates from the word 'Banca', which was a bench used to exchange currency which was set up in various city-states. The money changers had a higher social standing than the pawnbrokers as they made their money from manually exchanging currency and were not involved in any form of credit or charging interest; their function as a business was effectively to convert one currency to another and for that service charging a legitimate fee. Due to the terrible state of the coinage in the medieval period, its scarcity inspired the development in finding an alternative means of payment. The most prominent way of to do this was via 'payment in bank' where rather than handing over coins for goods, a payer could transfer a credit on the books of their bank, to the credit account of the payee, welcome to the world of modern banking. The ability for this system to function was down to the development of one of the simplest, yet most cost-effective systems in accounting, yet has transformed society to what it is today, the double-entry book-keeping system. The double-entry system was purely a way of recording business transactions, where for every entry into an account, there needs to be a corresponding and opposite entry into a different account. Although the early development of bookkeeping can be traced back to the ancient Mesopotamian Empire and the earliest concept of double entry bookkeeping has been recorded in the ancient Roman and Byzantium Empires, its modern format is attributed to the Italian merchants of the 13th and 14th Centuries. The first known documentation of the double-entry bookkeeping system was recorded in 1494 by Luca Pacioli, widely known as 'The Father of Accounting' due to his book 'Particularis De Computis Et Scripturis' which translated means 'The Rules of Double-Entry Bookkeeping.' Pacoli was a famous mathematician who became great friends with Leonardo da Vinci, who actually illustrated his book, the two spoke and debated quite regularly on the topic of mathematics and it is interesting to speculate he may have been involved in the development of the book, although there is no evidence of him doing so, it was well within his capabilities. The main purpose of the double-entry system is to ensure that a company's accounts remain balanced and can be therefore used to gain an accurate insight into the financial health of its financial position to both the management and external shareholders such as potential investors, current shareholders, suppliers along with any regulatory bodies. The equation is quite simply written as ASSETS = LIABILITIES + SHAREHOLDER EQUITY. In order to achieve the balance, accounts use the concept of debits and credits to record transactions, where a debit entry in one account must be equal to a credit entry in another account to keep the equation balanced. It is this system that was developed in the 13th to 15th Century that allowed for the transaction of goods in a time of the bullion famine, it also has given birth to modern societies' banking system to function.

The majority of money changers were established in Northern Italy in Florence, Lucca, Genoa and Venice, due to the geographical significance of trade with the Far East and Northern Europe, however, other centres did open up in the rest of Italy in cities such as Rome as well as other European cities such as Barcelona, Bruges, Champagne and Augsburg, the home of the Fuggers who are regarded as the richest family in history. The money changers handled coins and bullion in large quantities and, as a result, had facilities which enabled secure enough storage, they weren't, however, the only trade which performed the service of a bank, other professions such as goldsmiths, silversmiths, innkeepers, various religious establishments and certain government offices also offered the service, money changers were different from these other providers in one crucial area which transformed them into deposit banks were helping their customers to transfer payment 'title' to coins they had deposited with them, instead of paying with actual coinage. (Kohn, 99-03)

What deposit banks could be seen as is a place where local deposits and payments could be made and that it improved the efficiency of payment in coin, however another way of looking at their function is a system which uses debt as a way of making payments. Commercial transactions were rarely paid for on the spot in cash transactions, they almost always involved credit and deferred payment of some sort, which is no different to what occurs in modern society. Due to the scarcity of cash and the inconvenience of its use, it was common to settle debts, not by the use of coins or bullion but by assigning the creditor a debt owed to the debtor via the use of a third party. This system could only function effectively if the third party was known to the creditor and could be trusted. In the major commercial trading centres the trade would on the whole occur between strangers, this meant that trade could effectively only occur between these two people if the third party was involved, and both could trust that third party. The deposit banks became that trusted third party. (Kohn, 99-01, 99-02) Another advantage of the ability to assign debts meant there was a greater opportunity to enable the exchanging of one debt with another and as bank deposits happen to be a useful means of settlement, depositors were happy to keep cash in the bank rather than convert them immediately. The usefulness of deposit transfer as a way of making payments was further achieved by the willingness of the deposit banks to grant an overdraft facility. Credit, then as now is a vital lubricant which is necessary when making any payment settlements as it reduces the fear of the participants in the trade to meet their own obligations due to delays in payments which are owed to them; the overdraft facility which now became available enabled both the merchants and the traders to manage their liquidity with much smaller reserves than would otherwise would have been required, (Usher, 1934) this is where we can see the development of fractional reserve banking. Fractional reserve banking refers to the amount of reserves a bank keeps in ratio to its total deposits, for example if a bank has £100 million in assets and is required to hold 10% of those assets should its customers wish to draw their cash out for any reason, this leaves them requiring to hold £10 million and the ability to lend £90 million, the real risk is that if more than 10% of the money is required at one time then the banks have a real problem, as discussed in Chapter 1 this could then lead to a run on the bank, loss of trust and confidence, potentially leading to a collapse of the economy.

The growth of merchant banks as opposed to deposit banks grew from the fact that all merchants were involved in finance in one guise or another; they were either givers of credit, receivers of credit or as was usually the case, both. Credit sales were an intrinsic part of their commerce, so managing their finances was a large part of what they did, where to borrow, where and to whom to extend credit and how to ensure these obligations were to be met. For most of the merchants, finance was important but their main raison d'etre was still commerce; a few became financiers in their own right, this being the birth of the merchant bankers. They entered finance through remittance and transferring funds from place to place and in the process creating liquidity via the use of bills of exchange. (Kohn, 99-05) Bills of exchange developed from the 12th Century instrument of remittance 'Instrumentum ex Causa Cambii' or the cambium contract, which was a promise to pay, typically on a promissory note, drawn up formally by a notary where one merchant acknowledged the receipt from another of payment in local currency and promised to pay that person at a specific future time and distant place, in the currency of that place. The parties or agents were both required to appear at that place of payment for the transaction to be complete. (Blomquist, 1990) As business practices began to develop the 'Cambium Contract' was replaced by the bills of exchange and the letter obligatory, both serving different types of merchants.

The bill of exchange, unlike the 'Cambium Contract' wasn't a notarial deed only an informal letter of the transaction consisting of the amount outstanding and the date of payment. The advantage was the lowering of costs and the increased speed of transactions; the disadvantage was the bill of exchange was unenforceable in a civil court so instead had to rely on special merchants' courts for enforcement, to add some assurance to it, the letter usually began 'Al Nome di Dio' translated to 'In the Name of God' making default on the letter a blasphemous crime which could lead to excommunication. (People eventually found ways of getting around this by buying indulgences which netted the Catholic church a healthy profit to boot, a win/win except for the poor merchant who didn't get his goods or money!!) Its legal standing was established by being written in the hand of the taker, the taker on the bill of exchange was usually an international trading company, predominantly Italian that had branches in several cities around Europe on which it could draw. Only the branch manager or assistant manager had the authority to make out bills of exchange, it also required several specimens of their handwriting to be sent to all correspondents. The use of the bills of exchange and its reliance on the need for a physical presence led to the development of merchant banks. In addition, a system called 'Cedule Obligatoire' or 'Letter Obligatory' developed in smaller trading areas where the large merchant banks didn't have a presence. It was similar to the cambium as a promise, rather than an order to pay, however like the bill of exchange it was an informal merchants' document written in the hand of the taker and not a legally drawn-up letter. By the 14th Century, it was a common instrument for credit in England, France and the low countries, by the 15th Century had spread to Spain, with it playing an important role in the great merchant city of Antwerp by the 16th Century. (Bayer-Xambeau et al, 1994) The letter even became an instrument of consumer credit in the early 16th century in the Netherlands, when retailers used it to extend credit to their trusted customers (Van Der Wee, 1993) with the benefit of selling more of their products, we can see this as the medieval form of leverage. Leverage is simply the use of debt (borrowed capital) to use that debt to undertake an investment, business project or as the above example get more goods to sell to increase the profit ratio; the reason is to attempt to multiply the potential returns, in case of the merchants' example, they would use borrowed money to buy additional goods with a view to selling it, return the initial credit loan and make additional profit, the problem would come if the merchant couldn't sell the additional goods and didn't have the capital to pay of the credit owed. In modern trading on the stock exchange, an example would be an investor who has £1 million and wants to buy shares they believe are going to rise dramatically, will use that £1 million as collateral to borrow £10 million to buy additional shares, the debt-to-equity ratio is, therefore, 10:1; if the shares are initially worth £1 and double to £2 the investor has doubled his initial stake of £1 million, but also made an additional £10 million from the borrowed £10 million, (less any charges) this is all well and good as long as the shares rise if they fell to half that to £0.50 they would lose half their initial £1 million, but also an additional £5 million from the loss of the £10 million borrowed.

Merchant banks varied in size with some being enormous, banks such as the Bardi, Peruzzi and Acciauoli in the 14th Century and the Fuggers in the 16th Century. The Peruzzi had fifteen branches across Western Europe and the Levant. The most famous of these banks of this era are the Medicis of the 15th century, yet in terms of actual size were dwarfed in comparison to other similar institutions. They were seen in this period 'as first amongst equals' of the approximately 140 Florentine banks that operated in Lyon at the time. (Braudel, 1982) There are several reasons that merchant banks became so large and required an international presence; the first and crucial was to take part in the exchange process it had to operate in at least two places but preferably more, lending also required an international presence as the least expensive source of funds may be in one area, but the purchasing opportunity may be in another. Local offices also helped instil confidence in the banks' creditors and was also easier to keep an eye on the debtors. Lending to governments, then as now was based on trust and the relationships that are developed.

In their lending, merchant banks relied on two sources of funds; their own capital and the funds they borrowed from others which was then lent out at higher interest rates than it borrowed against. Most of their lending was via borrowing, they were financial intermediaries who borrowed in their own name and then proceeded to lend it out to their customers who were not only other merchants, but churchmen and other nobles. Usuary laws are also being chipped away at and finally come to head with the anti-usuary laws are repealed in Protestant Europe, starting in 1517 when Martin Luther posted his 95 theses in Germany; Catholic Europe liberalised when Thomas De Vio, Cardinal Cajetan, the leading theologian of his day and a favourite of the Pope and defender of the church against Martin Luther, changed its definition to excessive interest and this gave the church wiggle room, although technically to this day usuary is still sinful.

Although there were many sources of profits, a steady and stable source of income for the banks came from remittance in the financial exchange business, the big profits lay in trading and the use of arbitrage (simply taking advantage of differences in prices in two or more markets as well as trying to anticipate fluctuations in the exchange rates. (de Roover, 1949) Interest rate arbitrage was also another source of income stream to the merchant banks and although not risk-free any losses could easily be absorbed. The ability to provide both finance and good information by having a presence in many different marketplaces meant the merchant bankers were in a position to 'buy low and sell high' with the resources available to them they could readily exploit opportunities when they arose. "He could easily shift his capital from investment in bills to investment in trade" (de Roover, 1949) What they have effectively created is liquidity and the ability to exchange a bill of exchange for goods and payment easily. Liquidity is a vital component in lubricating the wheels of industry and commerce as without it, trade would essentially cease, an experience which almost befell the world in the great financial crash of 2008. The ability to provide both this finance and liquidity was a huge advantage in trade, especially in commodities such as grain, precious metals and wool which were the most profitable trade to be involved in, however, these commodities were often controlled by the crown and to obtain access to these commodities it was necessary to provide the crown with credit.

The ability of various sovereign and government states to control the most profitable commodities played a crucial role in merchant banks bringing these sovereign borrowers into the international money market, an alliance which became very unfortunate for many, as their involvement led to the downfall and bankruptcy of many as default was a regular occurrence. (Kohn, 99-05).

Despite the obvious pitfalls of default by a government or sovereign meaning the only way to get your money back would be to invade it, the main reason for lending was if it worked out, it was enormously profitable, the potential reward would justify the risk, the lending also came along with favours that the government or monarch bestowed upon them would include tax loopholes, commercial concessions, and monopolies. "There are no known examples of large-scale continuous financing of monarchs unaccompanied by important commercial privileges" (Hunt 1994) Lending to sovereign leaders could be seen as a loss leader, with the loans usually interest-free, however, the great Italian merchants of the 13th and 14th Centuries gained access to the grain of Naples and Sicily, along with the wool of England through their lending to respective leaders, whilst the Fugger's gained control of the mines of Central Europe in the late 15th Century via lending to the Hapsburgs, buying out the Medici's in the process, they were in turn succeeded by the Genoese who by becoming bankers to the Hapsburgs gained the control of the trade in American silver by the 16th and 17th Century. A final reason why the merchant banks engaged in lending to sovereign nations was the lack of good alternatives, which became especially problematic in times when trade was slack, usually because of war, which ironically quite often happened due to the sovereign states being lent the money had the resources to start wars, thus the banks became involved in a win-win situation, causing a circular flow of when there was a war, they lent money to fund it when there was peace, they lent money to fund the trade growth. An additional feature introduced by the banks to try and alleviate the problem of default debt was the introduction of short-term loans, with the ability to roll the debt over, this meant the government had to satisfy the banks of both their willingness and ability to pay the loan back to minimise the risk if the governments couldn't pay the loan back it would ensure banks made only a minimal loss.

The two other factors that came into play throughout the Middle Ages was firstly were the change in the population initially rising, falling then rising again throughout the Medieval era; initially, the growth was due to an increase in fertility not a decline in mortality, coupled with a long period of stability which meant women married earlier and decided to have more children, (Herlihy, 1976) leading to the subsequent medieval equivalent of the baby boom of the 1960s. The growth of the population-driven price rises was reinforced by several other forces; the expansion of trade, and the growth of commerce stimulated industrial development on such a scale that it has been described as 'The Industrial revolution of the 13th Century.' The rapid growth of commerce and industry, coupled with a lack of specie and increased population created some major consequences; These factors increased the velocity of money in circulation and once the price rises had begun it set a psychological shift in the population's mentality in that once they realised prices were rising over the long term, it acts as a self-reinforcing loop of price rises as people spend their money even quicker to buy goods before prices rose again. This then added to the strain on the money supply so demand would be met with debasement of the coins, leading once again to even greater velocity and yet more price rises. (Fischer, 1996)

Disaster now befell the people of Europe with several recurring disasters, in the summer of 1314 the weather turned cold and exceptionally wet, it rained constantly with crops rotting in the field, and grain harvests were also both late and dangerously short. The disaster at first just seemed routine to the people of 13 and 14th Century Europe, crops had fallen short before; in the winter of 1314 belt-tightening and prayers were the only solution yet in 1315 the next harvest was even worse, spring saw even more rainfall throughout Europe, stormy weather battered the continent for months with dikes collapsing in England and the Low Countries, entire fields being washed away in France and villages destroyed by rising rivers in Germany, this was not a crop shortage but a disaster with a complete failure of crops from Scotland to Italy and the Pyrenees to the Slavic regions. (Fischer, 1996) In England in 1315 the price of wheat rose by 800% from 5 shillings to 40 shillings, hungry livestock died, and impoverished peasants ate cats, rats, insects and reptiles, with many trying to survive on insect droppings. People in major cities such as London and Paris lay dying in the streets, with lawlessness breaking out as gangs of labourers roamed the countryside in search of food. (Kershaw, 1973) Most years now became known as the dreaded 'Dissette' and 'Grand Dissette', with Dissettes being the interval that came between the last grain of crop running out and before the new crop came in. Dissettes occurred even in normal times, but Grand Dissettes meant starvation. From 1260-1320 the fluctuation of grain prices shows the frequency of the Grand Dissette increasing. (Titow, 2010)

What has been a reoccurring theme so far is war and the plague, the Middle Ages are no different, in fact, they are synonymous with these tragedies. Not only did they have the Crusades but habitual and continuous wars throughout the whole period, they weren't evenly distributed throughout the centuries but came in clusters with both internal wars such as the War of the Roses in England (1455-1485), along with conflicts between countries such as England and Scotland, England and France, France and Flanders, with many smaller conflicts occurring between the Italian states, Germany and Switzerland. (Fischer, 1996) These endemic wars caused economic disruption both directly by the devastation it caused in the countryside by disrupting food production, and supply chains, which were already quite weak as well as losing manpower to work the fields, but indirectly as well with the burdensome cost and as large parts of public spending went into these wars, it was a cost Europe could ill afford. (Bradbury, 1977)

To add to the woes of the people of this period comes the plague, not just one of them but a whole host of them and just as virulent and deadly as anything the Roman empire saw, in some cases even worse. The deadliest popularly known as the Black death, its origins are disputed with it originally starting in either Central Asia or east Asia, what is known is first definitive appearance was in 1346 when a Tartar army besieged the Genoese colony of Caffa in the Crimea. The attackers were rife with the plague but converted their misfortune into a medieval form of biological warfare by catapulting its dead into the city to spread the disease. It worked; it was so successful that the Genoese abandoned the colony and fled via the Black Sea through the Aegean and the Mediterranean carrying the Black Death with them. By 1347 it had established itself in Sicily which quickly spread to Africa and the mainland of Europe. (Fischer, 1996) With the population already vulnerable due to war, poor harvests, the increase in population requiring substandard land being farmed being harder work, along with a lack of technology to increase food productivity and the inevitable rising food prices which made food unaffordable even if it could be found. All this led to malnutrition and poor health The plague was another nail in the coffin for the people of 14th Century Europe. (Zeigler, 1969) The total number of deaths will never be known, however amongst England's parishes where deaths were well recorded, it shows something along the lines of 45% of the population are known to have perished, with many historians estimating between 25 to 40% perished in Europe. The population in Europe fell from 80 million at the peak of the 14th Century to 60 million or less after the Black death in 1353. (McEvedy and Jones, 1978)

This huge loss of population had many economic consequences regarding the increase in prices, the price of food rose sharply during the epidemic years, then began to fall at a rapid rate as many died, meaning there were fewer people to feed. A counterbalance to this was the price of manufactured goods rose, partly due to the reduced number of artisans and craftsmen being able to demand higher wages, really a straightforward case of supply and demand coming into play. These countervailing trends of falling agricultural prices and rising industrial prices are called 'price scissors' by the 19th-century historian Thorold Rogers, in modern parlance it is known as bi-flation. For pure self-indulgence I would like to coin the phrase split-flation, which is where inflation splits into two or more groups of products, where certain groups can see price rises and others see prices falling, all in the same time frame. This terrible period was more than the collapse of medieval society, it was the death of the medieval civilization. (Fischer 1996) Inequality as would be expected also rose, by the late 14th Century with the economy of Western Europe struggling, inequality in wealth had increased with the Gini co-efficient showing in Paris in 1297 it being 0.69, rising to 0.79 in 1313, whilst in London in 1292 it rises from 0.70 to 0.76 in 1319. One bright glimmer of light in this tunnel of darkness was the emancipation of the serfs, no longer tied to any land as now they could simply up sticks and move to another landlord who previously wouldn't entertain them, but now welcomed them with open arms as they were all short of workers, that supply and demand theory is at work again. The servile dues rapidly withered away and all vestiges of the old obligations of the serfdom system were all but eradicated by the time of the ascension of Queen Elizabeth 1st in 1558. (Postan, 1973) By the 15th Century economic conditions began to stabilise in Europe, with price fluctuations ceasing and a long period of comparative stability began.

6. THE 18th and 19th CENTURY: A DIFFERENT KIND OF INFLATION

"I can calculate the movement of stars but not the madness of men" Sir Isaac Newton after he lost a fortune in the South Sea Bubble.

The Middle Ages saw wild swings of people's fortunes and wellbeing and depending on which period you were born in would determine how well you fared. The 18th and 19th Century were no less unpredictable, and as the chapter heading suggests we can explore some different forms of inflation and different kinds of revolution, with not all being bad. The inflation we see in this period is the first true hyperinflation, due to the first ever instance of mass money printing on an industrial scale, along with the creation of 'financial bubbles' such as the South Sea Bubble and the Mississippi Scheme and although it has no connection to the revolution in France the 'tulipmania' period for the Dutch has to be looked at as firstly it is the first truly market bubble crash and secondly it is a blueprint for all future bubbles that have occurred since. The revolutions being discussed are the American War of Independence, the French Revolution and the Financial Revolution with the creation of the first central banks, in particular the Bank of England, as we shall see all these factors are intertwined and interlinked with each other in some shape of form or other, it really is a most interesting roller coaster ride which has helped shape the 20th and 21st Century. As the purpose of this book is inflation it seems prudent to use the first-ever hyperinflation in history to be at the epicentre and how all the interlinking pieces played their part in creating this phenomenon.

The financial revolution which began in this period really revolves around the formation of the Bank of England as a central bank, although it actually wasn't the first central bank, that dubious honour goes to Sweden's Riksbank in 1668 and is still in operation to this day, (although the Dutch do argue they were technically the first true central bank due to the way it functioned) the English one has had the most pronounced effect on the modern world to this day. It may also seem a bit strange to use the formation of the Bank of England as one of the precursors to the French revolution but as we are becoming aware, history has many moving parts, some of them are unseen and the consequences unpredicted. On Thursday 21st June 1694 subscription lists for the Bank of England which had a capital of £1,200,000 opened, by the following Monday it had been fully subscribed, so began the start of public debt through borrowing by the government on behalf of its citizens to predominantly fund wars. The purpose was to lend King William 3rd unlimited sums at 8% interest per annum, to enable wars to be fought, in particular the conflict against Louis XIV of France, who did not have this ability to borrow, only tax. The crown would have to pay back interest of £96,000 plus a £4,000 administration fee. The bank also acquired the right to issue this £1.2 million in bank notes, without gold cover. (Irsigler, 1980) Britain had actually been on a bimetallic standard where the value of the monetary unit was defined between silver and gold but entered the gold standard quite by accident when in 1717 Sir Isaac Newton who by then had become the master of the Royal Mint set the exchange rate of silver to gold too low, thus causing silver coins to go out of circulation. (Eichengreen 2019)

It is somewhat ironic that the principle for the formation of the Bank of England and former founder member was a Scotsman named William Patterson, who was an interesting character, to say the least. At the age of 17, he left Scotland and settled for some time in Bristol, from there the opportunities were always available to travel to America which he did chiefly living in the Bahamas, where he was said to be a preacher, others record him as a buccaneer, a pirate by another name, how wonderfully ironic that in 1693 a former pirate wrote the original pamphlet entitled 'A Brief Account of the Intended Bank of England' which was to be the blueprint for the Bank of England. (Many would say the British have been robbed and fleeced by taxes to pay the debt the Governments have accrued purportedly on its citizens' behalf) He planned to establish the use of public debt borrowed from the bank, which was approved by Parliament, leading to the Bank of England being organised around the work of Patterson and formed in 1694. Patterson became one of the founding directors but resigned a year later citing policy disagreements. In reality, he had another project in mind the Darien scheme. The Darien scheme, which was a disaster for Scotland, involved the establishing of a 'New Caledonia,' a colony on the Isthmus of

Panama, located in the Gulf of Darien, with the plan being for the colony to establish and manage an overland route to connect the Pacific and Atlantic routes. It failed miserably with nearly 80% of the participants dying in the first year, Investors who were predominantly from Scotland lost everything and the scheme played a significant contribution to the 1707 Act of the Union, a Parliamentary Act merging the two separate states of England and Scotland (although they did actually share the same monarch) which were then "United into One Kingdom by the Name of Great Britain."

Where did most of this £1.2 million come from and what was its purpose? The money came from the people who were historically moneylenders and constantly being vilified for it, the Jews, which led to all 16,511 being expelled from Medieval England. After the passing of the Statutes of Jewry which abolished all usury in both 1233 and 1275, the Jews were finally expelled from England in 1290 by King Edward 1st on July 18th 1290 and any Jew who remained after 1st November 1290 was liable for execution, however if they paid a tax of one-fifth of the value of their movables and one-tenth of their specie, they could leave with any of their belongings that remained. (Goodson, 2014) In 1492 in Spain along with the expulsion of the Muslims by Isabella and Ferdinand, they also ran the Jews out of Spain which became known as the Edict of Expulsion, the Jews eventually settled in Holland. By the 17th century, the Jews in Holland began to lend money to the UK, actually affecting and altering the course of the whole of British history; the man they lent heavily to was no other than the beacon of Christian virtue, Oliver Cromwell, the Jews funded the New Model Army in the hope that should Cromwell be successful in defeating King Charles 1st, that they once again would be permitted to enter England. Despite Cromwell winning, having Charles executed and becoming Lord Protector, he was still unable to get the English to allow the Jews back in, he even convened a conference between 7th and 8th December 1655 in Whitehall to allow the Jews back in, yet although this conference was packed with his supporters, the majority of the delegates overwhelmingly rejected Cromwell's proposal. (Henriques, 1902) The Jews were finally admitted back into England when Jewish bankers financed William of Orange in Holland, who overthrew James II in 1689 to become William III, along with him came an entourage of Jews from the Dutch financial centre, who within five years funded the formation of the Bank of England.

The purpose of the Bank of England's formation was to provide sufficient finance for England to fight its wars against France. At the time France was the main world power both as a maritime force and its territorial possessions. In 1690 at the battle of Beachy Head, near Eastbourne, East Sussex, England, the French navy defeated an Anglo-Dutch alliance by sinking 12 ships, with a further 20 ships being exploded by their English crews to prevent them from being captured. The French under Louis XIV became engaged in the largest military conflict since the Crusades with the War of the Spanish Succession. (1702-1714) It was fought after Louis declared that he was going to place his grandson, Phillip, Duke of Anjou on the Spanish throne, if this had been successful it would have created a vast Franco-Spanish empire which posed a threat to the British Government; with the fractional reserve banking it had created via the bank of England, the English were able to build a large fleet as well as bank roll the Spanish to fight against the French. After a series of personal tragedies Louis XIV finally threw in the towel and signed a peace treaty in March and April of 1713, largely keeping its pre-war boundaries.

a) NETHERLANDS AND THE TULIPMANIA

We now enter the period of the first two most important financial crises that happened almost simultaneously in both London and Paris. They weren't the first to experience financial crises that occurred due to financial bubbles, we have the famous tulipmania in the Netherlands to bestow that honour upon. It was in a period known as 'The Dutch Golden Age' spanning between 1588-1674, in which Dutch trade, science, its arts and also its military, had become the most formidable in Europe. This period of growth was due to many factors but amongst them was the skilled Protestant workers who migrated there for religious reasons bringing along with them their work ethic, along with the wealth of corporate finance that the Jews provided. This was encapsulated with both the development of the Bank of Amsterdam and the first ever modern stock exchange, leading in 1602 to the foundation of the Dutch East India Company, the first ever truly multinational corporation. The Bank of Amsterdam was established in 1609 and was the first public bank to offer accounts which weren't directly convertible to coins, it is this function that can actually give it the claim to be the first central bank and was the blueprint for the formation of the other central banks in Europe, notably the Bank of Sweden in 1668 and the Bank of England in 1694, however, it neither managed the national currency nor acted as a lending institution except to the Government in emergencies, its purpose was to defend the coinage standard by correctly estimating the value of coins and in the process making debasement a lot less profitable. It also provided an efficient and trusted system for national and international payments as well as introduced the first ever international reserve currency the 'bank gilder' thus enabling it to hold the key central position in the financial world at the end of the era. (Quinn & Roberts, 2006) It was the formation of the modern stock exchange which ultimately precipitated the rise and finally the collapse in the value of the humble tulip and it is here we see the first ever speculative bubble which 'popped' leading to its spectacular collapse. Although there is no universally accepted definition of a bubble Schiller (2000) characterises it as "A situation in which temporarily high prices are sustained largely by investors' enthusiasm rather than by consistent estimation of real value"

Dutch commerce was flourishing in this period of the Golden Age creating wealth not only for the elites but an increasingly prominent and influential middle class; the level of risk-taking and what was seen as easy returns in the Dutch East India Company as they generated high incomes, led to a high level of high risk-taking in this period was one of several factors which led to the crash in the price of tulips. The history of the Tulip in Europe dates back to its initial entry into Vienna in 1554 via the Ottoman empire, then quickly spreading to other European cities, amongst them Amsterdam, its bright colours saw the popularity of the flower grow amongst an increasingly wealthy and ostentatious middle class, prices rose steadily and by 1634 speculators had entered the market which led to a continuing price rise throughout 1636, to the extent that any tulip bulb could fetch hundreds of guilders; it was in that year that the Dutch also created a formal futures market where contracts could be bought and sold. (Goldgar, 2007) By 1636 tulipmania had reached its peak with contracts changing hands up to five times, by February 1637 tulip bulb prices collapsed abruptly and the trade in tulips ceased, meaning the delivery of the bulbs was never fulfilled. The collapse began in Haarlem when buyers for the first time refused to show up for a routine auction, this was actually due to Haarlem suffering from an outbreak of bubonic plague. The fact that the bubonic plague was still present before the full outbreak may have helped create a fatalistic risk-taking attitude thus allowing the wild speculation to occur in the first place, (Garber, 2000) which makes it quite ironic that this fatalistic approach ultimately creates the circumstances for the bubble to burst. A major factor in the collapse was government interference in the marketplace and the catastrophic decision by the Dutch parliament to legally allow buyers to change the ways that the tulip contracts functioned. On February 24 1637 the self-regulating guild of Dutch florists made a decision that was ratified by parliament which announced "All future contracts written after November 30th 1636 and before the re-opening of the cash market in early Spring were to be interpreted as an option contract" (Thomson, 2007) in essence this meant all buyers of future contracts were under no legal obligation to pay the full amount that was owed but instead only pay the seller a small fixed percentage of the contract price, thus if the buyer saw the value of the bulb falling below the agreed purchase price they could avoid loss by simply paying a small fee, this essentially made it a futures contract, which is fine if both parties agree at the outset to this type of deal but being retrospective meant the buyers held all the aces and leaving the seller out to dry.

It is extremely difficult to get accurate data on the rise and fall in the price of the tulip, primarily due to inaccurate record keeping and buyers and sellers simply ripping up the contacts once the deal was done, most evidence cited is from Charles Mackay's book ' *Extraordinary Popular Delusions and the Madness of Crowds*' written in 1841, his evidence primarily comes from satirists from the period who were mocking the speculators, however, it is quite clear there was a rapid increase in prices which accelerated through December 1636 and January 1637 followed by a sudden and steep decline in February which contemporary accounts strongly suggest that these high prices were almost entirely sustained via investor enthusiasm rather than well informed and a rational estimation of the tulips real value, (Van de Veen, 2012) it has been estimated that the annualised rate of decline for the short period of December 1636 to February 1637 was 99.999% (Thomson, 2007)

Although Tulipmania wasn't a disaster for the Dutch economy per se, with the financial crisis affecting very few, the shock that Tulipmania had on the Dutch people was considerable and profound, with all the traditional values of thrift and hard work that had been involved in creating the Dutch Golden Age was thrown into doubt. In the 17th Century the idea of something as common as a flower could be worth more than somebody could earn in a year and could fluctuate wildly in winter even though it was a summer flower, really upended all belief in the value mechanism of goods and price. (Goldgar, 2007) It was a culture shock that affected the Dutch psyche for many generations, just as hyperinflation in Weimar Germany was to do after 1923.

Before we move onto the better-known bubbles of the South Sea and Mississippi Scheme, it really is worth mentioning a scheme which led to the ruin of a whole country which required its bailout by another country; that country was Scotland, and the scheme was the Darien scheme and led to the Act of the Union in 1707 between England and Scotland.

After the Tulipmania episodes, the next mania or bubble was a spectacular event and like buses you wait a while for one and then two come all at once. The outcome for the two countries was poles apart, one country went from strength to strength and solidified itself as an empire and world power for two centuries, whilst the other mania was the forerunner to a revolution, leading to much bloodshed, violence, and the upheaval of Europe. In 1720 Britain and France had their foundations shaken to the core with the South Sea Bubble and the Mississippi Scheme. These manias and crashes of the 17th and 18th centuries have initiated the phenomenon of financial manias which have overtaken financial markets on a regular basis ever since, Galbraith (1952) defined it as "Insanity born of optimism and self-serving delusion."

These two crises showed many similarities, the French Mississippi scheme peaked in the winter of 1720, with the British South Sea bubble peaking in the summer of 1721. Both revolved around large private companies which held monopolies to trade with the Americas, yet the most important similarity was both firms were involved in the refinancing and restructuring of the debts of their respective governments, along with having close ties to powerful political figures, the final similarity was both companies had were manic rises in their share prices, followed by catastrophic falls, ranging between 80-90% within a 90 day period, an even greater volatility than the Wall Street crash of 1929. (Frehen, Goetzmann and Rowenhurst, 2013) Yet despite the similarities in the respective bubbles, there were several major differences between the two countries in 1720, hence the dramatically different outcomes.

b) BRITAIN AND THE SOUTH SEA BUBBLE.

Although the British South Sea Bubble followed its French counterpart, the innovation of the Bank of England laid the foundations for both bubbles. It was the Whig Party-aligned entrepreneurs who were instrumental politically in the creation of the Bank of England and given the fact they were granted monopoly rights in return for making large loans to the government, emboldened the opposition party (the Tories) to form the South Sea Company in 1711. The principle behind it was to negotiate monopoly rights in regard to trade with the Spanish colonies in both Central and Southern America, in return for this monopoly right they were to share the profits with the Crown. The major problem the company had was their poor relations between Spain and Britain which meant the South Sea Company were forced to look elsewhere to be able to conduct its business.

By 1719 the government's total liabilities were £50 million, so by the spring of that year the government sought to lower its interest payments by consolidating and refinancing its debts. After several rounds of various bids, the South Sea Company's bid was accepted in favour of the Bank of England's bid, in essence, had things not turned out as bad as they did for the South Sea Company, potentially the Bank of England would have ceased to exist. The deal gave the government reduced interest expenses as well as promising investors returns if, and when trade between Britain and Spain's American colonies grew. Despite the big claims the South Sea Company was making, it did not have anywhere near the operating profits to pay the large dividends it promised to investors due primarily to the very poor trading deal the Spanish allowed the British to have. The result was an 18th Century Ponzi scheme where the company began selling newly created shares to new investors and using that money to pay dividends to the original investors, a sizeable proportion of whom just happened to be Tory party MPs. Initially the market manipulation, along with government bribes pumped up the share price, yet doubts began to appear as to the sustainability of the company once the company was prosecuted under the 'Bubble Act' (which ironically was the Act which gave the South Sea Company its Charter in the first place) leading investors to become aware of fraud, which inevitably led to the slump in its share price.

The Whig party now encouraged the Bank of England to buy out the South Sea Company, with the Bank of England extending its loan to the government along with making an equity investment in the South Sea Company to ensure it did not completely collapse, thus enabling the restoration of confidence in the broader market. This was probably the first rescue act of a central bank, bailing out a 'Too Big to Fail' company, in the process earning huge profits and its shareholders handsome dividends, whilst putting the taxpayer on the hook to this debt for several centuries to come, for the large part the owners of the South Sea Company shares didn't fare as well with many investors facing ruin. The Whig party pursued the corrupt and incompetent Tory politicians involved in the South Sea Company, this forced tighter restrictions in granting corporate charters. Despite all the upheaval and recriminations of 1720 Britain's financial sectors not only survived but grew, helping it to fund the Industrial revolution which made Britain the world's leading economic power of the 19th Century. (Bruner & Miller, 2020)

The South Sea Company did continue to trade under the umbrella of the Bank of England with its main function being managing government debt rather than trading with the Spanish colonies. It finally came to an end after the Seven Years' War with France. (1756-1763)

c) FRANCE AND THE MISSISSIPPI BUBBLE.

The French having noticed that the English could control vast sums of money effectively meant they lost the war not because of poor strategy or lack of firepower, but by a deficiency in financial credit, at this point entered another Scotsman, John Law. (Goodson, 2014) John Law is another genuinely interesting character who was the son of an Edinburgh goldsmith, becoming a mathematician and economist of note in the early 18th Century. He travelled to London after his father died and gambled away the family fortune. He became a fugitive from Scottish justice after killing Edward 'Beau' Wilson in a duel in 1694 over the honour of a woman. He was sentenced to death but after managing to escape from prison he ended up in Amsterdam. He spent around ten years travelling between Amsterdam and France dealing in financial speculation, spending most of his time studying finance and the principles of trade and in the evenings frequented the gaming houses where he started to become a successful gambler. (Macleod, 2018) This was mainly due to turning his back on wild speculation bets such as the outcome of wars (they actually did bet in vast sums on who would be the victor) and gambling on games where the odds could be calculated, which he became spectacularly good at. By 1715 Law made his home in the Place Louis-Le-Grand, a royal square where he hosted and entertained various Parisian nobles, gaining the attention of such notables as the Duke of Orleans, (Mackay, 1852) this was a meeting that not only both of them would come to regret, but the whole of France.

In 1715 John Law sought a state sanction to establish a French bank and trading company based on the South Sea model, envisaging a private bank which could issue paper currency backed by specie unfortunately for Law before King Louis X1V could make his decision, he died. On the death of Louis X1V in 1715, France's state finances (these in reality were the Royal finances) with royal debts of 3 billion livres due to endless wars in Europe and in particular the devastating Spanish Succession War. Combining this with an annual income from taxes of 145 million livres and an annual expenditure of 142 million livres, leaving only 3 million livres to pay 220 million livres of interest on its debts meant that France was on the verge of bankruptcy. The Duke of Orleans who was appointed as regent to the five-year-old Louis XV, was left to find a solution to this financial problem. His first attempt in 1713 was to debase the coinage by one-fifth, however, as we have seen the short-term gain of doing this led to inflation. In addition, the taxes collected were too little too late and filled with corruption and inequality. There were three groups in French society at this time, the nobility, the clergy, and the lower classes who were effectively everyone else from the peasants to what would be considered today as the middle class. Taxes were only collected from one of these groups and it doesn't take much stretching of the imagination to work out that it was the Lower classes who were the only ones to pay tax.

This coincidence of Law being acquainted with the Duke of Orleans enabled him initially to get promoted as controller general in May 1716 and because of this position was granted the right to form the *Banque Generale Privee* which began to do business in late 1716. The bank gained the confidence of its depositors with the commitment to convert on demand the bank notes into specie. (Murphy 1997) Banknotes did not exist before John Laws proposal for his bank, but once he had convinced the Regency of the circulating benefits of paper currency, but the notes could be used as loans to the King at 3% interest and not the 7 ½ % the Crown was currently paying, Law was up and running and although unbeknown to him and France set the wheels in motion for complete financial ruin.

The Banque Generale was set up as a private bank which could also issue bank notes. The livre was the most common name used for coins and units of account and it was in 1701 that the first French paper-backed currency was issued, denominated in livres tournois, yet as has always been the case ever since, it was devalued due to massive overproduction. Law found various ways to persuade the public to part with their specie for the paper notes, he was so successful in his endeavours that by April 1717 it was deemed that both taxes and revenues of the state could be paid in bank notes, by a happy coincidence it was John Law who was allowed to be the only issuer of these notes and an even happier coincidence he was exempt from actually paying any taxes. What Law managed to achieve was to free up the specie that had previously been hoarded when the Duke of Orleans debased the currency in 1713, mainly because of fear of further debasement of the specie. This has happened throughout history. By injecting confidence into the system Law increased the circulation and velocity much to the benefit of the economy, it was so successful he opened five other branches in France outside of Paris in Lyons, Rochelle, Tours, Amiens, and Orleans. Other private banks and money lenders now jumped on the bandwagon by using Law's banknotes based on extending credit; this success established his credibility with the

Regent, the French establishment and more importantly the trust of the commercial community. At this stage, no inflationary pressures could be observed as the banknotes had been issued against specie, yet it is clear that a loans business was beginning to be facilitated with leverage on the back of Law's paper money, leading to the inflation of the money supply, (Macleod 2018) the scene has now been set for the impending collapse.

In August 1717 Law's success allowed him to obtain the Charter for the Mississippi Company, this was a company which held a monopoly on trade between France and its Louisiana territory in North America. In 1718 Law arranged for a Royal takeover of the *Banque Generale Privee*, in essence affiliating it to the French crown, making it a prototype for the central bank and naming it the Royal Bank of France, the funding to form the bank was primarily from John Law and Louis XV. This bank held a monopoly on issuing and also converting the French money supply from specie into paper notes. In 1719 Law merged the Mississippi company and the Royal Bank of France into a commercial entity which controlled a large share of the French economy. The Mississippi Companies share took off into the stratosphere as it appeared to have rising dividends, the assurance of government protection, market manipulation and the easy money printing conditions that had been established, (Bruner & Miller, 2020) it would appear as history has repeatedly and continues to prove that all that glitters is not gold.

By now things were moving at breakneck speed with the French economy now hurtling itself into catastrophe, by the summer of 1719 Law acquired three other companies to merge with the Mississippi Company whose ventures each had individual exclusive trading rights to China, East Indies and Africa and became known as the *Compaigne de la Louisiane Ou d'Occident* (the company of the West) which now gave Laws Mississippi company effectively a monopoly on all Frances foreign trade. (Macleod 2018) To pay these companies' debts off and to build ships that were needed for transport the French government allowed Law to issue 50,000 new shares in the Mississippi Company at 500 livres each, with just a 75 livres deposit required as a down payment and the rest due in 17 additional monthly instalments of 25 livres each, this form of credit allowed many more participants into the market which helped to vastly inflate the price of the shares at a rapid pace. By the time permission for the share auction was granted the share value stood at 650 livres, predominantly funded by the banknotes issued by Laws Bank, existing shareholders could subscribe for one new share for every four they had previously purchased with an initial down payment of 50 Livres, the next payment then being deferred for over a month, creating instant arbitrage as the share could be sold for instant profit. To add even more fuel to the fire banknote issues continued without the corresponding acquisition of specie, combined now with private banks and moneylenders using it to expand credit, creating a recipe for disaster. The share price rose to 1,000 livres before the second instalment was even due, this created a frenzy amongst the ordinary citizens who flocked to Paris which in turn created even further demand and inflated the price of the shares even more. A bubble is well and truly being blown.

Due to this success, Law offered to pay off the National debt of 1.5 billion livres by issuing a further 300,000 shares at 500 livres to be paid for in 10 monthly instalments. At this time Law also purchased the right to collect taxes worth an estimated 52 million livres, with the view of replacing various taxes and consolidating it into just one single tax. This worked beautifully with the efficient streamlining leading to some products falling by up to 1/3rd in price. The stock market gains along with the tax efficiencies led to foreigners entering Paris to participate in the free-for-all and buying more stocks of the Mississippi Company. By mid-1719 the Mississippi Company had issued more than 600,000 shares and the par value of the company stood at 300 million livres, that summer the share prices rose from 1,000 livres to 5,000 livres, with the rise seeing no end in sight. It continued to rise until it realised the astonishing heights of 15,000 livres per share. It was in this period that the term millionaire was first coined. (Narron & Skeie 2014)

By late 1719 Law was finding it impossible to sustain this bubble that he had created, with the best part of 1 billion Livres now in circulation to ramp up the share price, regardless he was still held up in such high esteem that in January of 1720 he was promoted to Controller-General, his first act being to decree bank notes were the only permitted currency except for small transactions, with all old coins being either handed in or seized, he even went as far as banning the wearing of precious stones in case they could be used as barter or money. In the meantime, the bank notes continued to be printed and any pretence of it being backed by specie had been long abandoned. In September 1719 we also see the collapse of the livre with the exchange rate against the English sterling falling from nine old pence to 2 ½ pence. By the last three months of 1720, there were no prices quoted for the livre against sterling, essentially rendering them useless and all public confidence being lost. The bubble had well and truly been popped with anger and resentment leading to violence, bloodshed, and death. The fundamental difference between the two bubbles of France and the UK was that the UK had the Bank of England to come to the South Sea Companies rescue, but France did not. In essence, whereby Britain used competition to resolve the situation, Law used the state to actively crush competition leaving his company with no institution to save it when it got into difficulties. It could be even argued that the different experiences both countries had of central banks meant that Britain was allowed to flourish whilst France's development became stunted.

Law escaped to Brussels where he lived in impoverished circumstances, travelling between Rome, Copenhagen, and Venice, even moving back to London for four years where he had received a pardon. He died in Venice in 1729 of pneumonia, where he lived in poverty. The French Crown had essentially dodged the bullet as its debts had been cleared by Law, however, it didn't learn its lesson and all the anger and resentment would be compounded and stored which would ignite to create the French Revolution.

Before we move onto the actual economic causes of the French Revolution, it would be pertinent to look at some of the psychology behind the causes and this is rooted in the period known as the Age of Enlightenment which is sometimes simply referred to as 'The Enlightenment.' It followed the period of the Renaissance and was an intellectual and philosophical movement that dominated European thinking and is generally dated from the death of Louis XIV in 1715 and ending with the French Revolution in 1789, although many historians see the end as being in the early 19th Century with the death of Immanuel Kant in 1804. It included a broad spectrum of ideas ranging from how to value human happiness to the acquiring of knowledge by employing scientific reason and empiricism, (evidence of the senses) advancing the work of the Scientific Revolution by figures such as Francis Bacon, where developments in mathematics, physics, astronomy, biology, and chemistry, revolutionised the way society viewed nature. This ran alongside notions such as liberty, progress, toleration, having a constitutional government and the separation of the state and church. (Outram, 2006) Early influences came from across Europe with philosophers such as Francis Bacon, Rene Descartes, David Hume, Immanuel Kant, Gottfried Wilhelm Leibniz, Adam Smith, Voltaire, and Jean Jacques Rousseau contributing to the Enlightenment. Within this group are clustered a wide range of disciplines such as philosophy, science, sociology, psychology, economics, law, and politics. Even though the Enlightenment took hold in most European countries and influenced nations globally, each nation adapted and adopted different formats, for example in France it became associated with anti-monarchy, anti-government, and anti-church, whilst in Germany it expressed itself in a spiritualist and nationalist form without threatening any of the establishment's structures. The two were probably the most influential in sowing the seeds in the minds of the people and triggering both the American War of Independence and the French Revolution, the latter it could be argued was caused by the French philosophers, Voltaire, and Jean Jaques Rousseau.

Before we look at the downfall of the French monarchy and its involvement in the American War of Independence, it is worth looking at America and its financial development from the 17th Century and how it was the first Western country to start printing fiat money.

The modern-day America started as thirteen colonies belonging to the Kingdom of Great Britain with coin being very scarce in mainland America for two reasons; firstly in the 17th Century they had no gold or silver mines (this would change with the California gold rush in 1848) meaning they effectively had no national supply to draw upon and secondly, they had major trade deficits as there were no real industries that had been developed, this meant they literally had to import everything, they did have some exports such as tobacco, but this nowhere near compensated for the deficit spending leading to a huge trade deficit.

The colonists experimented by using alternative commodities as money for example Virginia used the alternative of tobacco as money and we see that settlement of accounts and bookkeeping in Jamestown by the late 1610's being kept in Lbs of tobacco. Government ministers, church ministers and even the Governor of Virginia all received their salaries in tobacco, records show that by the 1650's the Governor received a salary of 25,000 Lbs of tobacco. Payments were obviously not made physically but as a credit in a bookkeeping account. Taxes could also be paid in tobacco and this system continued until the 1750's when Virginia finally abandoned tobacco for paper currency. Other colonies such as New Netherlands/New York used beaver skins as money. New England used food produce as money and called it 'country pay' with bushels of corn being the main medium again government officials, Governors, etc received their salaries in corn, however, other foodstuffs such as barley and wheat were also used. It is quite interesting to note that Harvard was financed by bushels of corn with fees paid for by country corn. (Barth 2021) They did have defects as mediums of exchange, such as the deterioration in quality, it was less portable and a very bulky medium of exchange.

Some coins did make it to the mainland, these were predominantly procured in port cities in part due to the trade with sugar islands of the Caribbean as the lands on these islands were almost 90% cultivated to grow sugar and therefore needed to import food stuffs such as cattle and cereal goods which were paid for in gold and silver coins. The biggest source of coins for the Americans, especially in the 1680s and 1690 was via piracy. (This is where William Patterson one of the founders of the Bank of England plied his buccaneer's trade) Plundered coin needed to be spent and going back to England was out of the question so the North American colonial ports were where the money was spent lavishly in the taverns and brothels along with any ship repairs and supplies required.

The colonists had a real problem, little specie and being under the rule of an empire, they couldn't mint their own coins as Britain saw it as too risky and encroaching on the crown's prerogative. The main reason was the theory of mercantilism which was a policy whereby a country accumulates bullion, establishing colonies and a merchant marine with the view to developing industries and wealth in these colonies to acquire a favourable balance of trade. The Navigations Act of 1651 was an act of parliament which compelled American colonists to only buy goods from England and reciprocally only sell goods to England causing a lot of resentment amongst the colonists. To overcome the shortage of specie and increase trade, in 1686 Massachusetts established the first American land bank, this has been argued that by default became the first Western Nation to create fiat currency, however as the money was backed by land which can be construed as a commodity it would make sense by the definition of money to actually call it money, the real fiat currency would follow a short four years later. The other colonies would very quickly and eagerly follow the Massachusetts Land Bank model as they had reasoned that although specie may be scarce, land certainly was not so they hit on the idea of backing paper currency by land instead of gold or silver, this had actually been thought about in 1650 in England, but the idea didn't catch on. The land bank was not a bank in the conventional sense that it accepted deposits, the only thing that it did do was to lend paper notes to anyone with land to mortgage; the value of the land would be ascertained by an assessor from the land bank. Once the borrower had received the paper notes they could use it to invest in farming equipment, etc. The borrower then paid back the principal along with the interest, again with paper notes, if the lender was unable to pay the loan back, the land bank would sell the property which had been used as collateral. (Barth 2021)

In 1690 Massachusetts inadvertently created the Western world's first type of fiat currency called 'A Bill of Credit' all due to it being involved in 'King Williams War' (1698-1697) when a raiding party attacked French Quebec but failed miserably. The back story is the Massachusetts treasury had no money to finance the war to pay for the soldiers, etc, however, the troops were confident of victory and believed they would be handsomely rewarded with the plunder. Unfortunately, the mission was a huge failure and with the soldiers on the point of mutiny after not being paid; the Massachusetts government was in a desperate position so as a last throw of the dice the government in December 1690 printed up 'Bills of Credit' to pay the soldiers with, it was essentially a paper note saying the soldiers were owed so much money, a kind of an IOU. The government printed up the equivalent of £9,000 in sterling and was seen as a 'temporary measure', however, this temporary measure didn't last very long and by the 1750's the government as issued £100,000 paper bills. These notes were used to pay out any government expenses such as war, ship construction and road building, what gave it value was that people could use these bills to pay their taxes in place of specie which meant that most of the paper money printed would eventually return back to the state. (Barth 2021) The term 'temporary measure' has been adopted by many governments and many nations globally ever since to fool the public, and yet as the economist Milton Friedman once noted "There's nothing more permanent than a government temporary measure."

The essential difference between the Land Banks loans and the Bill of Credit is that land bank notes entered circulation via the Land banks themselves whilst Bills of Credit notes entered circulation through the treasury creating and spending new currency. As is the pattern with governments overprinting it became an issue thus devaluing the worth of the currency although some colonies did show restraint; the worst offenders were New England where the Massachusetts currency required five-shilling paper notes for one silver coin, Rhode Island fared even worse with eleven-shilling notes required for one silver coin. In North Carolina, ten Shilling notes were required for one silver coin, whilst in South Carolina 6 were required. The most stable currencies were the Middle colonies with Pennsylvania having an exchange rate of 1.25 Shillings for 1 silver coin and New York requiring 1.50. Inflation helped the debtors and hurt the creditors and corruption started to take place; in Rhode Island people who were large debtors, got elected to and occupied seats on the legislative where they continued to print excess currency in order to intentionally create inflation and thus pay off their own debts. (Thayer, 1953) In the early period of money printing, the UK was quite supportive as the printing was done primarily to fund wars against the French, however by the 1720's the British stance was very aggressively against the currency thus sowing the seeds for revolution and the American War of Independence.

Following the King William War, the printing financed the Queen Anne's War (1702-1713) and the stock of paper currency increased by approximately 39% per annum. (Compound Annual Rate) Other colonies soon followed suit and in this period of the war paper currency across the colonies had increased at least 34-fold, yet initially, it didn't cause any price rises as one would assume it might, figures show the price of silver in Boston which measures the depreciation of the Massachusetts Pound, rose from only 7 shillings to 8 ½ Shillings. (That is an increase of 21.4% in 10 years equalling just 2.14% per annum) The reason for the lack of price rises in the specie concerning the paper currency is the currency only circulated in New England and the specie circulated globally, therefore when a colony issued paper currency it tended to lose its specie, and the loss had the effect of off-setting fiat currency expansion and reduced the inflationary consequences of this expansion, however, this can only work for a short time and if stability isn't eventually restored and specie returns, price rises will occur.

At the end of the Queen Anne's War in 1714, Massachusetts, Rhode Island and Connecticut reduced the stock of paper currency for a short period, this unfortunately had the effect of depressing the economy. Massachusetts started to print money again but at a modest 3.2% per annum. Rhode Island started up the printing presses again and increased its bills by 12.5% per annum; on the back of this we start to see price rises becoming a problem which exploded during King George's War, (1743-1748) in order to finance this war, New England's colonies increased the amount of currency printed by 24.3% per annum, (compound annual rate) the specie left the colony (remember Gresham's Law) and once the specie had gone price rises were inevitable with silver in Boston rising by 11% per annum. (Compound Annual Rate) (Humpage, 2015)

The UK saw the colonial money as an asset as it was used to help the colonies fight wars against the French, land banks performed no such function so by the 1720s and 1730 the crown instructed its royal governors to veto any colonial legislation for land banks, the colonists being quite shrewd the wealthy merchants bypassed the legislation and made the land banks private which meant it didn't need any state or authoritative legislature, the crown responded by outlawing private land banks by passing the Currency Act in 1741. This is now developing into a huge problem as a combination of mercantilism, no silver, no land banks, no private banks and wars with France (1740-1763) led to political upheaval and the earlier seeds that had been sown for Independence were now starting to germinate. A great global conflict known as the Seven Years' War erupted in Europe which ran between 1756 and 1763. It was a major world war including many powerful European countries and several smaller ones, with the main protagonists being England, France, and Spain. Many battles took place around the world with the major conflicts erupting in North America, Europe and India. The consequence of the seven-year war for France was that it had ceded all the dominance it had in North America to the British and although Spain held some regions, it also ceded Florida, along with France losing all control of India, this essentially making Britain the major power globally, however both France and Britain were now facing huge debts incurred by the war. At the end of the Seven Years' War, parliament prohibited the colonies from any further printing of paper currencies legal tender with the Currency Act of 1764 as it began to see the possibilities that the colonies may start to become aware of the possibilities to self-govern, the British government's actions and the law of unintended consequences ensured that independence would eventually happen.

In addition to the Currency Act, there were a raft of other legislations which upset the colonies, but the one which sent them over the edge was the Stamp Act of 1765. After the Anglo-French wars (1740-1763) finished the British National debt had ballooned up. In 1714 it was £36 million by 1764 it had reached £146 million. (That equates to a rise of 305.55% in 50 years, or 6.11% per annum) The Prime Minister George Grenville announced the colonies had to pay their share, this was not an unreasonable request as most of that debt was to help the colonies fight the French and up to the point the colonists had paid little or no taxes. The Stamp Act was the first direct tax by Parliament on the colonies; in the UK the citizens had been paying this tax for decades, however, the Americans did have a grievance against this as in law they didn't have the same rights as their UK counterparts, an example of this would be the violation of due process where an offender could be imprisoned without a jury and also presumed guilty and had to prove their innocence and not the other way round. Their biggest bugbear was the tax had to be paid in silver and with the combination of silver flight due to excessive currency printing and mercantilism, they didn't have any silver to give, it was all these factors that led to the famous slogan "No taxation without representation." Benjamin Franklin one of the founding fathers of the United States of America went to England to oppose the legislation, proposing a Continental Land Bank where the interest payments would go to the UK government, Parliament rejected this as they feared it might unite all thirteen colonies, oh the irony!! The Stamp Act didn't succeed as riots, protests, and attacks on the governor's mansions in Massachusetts led to Parliament repealing the Act in 1766. By now the seeds of Independence that had been earlier sown were starting to take root.

In Boston Massachusetts on March 5th, 1770, nine British soldiers were confronted by an angry crowd of approximately three to four hundred people who were abusing them, fearing for their safety they opened fire and shot five Americans dead. It was described by patriots (also known as revolutionaries who opposed British rule during the American Revolution) such as Paul Revere and Samuel Adams as a Massacre, eventually becoming known as the Boston Massacre. The massacre took place due to the Townshend Act in 1768, which put tariffs on a variety of common items that were manufactured in Britain and imported to the thirteen colonies. The Boston Massacre is regarded as one of the most significant events that turned colonial sentiment against both King George III, and the British parliamentary authority as a whole. John Adams, who was an American statesman, attorney, a diplomat who went on to become Vice President twice under George Washington and actually served as President for one term in 1796 one of the founding fathers of the United States said of the massacre that it was where the "Foundation of American Independence was laid." Adams along with Jefferson also helped draft the Declaration of Independence in 1776, ironically within the declaration was the right to counsel and presumption of innocence and against anti-British sentiment successfully defended the British soldiers against the murder charges they faced for their part in the shootings of the Boston Massacre. Other events such as the Gaspee Affair, the Boston Tea Party, and the Westminster massacre on March 13th, 1775, led to the Battle of Lexington on April 19th, 1775, which would eventually lead to the colonies signing the Treaty of Paris on September 3rd, 1783, which formally saw America being recognised as an independent country.

When the American War of Independence began there was a major concern that the French support for the American revolutionaries would bring about a new financial crisis as the one that had occurred in the Mississippi bubble, those that had believed this was the worst possible scenario that could happen again were soon to find out how spectacularly wrong they could be and it was to be much, much worse than they could have imagined.

The budget for 1780 had a total expenditure of 625 million livres covered by revenues of 501 million livres and borrowings of 124 million livres. By 1782 the cost of funding the American War of Independence had pushed the French finances to an unstainable 1.066 billion livres, funded with total borrowings of 997 million livres. This was unsustainable and forced interest rates even higher, making the debt even harder to finance, taxes which needed to be raised weren't and by 1785 the peacetime budget was wholly financed by the issue of new debt. In 1788 a poor harvest led to a further drop in tax receipts, with the master of the finance issuing a partial default on its debts. Unable to borrow money from the markets the government covered its deficits by borrowing from its only discount bank the *Caisse D'Escompte* (discount banks are financial institutions that act as money lenders or serve as intermediaries between commercial lenders and borrowers, the *Caisse D'Escompte* was a bank formed in 1767 to purchase commercial and government securities, paying 4% interest and charging 2% commission, it also had a monopoly on the issuance of coinage, which effectively performed the role of an independent central bank) whilst waiting for the Estates-Generale to hopefully raise taxes to solve the crisis. The taxes were not raised, people simply refused to pay them, and the monopoly bank of issue was forced to suspend payments in 1789 when a run on the bank turned the bank notes into fiat money. (Bardo and White, 1990) France was in a financial doom loop and revolution was just around the corner. The loss of the Seven Years' War to Britain had left France feeling humiliated, and the desire for revenge at all costs, led to totally un-fundable loans, once the war was over the French were hoping to start receiving payment from the Americans who neither had the finances nor the will to repay these loans, in essence, America started as a nation that defaulted from the very beginning.

The French Revolution started in 1789 and once the revolutionary Government was in place, the Government depended increasingly on borrowings from the *Caisse d'Escompte*. The problems of the new government became apart as new loan issues failed and tax receipts continued to fall leading to a run on the Caisse, forcing it to suspend payments in September *1798*, thus turning its banknotes into fiat money. Ruling out an increase in taxes as two of the three influential groups in society the clergy and the nobles who made up only 2% of society but controlled over 60% of the wealth refused to pay. Default was also ruled out therefore the assembly found a small but extremely wealthy group who couldn't fight back and were forced to pay. In November 1789 the legislators took control of the Catholic Church's lands. To sell the lands they created the Assignat, which was a monetary instrument, initially issued as a government bond backed by the church lands that it had seized, once this objective didn't work it was re-released as currency. It was used over three periods of the Revolution; the first was before the Reign of Terror (1793-1794), the second coincided with the terror and the third and final period was at the end of the 'Terror'. The first period saw the growth of inflation, the second period was when violent measures were used to counteract the negative effects of inflation and the third period signalled firstly the discredit and then the end of the system of revolutionary paper money (Hawtrey 1918).

To reduce the debt burden, the Government sold the assets of the church by issuing assignats alongside the livres, to quickly obtain funds without it appearing to be a fire sale and thus reduce the value of the sale, the National Assembly declared the first issue of 400million livres of assignats on December 19th and 21st 1789, printed in denominations of 1,000 livres and carrying a 5% coupon, (interest) with the most important asset being they were backed by the future sale of church properties. (Levasseur 1894) This method was seen by its proponents as a painless way of solving the fiscal problems due to a special fund being established to destroy the assignat once it had been accepted for either payment of land at the auctions or the payment of taxes. If this was to happen it was seen as a way of solving the potential problem of inflation which the people who derided the scheme were most afraid of, the memory of John Law's was deeply ingrained and fresh in the psyche of many French people.

The absence of tax revenues forced the Government to order a second round of assignats on September 29th, 1790, which continued to be issued with a total issuance of 1,742 million livres in December 1791. The interest rate was lowered, and the denominations were reduced to 50 livres, effectively making it legal tender. The key problem with all the new issues was to ascertain if there was enough land to sell to enable debt reduction to bring the budget into balance along with the interest payments which were needed to be made to maintain credibility. The land also needed to be marketable with property rights enshrined in law, giving security that the land wouldn't be repossessed at some later stage. New tax systems were required to be put in place to help raise sufficient revenue to help reduce the debt. The value of the land was believed to fall between 2,000 and 2,500 million livres, which meant in theory all the debts could be paid yet persistently falling tax revenues after the fall of the Bastille and attacks on tax officials in late 1789 meant tax collection was lower than normal meaning the budget deficit rising from under 100million livres in 1788 to 340 million livres in 1790. On August 27th, 1790, the Assembly decided to issue 1.9 billion assignats to become legal tender, this was an astronomical amount, however, the highly regarded finance minister Necker voted against this transformation, managing to get the number down to 800 million lives, but forced to resign in the process. (Stael, 1818)

In 1792 the war with Austria dramatically increased expenditures resulting in the Government becoming almost totally dependent on money creation for the next two years. For 1792 expenditures ballooned to 1,363 livres leaving a deficit of 998 million livres needing to be covered with the assignat. Faith in the assignat was ebbing by mid-1792 and more land was needed which was duly taken from the nobles and the clergy; people were less secure in the title deeds from these lands than they were from the lands of the church, fearing they could be reclaimed by their original owner at a later date. The answer was to export the revolution and seize foreign lands and resources, with success being self-financing, the invasion and victory over Belgium offered some hope of extracting resources, yet the yield was much lower than the French had hoped for with 109 million Livres demanded but at most receiving 50 million. As these foreign transfers were limited, the domestic struggle intensified, and radicalisation in the assembly led to the abolition of the monarchy and the establishment of a Republic.

Price rises led to the urban workers, shopkeepers, and middle class (who made up 98% of the population and were all deemed the peasant classes) demanding price controls. The rentiers (people who predominantly earn income from interest and investments) were forced to take in modern parlance 'a haircut' totalling 100 million livres, however due to the huge expenditure this accounted for a modest amount. The increasing alarm in the growing number of assignats led to the economic phase of the terror, the price of grain was made uniform throughout the country, abandoning its *laissez-faire* approach to the market, draconian penalties were set for infractions of the rules and armed militia scoured the countryside to force producers to exchange goods at the fixed assignat prices, unfortunately, all these measures achieved was to create even more shortages. The success of the peasant classes in initially shifting the burden of government finance to the nobles and clergy was short-lived, as firstly they didn't pay and secondly the government now not only needed money but men to fight the wars, so a revolutionary conscript law was passed in 1793. By early 1794 the price controls were losing another important effect as prices began to rise, as the value of the livre fell.

By 1795 there were signs of hyperinflation as although tax receipts began to rise between September 1794 and April 1795, it only covered 54% of the 5.7 billion livres of expenditure which the inevitability of requiring more assignats After April 1795 government records appear to have conveniently disappeared, but data of issued assignats show it rising between 100-250 livres monthly. By definition of modern standards, hyperinflation followed reaching 80% per month by June 1795, peaking at 130% for the month of December. The increasing issuances of assignats were now being outpaced by inflation, meaning the revenue due to inflation falling sharply. The government needing to prove fiscal responsibility, decree a limit of 40 billion livres and when the number was reached the printing plates would be destroyed. This worked for a while and confidence was restored. The government although having a secret store of pre-printed assignats kept their word and destroyed the plates and printing equipment, the problem now became what was going to be an alternative source of revenue and the solution was the *mandats territoriaux* with assignats being redeemed at 30:1. Having printed 2.4 billion mandats and 36.4 billion assignats outstanding, it meant half the issue would be absorbed immediately. It was doomed to failure, the government only survived by success on the battlefield, however even with all the indemnities from the Dutch, Austria, Venice and the Papal states as well as Egypt, it still only came to 360 million livres, which only half the peacetime pre-revolutionary budget, although money creation had become exhausted, the battlefield victories delivered specie (physical coins usually gold and silver) to pay the troops (White, 1995).

Discontent within the government continued with a coup taking place on September 9th, 1797, that purged the legislature and on September 30th, 1797, the new legislature passed a law known as the bankruptcy of the two-thirds, along with a cut in interest payment on the debt. Even now with the default confidence was not restored so new harsh laws were introduced with fear sweeping the nation in anticipation of a new terror. Finally, at the peak of the crisis, Napoleon led a coup on November 9$^{th, 1799,}$ and drawing on his experience of paying his troops in specie, France officially returned to the bimetallic standard. Napoleon was to change the face of modern Europe in ways he wouldn't even begin to comprehend, by ending the Holy Roman Empire after defeating the Austrians in the Battle of Austerlitz in 1805, combined with beating the Prussians at Jena-Auerstedt in 1806, he initiated a chain of events that led to the formation of a nationalist German state, which was militaristic in its outlook.

The hyperinflation of the French economy during mass printing of the assignat was the first true example of hyperinflation; coupled with the usual suspects of war, economic collapse, food shortages and riots; along with the writings of famous philosophers such as Jean Jacques Rousseau, whose famous quote "Man is born free, but everywhere he is in chains" spurred the French to violently overthrow their monarch Louis XVI, along with the traditional order of its society and create a republic. The fundamental difference between the French and American Revolutions was the French Revolution fundamentally sought to change wholly change society, whilst the American Revolution wished to maintain the traditional structures but gain the right to secure autonomy in decision-making.

7. GERMAN UNIFICATION AND THE WEIMAR REPUBLIC

"Eisen und Blud" (Blood and Iron) Ending of speech by Otto Von Bismark on 30th September 1862 as Prime Minister of Prussia about the unification of German territories.

Perhaps the most famous example of hyperinflation in history is that of Weimar Germany in 1923, to understand this episode we need to understand the psyche of the German people in the build-up to the First World War and to understand this we need to have a brief overview of the history of Germany, in particular Prussia which became the dominant force after unification.

The concept of Germany as a distinct region in itself can be traced back to when Julius Caesar marched his forces to fight the Celtic people of Gaul in the Gallic wars. Gaul at the time incorporated all the areas of present-day France, Switzerland, Belgium, and parts of Germany. Caesar categorised the people that he encountered in battle as 'Gauls' 'Aquitani' 'Belgae' and 'Germans' and referred to the area which had been unconquered East of the river Rhine as Germania, also using the river Rhine as a boundary between Germania and Gaul.

In 9 AD. at the battle of Teutoburg forest where an alliance of Germanic people led by Arminius, a Germanic officer from Varus's auxilia, ambushed a Roman legion and their auxiliaries led by Publius Varus. This defeat is regarded as important historically as it is seen as the end of the triumphant period of expansion under Emperor Augustus. It showed the Germanic people as an organised warrior-like race and persuaded the Romans (all be it temporarily) from attempting to conquer Germania and settling for the lands West of the Rhine, whilst the lands East of the Rhine would remain independent of Roman control. This remained so until the series of wars known as the Marcomannic Wars between 166-180 AD under Marcus Aurelius. Although the wars brought victory to the Romans, it was ultimately a Pyrrhic victory as it not only led to the Antonine's Plague, (mentioned in Chapter 3 on the Roman Empire) the war exposed the weakness of Rome's Northern frontier, which required half of its legions (16 out of 33) to be stationed along the Danube and the Rhine, drawing on huge reserves of the Roman Empires wealth and resources. The ultimate irony would be that it would be a German 'Barbarian' King Odoacer who in 476 ADS deposed the last reigning emperor Romulus Augustulus. On the fall of the Roman Empire, Europe broke up and fell into numerous small feudal states, amongst them a collection of ever-shifting entities became known as 'The Holy Roman Empire'.

The history of the Holy Roman Empire stretches back to the invasion of the Iberian Peninsula (an area which covered most of Spain, and Portugal along with a small area of France, Andorra, and Gibraltar) by the Umayyad Caliphate. The Umayyad Caliphate was the second of four Islamic Caliphates founded in Arabia after the prophet Mohammed's death. They ruled the Islamic world between 661-750 BC with the capital city being in Damascus and it stretched from Central Asia through to the Straights of Gibraltar. (Szczepanski, 2021) It invaded and conquered the Iberian Peninsula from the Visigoths and looked on course to overrun the whole of Western Europe with the Frankish army being the only obstacle for the Caliphate to overcome. In the battle of Tours in 732 AD Charles Martel, the King of the Franks led his army to victory against the Umayyads and although the caliphate remained in parts of the Peninsula until 1031, it was effectively ended when it was dealt a shattering blow with defeat in Constantinople in 740 AD. With his victory, Martel laid the foundations for the Carolingian Empire which was the first phase of the Holy Roman Empire.

The Holy Roman Empire was initially formed as an alliance between the Pope and the Frankish Empire and as Voltaire succinctly puts it "It was neither Holy, nor Roman, nor an Empire". The Empire never took steps towards nationhood unlike France or England and throughout its long history was an amalgamation of different feuding states, all having their own identities, cultures and laws, states also grew and shrunk throughout the period, until the growth of two major super players Austria and Prussia, with Prussia eventually becoming the dominant power to form the nation of Germany. It was throughout most of its existence a set of Kingdoms loosely set of ideological principles rather than one political entity backed by a state, it was also largely Germanic with no claim to Roman ancestry. In 795 Pope Leo the Third was forced out of the papacy for the sole reason of not being a part of the elite establishment but a commoner. In 799 he returned with the Franks under their King Charlemagne. With the powerful force of the Franks backing him, Leo became Pope once again and to reward Charlemagne anointed him 'Emperor of the Romans' creating the concept Holy Roman Empire, (although he was still technically the King of the Carolingian Empire) this was done to ensure the Papacy would receive the support of the Holy Roman Empire should it be required. (Wilson, 2017) It is interesting to note that the term *Sacrum Romanum Imperium* (Holy Roman Empire) was not officially used until 1254, although the term Holy Empire dates back to 1157, the term Empire goes back to 1034. The term Holy Roman Emperor dates to 964 ADS under Otto 1st (Barraclough, 2022).

The Prussian state was to dominate the region of the Holy Roman Empire and eventually led to the unification of Germany and it dominated the new state. Its early history was greatly influenced by the Teutonic Knights who were a member of a Catholic military order 'Deutscher Orden' or Teutonic Order and officially formed in 1198. Its first mission was to help retake Jerusalem from the Arabs in the Third Crusade, when this ultimately failed, the Knights became based in Acre within the Kingdom of Jerusalem where their function was to accommodate German Crusaders to the Holy Land, collect port tolls, running hospitals and guarding pilgrims. The Knights left in 1211 after the Kingdom of Jerusalem fell, they went to the Kingdom of Hungary to help fight and successfully defend the Hungarian borders firstly against the Cumans and then the Ayyubids in 1217 and 1218. In 1225 they were themselves expelled by force from Hungary by King Andrew the Second after they started to try and build their state in Transylvania. In 1226 they joined forces with Poland to fight the pagans in Lithuania and Prussia, and eventually won a degree of independence in Prussia by conquering the original inhabitants of the area in what has become known as Old Prussia, the people of which were Baltic pagans not Germanic in any way, thus making them an easy target for expansion. The Knights's arrival in Northern Europe saw the start of a shift in power in the continent and the rise of Prussia as a great power.

In 1525 the Grand Master Albert of Prussia converted to Lutheranism and ended the ties to Catholicism (although not the Holy Roman Empire, this was to come several centuries later), declaring himself the first ruler of the Duchy of Prussia making himself a feudal ruler. He already had some family members in power as the House of Hohenzollern, ruling in Brandenburg, a small German state based around Berlin. In 1618 when the Prussian ruler Albert Frederick died childless, John Sigismund of Brandenburg took the opportunity to inherit the Duchy of Prussia and form the Brandenburg-Prussia Duchy. In the same year began probably the most destructive war ever fought in Europe known as the Thirty Years War, between 1618 1648, where it is estimated that between 5 and 8 million people died as a result of battle, disease, and famine. When it ended Prussia had added another five states, although they were all geographically disconnected and each principality having its own laws and customs.

In 1701 Frederick the First (1701-1712) became the first King of Prussia and formed the Kingdom of Prussia; under his son Frederick Willhelm the First (1712-1740) who became known as 'the soldier King' due to one every nine men serving as a soldier. He also allowed immigration on a large scale and incorporated the new arrivals into society, it is estimated that by 1710 one-third of Berliners were French Protestants, he also accepted waves of protestant refugees escaping religious persecution from South Germany. Frederick the Great increased the army from 83,000 under his father to 100,000 which doubled to 200,000 in times of war. They managed this expenditure through what was known as 'Prussian Thrift' coupled with the strong Protestant work ethic and taxes, four-fifths of all the revenue collected was spent on the army. Voltaire famously said, "Where some states have an army, the Prussian army has a state", Prussia continued to expand until Napoleon defeated it in the Napoleonic wars of 1802-1815, in particular, the defeat of Jena-Auestedt (October 14th, 1806) saw Prussia lose half its territories and also the Holy Roman Empire ceased to exist and became known as the German Confederation which was an amalgamation of thirty-nine sovereign states, the most powerful of these states being Prussia and Austria, with its first leader being Emperor Franz Joseph the first. By 1815 Prussia sided with the British and helped to finally defeat Napoleon at the Battle of Waterloo for this was rewarded by having much of its territories returned and for those parts it lost, some new ones were added, including 40% of the Kingdom of Saxony and much of Westphalia and the Rhineland. (Haffner, 1980)

In the aftermath of the Revolutions sweeping Europe in 1848, which were a series of upheavals occurring throughout Europe, that eventually saw up to fifty states or countries involved, the aims of which were to implement the political removal of monarchical states to create various independent, democratic nation states, the German Confederation, whom before this were embroiled in its own political turmoil as to whom should be the leading nation of a unified Germany, the two nations involved being Prussia and Austria. The Confederation were ahead of the game with regards to some of the Revolutionary ideals, it was quite liberal and tolerated different religions and encouraged immigration, also not minding what you did in your private life, so long as you paid your taxes and or served in the military. It even had the first freely elected parliament for all the German states called the Frankfurt Parliament, which offered King Frederick William IV of Prussia the crown of a united Germany; he refused the offer, firstly because he saw the Parliament as a revolutionary assembly and thus had no right to offer Royal titles, but he also felt the formation of a German Empire would end Prussian independence within the German states.

Due to a lack of cohesion and co-ordination, the 1848 Revolution fizzled out, however in the same year Denmark embarked on a war with the German Confederation over two Duchies; Schleswig and Holstein, it lasted between 1848-1851, culminating in a victory for Denmark. In 1861 Prince William Isucceeded the Prussian throne and appointed Otto Von Bismark as the Prime Minister the following year. Bismark was to be the prime mover in the unification of Germany, ultimately leading to World War I and the Hyperinflation consequences of Weimar Germany which followed. Before the calamity of World War I Bismark embroiled Prussia in three wars, the Second Schleswig War (1864) where the Danish were soundly defeated by Prussia with the aid of Austria; the second war was the Austro-Prussian War in 1866 (also known as the seven-week war) which was fought against

Austria in a dispute over how to divide the administration over the captured Schleswig and Holstein territories; Prussia crushed the Austrian led coalition, leading to it taking possession of the Rhineland and Westphalia. Prussia was now starting to geographically connect all its territories for the first time. The third and final war which led to the unification of Germany was the Franco-Prussian war (1870-71) where Bismark skilfully manoeuvred Napoleon 3rd into declaring war with Prussia, this not only persuaded all the German states (less Austria) to act together as the memories of Napoleon I still loomed large, but it also aroused patriotic fervour against France in the whole of Germany. Collectively they swiftly defeated the French and followed on January 18th, 1871, by proclaiming William I asthe first Emperor (Kaiser) of a united Germany in the Hall of Mirrors at Versailles.

It is fitting to end the history of Prussia and thus Germany to get a perspective on how Prussia which had been reasonably liberal in its outlook and the role Bismark played in this and the decades he spent shaping its future as originally, he had believed as had most of Prussians that an independent Prussia was in its best interests. In the 'Eisen unt Blut' (Iron and Blood) speech by Otto Von Bismark on 30th September 1862 as Prime Minister of Prussia on the unification of German territories he said, "The position of Prussia in Germany will not be determined by liberalism but by its power......Not through speeches and majority decisions will the question of the day be decided but by iron and blood" (Steinberg, 2012). Germany has now turned from a nation with all thoughts of liberalism swept away from its identity into a nation which was increasingly militaristic, and imperialistic and that unquestioningly followed the state. This attitude would lead to the First World War with millions slaughtered and eventually the collapse of the state through the first true hyperinflationary period ever experienced in the world during the Weimar Germany.

WORLD WAR ONE, AND THE WEIMAR REPUBLIC

The unification of Germany saw it grow to become one of the world leaders of production and manufacturing overtaking the United Kingdom and rivalling the United States of America. In 1760 the Industrial Revolution started in Britain, lasting until around 1820-1840, with huge developments in chemical manufacturing, iron production processing, technical innovation, and the textile industry. (Horn, Rosenbrad & Smith, 2020) Between 1880-1913 the British share of world trade had declined from 38.2% to 30.2%, whilst Germany had increased its share in the same period from 17.2% to 26.6%. (Balfour, 1968) Between 1890 and 1913 Germany's export tripled and by 1913 Germany's share of overall world manufacturing had overtaken Britain's, whilst in 1914 German steel output was 17.6 million tons, which was larger than the combined production of Britain, Russia, and France. (Kennedy, 1989)

If you add to this astonishing output and economic performance, the fact that Bismark had also introduced the Health Insurance Act in 1883, making it the first national system in the world where both companies and employers contributed (Boissoneault, 2017) it will seem rather strange that Germany and the German people would willingly embark on a journey of self-destruction, but embark on it they did; to understand why we need to look at the causes.

The short explanation that we are usually taught in school is that World War One started in August 1914 with the assassination of Archduke Franz Ferdinand in the city Sarajevo of Bosnia and Herzegovina by Gavrilo Princip, a Yugoslav nationalist and member of a terrorist organisation called the Black Hand, which wanted the occupation of the Balkan states by the Austrian Hungarian empire to ended and the formation of a united Yugoslavia, this is a simplistic explanation for the cause of a war which devasted Europe and the assassination was really only the excuse that was required that had several long term issues building behind the scenes for several decades, war was coming, the whole of Europe knew it so it wasn't a matter of if but when.

There are four long-term causes of the war and have been given the anachronism M.A.I.N.

MILITARISM- This was not just in Germany and a legacy of the Prussian Empire but throughout Europe there was a massive increase in army training and equipment, compounded with industrialisation and new technologies everything from warships to rifles could be built on an industrial scale and not only more but also more devastating, like the world had never seen before. By the time the war had begun, Europe had massive arsenals and military resources which would wreak devastation like never before.

ALLIANCES- During the late 19th and early 20th centuries, countries throughout Europe formed mutual defence alliances which required the participating parties to support each other should there be a war in case of attacks by other alliances. The two main alliances were the Triple Entente of Great Britain, Russia and France, whilst Germany, Italy and Austria-Hungary formed the Triple Alliance. The war began after Austria-Hungary declared war on Serbia after the assassination of Archduke Franz Ferdinand, Russia rose to defend Serbia, and Germany then followed suit by defending Austria-Hungary, which in turn led to Britain and France being sucked into the conflict.

IMPERIALISM- A simplistic definition of Imperialism is to regard it as the expansion of a government's power through the conquest of other territories. The British and French had the largest areas, whilst Germany which had only recently unified came to the party quite late on in the game and were scrambling to add to their empire. When the war began, the colonies became recruiting grounds for the major powers which turned a European war into a worldwide affair.

NATIONALISM- each nation in Europe saw the rise in nationalism, all spurred on by pride in nationhood, empire building and by either winning a war against another power, giving a sense of superiority, or losing a war which led to resentment and grudges, non-more so than the Franco-Prussian war, leading to the unification of Germany.

Although Bismark died in 1898, it can be argued he was the architect of the war and shaped Europe into what it is today; he was the most brilliant statesman and foreign diplomat of the 19th Century and his tangled web of intrigue and deals with which his skills were able to control, it was, unfortunately this skill he had, that others were not able match which brought these four long term causes together in 1914, leading to such brutal and devastating consequences and which would ultimately contribute to the rise of Adolf Hitler and World War Two.

Another major factor that is often overlooked but is vital in laying the groundwork for World War One was the First and Second Balkan Wars of 1912-1913, where after centuries of the Ottoman Empire controlling the Baltic peninsula by the 19th Century a dramatic change was taking place, the empire was growing weaker, nationalism was on the rise, new states began to emerge and nations such as Greece, Serbia, Montenegro, Rumania and Bulgaria gained independence, this was only achieved with uprisings and bloodshed. Turkey's defeat to Russia in the Russo-Turkish Wars of 1877-1878, ensured the independence of the Balkan states but also created a great deal of mistrust from the major powers of Russia with the creation of a large and Russian-friendly Bulgaria. The major powers met in Berlin to modify the Treaty of San Stefano which had been agreed between Russia and Turkey after the war to limit Russian influence in the area. The major modification to the treaty returned most of Macedonia to the Ottomans to the anger of the Bulgarians, they weren't the only ones unhappy and brief wars were fought between Greece and Bulgaria in 1885 as well as between the Greeks and Ottomans in 1897. By the start of the 20th Century tensions were running high, with all these states now hoping to expand at not only the Ottomans but each other as well, the major powers were getting increasingly concerned over the balance of power in the area. The Ottoman Empire was in crisis both internally and externally, territorial losses due to defeat on the battlefield led to violent instability at home, leading to the Young Turks' constitutional revolution in 1908 with a desire to modernise the constitution, the empire, the army and create an Ottoman identity and to preserve its territory, in particular Macedonia.

In 1911, Italy saw the weakness of the Ottomans and occupied Libya, the other Balkan states watched to see how everything was going to be played out, previously to maintain stability the major powers had supported the Ottomans, not this time and the Italo-Turkish war took place. By March 1912 Serbia and Bulgaria had agreed to a defensive alliance, but by May that had changed to an offensive alliance; Montenegro and Greece also joined, and they formed the Balkan League to make war on the Ottomans, knowing they were bogged down in Libya and the major powers were not going to intervene, they formally declared war on October 16th, 1912.

Bulgaria had some huge victories very quickly and made great inroads into Thrace and even almost entered Constantinople. In Macedonia the Serbs initially defeated the Ottomans, eventually taking the battle to the Ottomans and routing them, the Ottomans withdrew to Southern Albania.

In the South of Macedonia, the Greeks headed for the strategically important seaport city of Salonika. (Now Thessaloniki) The Bulgarians were incensed as they had lost men in the campaign in Macedonia and moved towards Salonika asking the Ottomans to surrender to them, they were unfortunately for them too late as they had already surrendered to the Greeks on November 8th. The Bulgarians entered the city and an uneasy peace ensued. To add to this melting pot of confusion religion is added with atrocities of Christians on Muslims and Muslims on Christians taking place creating more anger, hatred, resentment, and desire for revenge in the region.

Before the first war ended on the 30th of May 1913 all members of the Balkan League as well as Romania started to argue amongst themselves over who was to get what lands, with no one wanting to honour any pre-war agreements, even the arrangement before the conflict started that Russia was to mediate any disputes fell by the wayside. Bulgaria felt the most hard done by and all this friction led to the inevitable Second Balkans War on June 29th, 1913, more atrocities this time by Bulgarians on Greek, Serb and Turkish civilians took place, whilst atrocities were committed against Bulgarians. The Bulgarians were facing defeat when Romania entered the fray and took the opportunity to take Southern Dobruja, 250,000 Romanian troops poured into Bulgaria via the Danube and headed towards the capital city Sophia. Bulgaria offered no resistance. The Ottomans also saw an opportunity and entered Thrace on July 12th, with Bulgaria offering little resistance, many Bulgarian citizens fled creating a new wave of refugees entering Sophia. The Russian government who had previously been friendly to Bulgaria now refused to help; the Bulgarian pro-Russian government was then replaced by a pro-German one. Fighting continued with Bulgaria in defensive battles against both the Serbs and Montenegrins in the North and the Greeks in the South. With no breakthrough, the Greeks formally asked for an armistice and the Second Balkan War ended on 10 August 1913. (Hall, 2000) The map of the Balkans was redrawn again mainly to the disadvantage of the Bulgarians. This whole war left a legacy of mistrust, anger, and a desire for revenge in the region and helped create the catastrophe which would eventually be played out just a year later.

By 1914 the Germans seemed to be leading an enviable idyllic life, yet that life was fast approaching the end and this year was going to be the last year when they would know real peace and be fully solvent until the later part of the 20th Century. The war, which seemed to promise so much for both the Kaiser and the German people would end four years later in defeat, humiliation, economic ruin, and a human catastrophe, leading to Hitler, Nazi Germany and more of the same a mere twenty-one years later. All this seemed totally inconceivable at the start of the war as Germany boasted rich iron and coal deposits, a booming industrial base, 68 million people who were both skilled and industrious and even before any general mobilisation the Prussian influence in the army meant they had 500,000 men under arms with millions more former trained conscripts which could be called upon.

Most Germans knew their strengths, but what is probably more important to know is your weaknesses and Germany had several major flaws which was unacknowledged by its leadership. Firstly, Germany was tied to the Austro-Hungarian Empire which was described in Berlin as 'being shackled to a corpse'. Secondly, despite attempts to rival Britain's naval power, it is a country that is essentially landlocked and thus susceptible to a British blockade, a situation the British exploited so ruthlessly that by the end of the war, the German population was reduced to a state of semi-starvation and thirdly and probably the most important weakness was that despite its confidence, Imperial Germany was not only short of the money needed to fight any prolonged war with the Triple Entente, it equally lacked any means of acquiring it.

The military side of the Imperial General staff's plan to deal with this was to have a massive, no-holds-barred attack against France through neutral Belgium, the aim being to deliver a swift knockout blow that would then allow Germany to turn its full military attention to dealing with the Russians in the East. The original plan had been developed ten years earlier by the Chief of the Prussian General staff, Field Marshall Count Alfred von Schlieffen and became known as 'The Schlieffen Plan'. On the economic side the financial mandarins that ran the Reichsbank (the German national bank) which was formed after the unification of Germany in 1871, were fully aware of the financial problems that would occur if Germany undertook a major war against the Triple Entente. The expectation of a quick end to the war was based on experiences such as the Schleswig Wars which were over in a matter of months if not weeks. Industrialisation had changed warfare with new weapons such as the machine gun and artillery changed the way future wars were to be fought, the Germans became bogged down on two fronts as the breakthrough on the Western front never materialised and they became mired in a war which spanned miles of trenches, whilst simultaneously fighting a war on the Eastern front, which although successful when the Russians had their second revolution at the end of 1917, known as the October revolution on the 25th October (the West recognise the date as the 7th November as the Russians use Julian calendar, whilst the West uses the Gregorian Calendar) which did free up resources, it was too little too late.

As war was becoming increasingly certain, the international monetary markets were becoming unsettled so the mandarins in the Reichsbank developed a secret blueprint that would enable the nation to overcome its financial limitations, the first part of this plan was to abandon the gold standard. The wheels had now been set in motion for the world's most famous hyperinflationary episode that was to take place in 1922-1923 in Weimar Germany. For decades the German paper currency could be converted into solid gold or silver, with one-third of all the currency printed having to be backed by gold, it was this system of convertibility that had led not only Germany but all the other major countries' currencies stability throughout the decades. So, why was it that the Reichsbank suspended the gold standard? Firstly, as Germany stood on the brink of war its citizens started to become increasingly alarmed in early July by the headlines of war and as the prospect of the reality of war and its consequences began to dawn on the population that by the end of July, they began to form queues, initially outside the doors of the private banks then finally at the Reichsbank itself. The fear of war had revived old anxieties about paper currencies, the people were losing confidence and trust in it so they wanted something more tangible that they could rely on, they wanted gold and silver which had stood the test of time over several thousand years.

On Friday 31st July 1914, the doors of the Reichsbank were closed (with the private banks having suspended the currency exchange for gold and silver three days earlier) and weren't opened until Tuesday 4th August 1914, by which time it had become pointless to queue and demand gold for paper currency because the banks simply refused. On the 4th of August a raft of emergency legislation declared convertibility of paper currency to gold was suspended for the duration of the war; fiat currency now became the only currency in circulation, gold as always happened in the past was either hoarded or became the property of the government as it was recognised that gold was the only thing they could use to trade internationally for precious minerals and resources which were required by the military. In addition, the most important factor, in the government's collection of gold is that under the Loan Bureau Law which was included on the 4th of August measures meant that the more gold they had the greater the illusion of gold-backed currency. Under the Labour Bureau Law, the Reichsbank was no longer limited in its ability to print paper currency and have it restricted to the amount of gold it held. (Taylor 2013)

The Loan Bureau Law had another function which proved to be pivotal in the creation of huge price increases during the war years and the springboard for the hyperinflationary period of 1923. The Law relieved the Reichsbank of its previous duty to provide credits to individual German states, in its place the law set up a system of bureaus that would provide the states a three-month credit note (in reality, they were continually renewed so never actually cashed in) which was backed by either goods or securities, acceptable forms of securities were Treasury bonds issued by the German states and also crucially war bonds. At this point all is straightforward, unfortunately hidden in the Law was a stipulation that the Loan Bureau could issue Bureau notes and although not truly legal tender, were rapidly accepted as such and started to be used in general circulation alongside the paper currency issued by the Reichsbank. What in essence this meant was an endless financial doom loop of unlimited borrowing as there was nothing to stop the state or communities from using the war bonds to acquire loan bureau notes, which in turn could be used as security to buy more loan bureau notes, ad infinitum. In conjunction with this, the Reichsbank would increase its ability to print money that could be then funnelled into the war effort. The Law on the 4th of August had at least tried to cover this eventuality by putting a ceiling on the issue of Loan Bureau notes to 1.5 billion marks, but by November 1914 it had raised the ceiling to 3 billion marks to coincide with the first-ever war bond drive. After that point, the ceiling became irrelevant as it would continually be moved up as and when required and so by the end of 1918 the amount of loan bureau notes produced was 15.15 billion marks of which more than a third was owned by the Reichsbank, which meant it was allowed to print 15.7 billion fully legal and valid marks based on this so-called war bond 'security' in reality it was worthless and meaningless and just an exercise in self-delusion, this self-delusion not only prolonged the war but was the very bedrock for the hyperinflation that was to come. (Taylor, 2013)

The effect of this excessive expansion of the money supply in Germany was two-fold, firstly throughout the war the German people started to see the value of the Mark fall by half between 1914 1918 and then by August 1919 it halved and by early 1920 the Mark had one-fortieth of its purchasing power left; this was making imports of goods increasingly more expensive. The war didn't equally affect all Germans' finances, those who worked in defence-related industries did relatively well compared to their counterparts who worked in the non-industrial and service sectors, the male defence industry workers saw their daily wages increase by 152%, the women did even better with wage rises of 186%, those employed outside of these sectors saw rises of 82% for the men and 102% (Feldman, 1992) for the women add to the fact that there were millions more women at work due to many men being conscripted to military service, this was a recipe for massive price rises and the erosion of purchasing power. It is estimated that through the war years prices had roughly trebled during the course of the war. By 1918 the German Mark had recovered considerably, yet this wasn't reflected in the cost of living and as standards of living had declined the German people started to notice it; in Hanover, by the summer of 1918 a woman's weekly wage could only purchase two kilograms of butter. (Bessel, 1993)

The people who suffered the most throughout the war years were the older, retired middle classes. Before 1914 they were respected members of society, whose great virtue was the aptitude for hard work, thrift and savings, qualities which enabled the newly formed Germany to grow so rapidly in its early years, however once on fixed income pensions the rising prices eroded not only their income but their savings as well. The difference in wealth between the middle classes and working classes was narrowing and not because the working class were getting richer but because the middle classes were getting poorer (Taylor, 1993), thus the war had inadvertently created a more equal society, everyone was getting equally poorer and getting equally angrier, this was to be the catalyst that would eventually not only contribute to Germany losing the war but to help in the rise of the Nazi party approximately 20 years later.

To add to the supply side woes of the German economy, military production kept being ramped up, so much so that by late 1916 the 'Hindenburg Programme' was introduced to accelerate the armament production with caution being thrown to the wind with regards to the material and resources which would be required. (Bessel, 1993, P13) (Feldman, 1992, P154) Little consideration was taken in the decision-making process and even farmers were taken off the land to join in the production effort, along with the shortages of imported fertilisers due to British blockades, the problem of food shortages was acerbated with it resulting in the halving of wheat production, driving prices even higher, this policy not only lowered food production but Industrial production as well as we can see from the graph below.

Indices of Industrial Production (1914=100) (Ferguson, 1999)

GERMANY BRITAIN RUSSIA ITALY

1914 100 100 100 100

1915 81 102 115 131

1916 77 97 117 131

1917 75 90 83 117

1918 69 87 83 117

The whole economy was so distorted by the end of the war that when the Armistice was finally agreed and Germany was forced to make reparations at the Treaty of Versailles, it wasn't in a good place to do so.

Despite all the hardships the German population were suffering, by the Spring of 1918, there was a renewed optimism that the tide of the war was moving in their favour as a continuous stream of press reports about the successes of the German army kept morale and hopes high. This was to change suddenly and with a violent reversal of fortunes on August 8th, 1918, when a British counterattack at the town of Amens saw seventy per cent losses for the German army, the main losses were not from the dead or injured but in the numbers being made prisoners, the soldiers were surrendering which is a major indication of a collapse in morale amongst the rank and file. (Jonke, 2008) The press reporting had set up expectations of Germany winning the war and almost overnight the people of Germany were now facing the inevitability of defeat making the shock and confusion an even more difficult and bitter pill to swallow.

By late October the German frontline had been pushed back over 50 miles, which in a war that over the years distances gained could be measured in yards was an enormous distance. In early October 1918, General Ludendorff who had become the chief policy maker and by de facto led a military dictatorship that dominated the German government announced that an armistice had to be obtained on virtually any terms offered, assuming it would be predominantly based around the American President Woodrow Wilsons fourteen points, which attempted to secure a just peace, which included economic free trade, decreased armaments amongst all nations, open diplomacy without secret treaties, Belgium to be evacuated and restored and the return of Alsace-Lorraine and all the French territories back to France, the creation of an independent Polish state and Austria-Hungary to be provided with the opportunity for self-determination. Unfortunately for the Germans, the Entente had other ideas for the settlement and in late October Ludendorff had changed his mind and declared these conditions unacceptable but by now his power and influence were diminished and soon was dismissed by the Kaiser and replaced by General Wilhelm Groener. Ludendorff was to become a major antagonist after the war, feeling bitter and betrayed about his dismissal, he became a prominent nationalist and took part in both the Kapp Putch in 1920 and the Munich Beer Hall Putsch in 1923, eventually leaving politics after losing to Field Marshall Hindenburg to become the President in 1925.

With Ludendorff gone and the dictatorship subsiding, the coalition government of Majority socialists, (SPD) Progressives and the Centre, which had struggled to hold together since 1916 found itself in the position of being in charge and being responsible for sorting out the mess that the military had made, unlike countries like the UK and USA which had developed democracies over the centuries so had experience to fall back on, the fledgling German democracy was faced with genuine problems of enormous proportions and no experienced democratic leaders to steer them through the storm. They were torn between the Spartakists/Communists on the left who didn't want any form of government but revolution instead and on the right, they faced a group who firstly had no love of republicanism and secondly loathed the fact that it was the leader of the Centre Party Mathais Erzberger who had signed the humiliating Armistice deal on November 11th, 1918. (Ferguson, 1975)

Before the armistice deal the Kaiser, who is traditionally thought to have left Germany on November 9th, had in fact left for Spa on October 30th and only left for the neutral Netherlands once it was made clear that he did not have the support of either the German government or crucially the military. The November Revolution was triggered by the Kiel mutiny in early November when the naval command seeing Germany faced defeat still insisted on a final suicide mission by engaging in a pitch battle with the Royal Navy, however quite understandably the sailors who had been effectively locked down since 1916 in harsh conditions since the inconclusive Battle of Jutland, saw no reason to continue, the Kaiser was also informed by Groener that the returning army would march home in an orderly fashion for Hindenburg but would not fight for him, the Kaiser realising the game was up left for Holland and renounced his throne on November 9th. The German Revolution or November Revolution started after a general strike had been called on November 9th and lasted until the adoption of the Weimar Republic in August 1919. The January uprising was another general strike in connection with the November strike, but this time accompanied by an armed struggle. It took place in Berlin between the 5th and 12th of January and became a power struggle between the SPD led by Friedrich Ebert who favoured social democracy and the Communist Party of Germany (KPD) led by Karl Liebknecht and Rosa Luxembourg who wanted to set up a council similar to the one set up by the Bolsheviks in Russia. The revolution was quickly crushed by both government and paramilitary forces the Freikorps. Both Liebknecht and Luxemburg paid a heavy price for their part in the revolution, upon being discovered by the Freikorps, they were first tortured and then shot in the head. These outbreaks of violence were not the only uprising taking place, with revolutions erupting throughout Germany, this led to the relocation of the parliament from Berlin to the small but relatively stable Weimar and the start of the Weimar Republic which lasted from 1919 until 1933 when the Nazi party took power.

8. WEIMAR GERMANY: TREATIES, TREATIES AND MORE TREATIES

"Sauve Qui Peut"- Save himself who can, or loosely translated "Every man for himself".

The armistice came into force at 11 a.m. on November 11th, 1918, yet this was only a cease-fire for 36 days which would roll on until the actual treaty was to be signed, up until that point that the Germans signed the war could resume. The Treaty of Versailles was signed on June 28th, 1919, and became effective on the 10th of January 1920. The terms of the treaty were harsh on the Germans, they found it a very difficult pill to swallow, so much so that Germany's first democratically elected head of government Phillip Scheidemann resigned rather than sign it. After his resignation, a new coalition government was formed under Friedrich Ebert, although he shared his countrymen's disgust at the terms knowing he was in an impossible situation that if he refused to sign Germany could be invaded from the West, Ebert asked Hindenburg if there was any possibility the army was able to mount any form of meaningful resistance should the allies invade, and if there was then Ebert would have recommended against ratifying the treaty. Hindenburg along with Groener informed him they could not continue with another war no matter how limited. It was on this news that the government recommended the treaty be signed. It is interesting to note that the supreme army commanders made sure that no one from the military was present at the signing of the treaty.

What was in the treaty that made the Germans so shocked and so angry was that it caused political upheaval and essentially turned a once united German people against each other. After the armistice was signed in November, a conference was convened in Paris known as the Paris Peace Conference in January 1919 to work out the exact terms and officially end the conflict. Nearly thirty representatives attended but the 'Big Four' who drove the terms were America, Britain, France and Italy, the defeated nations of Germany, and their allies Austria-Hungary, Turkey and Bulgaria were not allowed to attend. The final text, which was signed on June 29th, 1919, had 240 pages which contained 440 separate articles, 116 related to the League of Nations, the rest around the terms Germany needed to sign to declare peace. The treaty was long and harsh, but the most brutal parts which the Germans found so reprehensible were: - Article 40-45 which compelled Germany to hand over Alsace-Lorraine along with the coal mines in the Saar basin to France, a plebiscite was to be held after 15 years to decide whether the people wanted to remain French or become part of Germany again. (In 1935 90% voted to be part of Germany) Article 87-93 gave what had been German West Prussia and other territories which had German ethnic inhabitants to a newly independent Poland. Article 159-163 was to reduce the size of the German army which at its peak had reached 1.9 million troops, to just 100,000 and that force was mandated to only maintain order within its borders. Articles 164-172 disarmed the German military regulating even how much ammunition it could have, whilst articles 181-197 reduced the naval forces and articles 198-202 prohibited Germany from having an air force, in essence, the German military was effectively neutered. Article 227-230 authorised the Allies to carry out war crimes trials, article 227 specifically called for a five-judge tribunal to put the abdicated Kaiser Wilhelm on trial (this never happened as the Dutch who were neutral refused to extradite him and there was no real desire from the British to follow it through. (He eventually died in Holland in 1941), 17 Germans were put on trial ranging from looting to sinking a hospital ship, but most were acquitted whilst the others who were found guilty received light sentences. The problem with the treaty is that the 'Big Four' all had different agendas, France wanted revenge and to ensure Germany was to never be a threat again, Italy was just looking for any opportunity to expand its empire, America was hoping for peace and consolidation between everyone whilst Britain seemed keen to punish the Germans somewhat but not so much as to destroy them. It is interesting to note that the Americans never signed the treaty along with China, who were angry at being unable to recover the lands held by Germany before the war instead they were turned over to the Japanese.

These conditions were seen as bad enough the but the real source of controversy and later much resentment was Article 231 which is commonly known as 'The War Guilt Clause' which meant Germany had to acknowledge and accept all responsibility for the loss and damage inflicted on the allies the amount was to be determined at a future date at future conferences, the ultimate figures were decided at the London Schedule of Payments. This clause then became the basis for the demand that Germany pay reparations and was originally set at 226 billion gold marks in January 1921, it was reduced in May of that year to 132 billion gold marks, the equivalent to $442 billion or £280 billion in 2022 prices. The price of 132 billion German gold marks which set at the London Schedule of Payments with the figure divided into three bands: A, B and C. The total of the A and B bands was 50 billion gold marks whilst the remainder (82 billion) was in the C band, which was interest-free, the payment of the C band was contingent on the Weimar Republics' ability to pay which was to be assessed by the Allied Committee at a later date. The sum was a compromise set by Belgium, as both the French and Italians wanted higher reparations, (the French as they suffered the most on the western front and wanted not only the money to rebuild its economy but also as a way of extracting revenge and to also stop the Germans from being a threat again, the Italians wanted to destroy Germany for political purposes so it could have one less rival in its Empire expansionist programme) the British and Americans wanted lower payments to offer a more conciliatory tone and also be more realistic, none believed that the payment could actually ever be made and the figure became based not on what was realistic payments for war damages but was the lowest amounts governments felt they could get their public to tolerate and accept as a justified punishment. (Marks, 1978) The figures that were eventually agreed on were in essence totally misleading, they were a tool to mislead the public into believing the Germans were being punished financially. Allied experts knew that there was no way the Germans and their allies could ever repay the amount, therefore the sum of bands A and B were the realistic figures that were felt could genuinely be paid, they also took into account the 9 billion paid between 1919-1921 thus leaving a total of 41 billion gold marks, which could be paid for in either cash or kind with commodities such as coal, timber, chemical dyes, factory machinery, etc, the C category was always meant to be conveniently forgotten about as time passed. (Fergusson, 1998) The Four other treaties were signed in the coming years which involved each of the German allies, all were based on the Treaty of Versailles, which was used as a blueprint, each in its way had profound effects on the destiny of Europe for the rest of the 20th Century.

The Treaty of St Germaine was signed by the Austrians and allies on September 10th, 1919, and came into force on July 16th, 1920. The treaty registered the break-up of the Hapsburg Empire which ensured the independence of Czechoslovakia, Poland, Hungary, and the Kingdom of the Serbs, it also forbids any union with Germany. The military clause allowed for only 30,000 troops and a break-up of the Austro-Hungarian navy, which was to be distributed amongst the allies. The war reparations became a difficult matter for the Allies to decide, one of the problems was in 1919 Karl Renner's Socialist Party won elections with a mandate to create a new constitution and lead the peace negotiations with the Allies. The Austrians were looking for Anschluss (union) with Germany as they thought that would help them economically, however, this was forbidden, especially by the French who thought it unthinkable that further resources and manpower, could be put into the German hands. The real problem for the Allies was who was to pay the Austrian-Hungary reparations as the country didn't exist anymore. Once Austria had been broken up the oil-rich areas of Galicia went to Poland, the farmlands went to Hungary, the biggest factories went to Czechoslovakia, and they had no access to maritime trade combine this with a demoralised and exhausted people, it was difficult to see where the payments were going to come from anyway, the capital city Vienna which had been the fourth largest in the world and had a thriving economy was now filled with starving people all looking for work which wasn't readily available. Francesca Wilson a British humanitarian worker noted,

"This is how an empire ends, not with a bang, nor even... a whimper.... Nothing here but hunger, cold and hopelessness. It would appear that Austria, however improbable, had received harsher terms than the Germans, the map of Europe was being radically redrawn". (Sargent, 1982)

On 27 November 1919, the Treaty of Neuilly was signed between Bulgaria and the Allies, coming into force on August 9th, 1920. Bulgaria joined the war in 1915 with the Central Powers essentially to get the lands back that they had lost in the Balkan wars two years previously, they were the first powers to ask for an armistice as they were completely weary of war, uprisings and demonstrations, rebellions, and economic ruin. The armistice terms meant they had to evacuate the lands captured during the war, whilst several port cities were to be occupied by British and French troops, this at least spared them the insult of being taken over by Greek, Serbs their Balkan rivals. This was also crucially important as the Bulgarians had committed atrocities on civilians and feared reprisals, nevertheless, 100,000 Bulgarian speakers fled the disputed regions, thus exacerbating the desperate refugee crisis. The Bulgarian's hopes were pinned on Wilson's fourteen points and the right to self-determination, rather than be broken up, they also argued that Bulgaria was never formally a war with America and was forced into the war by Germany and Austria. As in the previous Balkan wars various factions made claims to various lands, drawing in the allies, who again all had different political reasons for whom they supported. In the end, the British and French won the day with the army being reduced to 20,000 and the air force to be disbanded. With regards the lands of Western Thrace were under the control of the allies who had agreed to give it to Greece, Yugoslavia received several small but strategically important areas along the Bulgarian borders; a population exchange was also implemented which saw 50,000 Bulgarians leave Greece, whilst 40,000 Greeks left Bulgaria. The repatriation costs were 2.15 billion gold Francs, a figure that was higher per capita than that imposed on Germany, although as with the German war debt it was eventually forgotten about. The war atrocities committed by the army in its occupation of Serbia were not dealt with. (Sargent, 1982).

One Treaty that had long long-lasting impact to this day was the Treaty of Trianon which dealt with Hungary, was drawn up at the Paris Peace Conference and was signed on 4th June 1920, it drew up new states and strengthened old neighbours as the old Kingdom broke up. The Kingdom of Hungary was approximately half of the Austro-Hungarian empire with Emperor Franz Joseph of Austria functioning as the Monarch. Post-armistice was a revolutionary period for Hungary and in 1918 Hungary declared itself a Republic, other areas also did likewise which led to conflicts as to where the borders lay. The Austrian-Hungarian empire was a very multi-ethnic state and multilingual; The Kingdom of Hungary was extremely diverse, with a 1910 census showing 54.4% of the population being ethnic Hungarian with the rest being made up of German-speaking Austrians in the West, Slovaks in the North, Romanians in the South and East, with Slavs also being in the South; some areas consisted of areas where the majority were Hungarian speakers. When the empire broke up the different minorities started to make claims to the lands as new states emerged. Throw into the melting pot instability and violence in 1919, along with the threat of a Bolshevik Revolution, several border wars with neighbours, in particular Romania, made sorting out a peace all could agree on almost impossible. At the end of 1919 Admiral Miklos Horthy established control in what remained of Hungary's borders, provided some stability but used the 'White Terror' which was violence against both the leftists and Jews to achieve this. The allies who saw that there was at least some stability managed to get the treaty signed with Horthy, the treaty ensured the three regional powers all ended up with new territorial boundaries, the Czechs took control of Slovakia, (also known as Upper Hungary) the new state of Yugoslavia took control of Croatia and parts of Southern Hungary and Romania controlled Transylvania and several other provinces, despite the new borders all the old divisions and conflicts were still there, which resonate in this region today, where a study in 2020 showed 66% of Hungarians agreed that parts of neighbouring countries belonged to them. (Sargent, 1982)

The consequences were dire for Hungary, in all it lost 72% of its territory, its access to the sea, half of its ten biggest cities and all its precious metal mines. 3.5 million ethnic Hungarians also found themselves living outside the boundaries of their Motherland. (Tapon, 2012) The economic consequences of Trianon were especially harsh on the Hungarians, with it losing 90% of the engineering and printing industry, 89% of its timber industry, and 84 % of its iron industry. If this wasn't bad enough, it lost 61% of its arable land, 74% of its public road, 65% of its canals, 62% of its railroads, 83% of pig iron output, 55% of industrial plants and 67% of credit and banking institutions. (Tucker & Wood, 1996) The initial result was high unemployment and industrial output which had been increasing before World War One, falling by 65% and the production of grain fell by 70%. (Rothschild, 1946) To add to this, further conditions were imposed where the army was restricted to 35,000 men, the Danube fleet was confiscated, tanks, aircraft and warships were forbidden and the one that Germany felt most aggrieved concerning the war guilt clause and repatriations, the amount to be paid back was to be decided at a later date, however, it was suspended due to the weakness of the economy and never paid. The size of Hungary by the end was one-third of its size and had seven million people as opposed to 20 million and 3 million ethnic Hungarians living in what was now another country, with 400,000 returning to Hungary as refugees, (Ra'anan 1991) turning a very difficult economic situation to a desperate one.

The Treaty of Lausanne was the last of the peace settlements and the only one to endure to this day. At the San Remo conference held in April 1920, Britain and France shared the former Ottoman Empire's territories, using the League of Nations as a 'fig leaf' cover. In August 1920, the Treaty of Sevres partitioned the Empire's Anatolia heartland, assigning lands to Greece, Italy and yet more to France. The forces of the Turkish Nationalist Movement refused the terms and under Mustafa Kemal Pasha (later Atatürk) expelled French forces from Southeast Anatolia. The Turks kept fighting eventually forcing negotiations at the Swiss resort town of Lausanne between November 1922, finally signing on the 24th of July 2023. The treaty recognised the boundaries of the modern state of Turkey, whilst Turkey made no claims to its former Arab provinces. The allies also dropped their demands for autonomy of Turkish Kurdistan, and Turkish cession of territory to Armenia which had previously been agreed upon in the Treaty of Sevres, it was also a blow to Wilson's policy goal which was the right to national self-determination. The Turkish Straits between the Aegean Sea and the Black Sea was also declared open to all shipping. Crucially for Turkey, no financial repatriations were made as well, and no responsibility was admitted for the Genocide against Armenians. Out of all the follies of the negotiations made after World War 1, this must surely rate as the most scandalous; the systematic deportation of and killing of Armenians by the Turks of the Ottoman Empire that began in 1915 and which, and by the early 1920's, when the genocide finally ended, between 600,000 and 1.5 million Armenians were dead. The Turkish government to this day does not recognise the scope of this event. The Kurds have also fared badly ever since, fighting separate guerrilla campaigns to this day in Turkey, Iran, Iraq, and Syria to achieve autonomy. (Sargent, 1982).

Weimar Germany and its hyperinflation period are regarded as the most famous example of this economic phenomenon in history, yet at the same time, four other countries also suffered on a comparable scale, all newly formed, and all going through the same type of pain, the four being Austria, Hungary, Czechoslovakia, and Poland. (Sargant, 1982)

Austria suffered food scarcity throughout the war, primarily due to the effective allied blockade. Once the treaty of St Germaine was signed and new national boundaries were imposed, it effectively cut off Austria's food sources from its former empire, in addition the government of Austria reabsorbed a large number of Austrian Imperial bureaucrats who were no longer welcome in the new states that they happen to find themselves in. It also faced a large-scale unemployment crisis originating from its need to reconvert its economy from the wartime footing it had been on for the previous four years to peaceful activities and producing goods that were actually required both nationally and internationally and if this wasn't enough problems that they faced the repatriations they owed were still actually unknown at the time but considered to be substantial, in effect the reparations commission held a blank mortgage against the assets and revenues of the Austrian government. Austria's response was to make large expenditures in the form of food relief and payments to the unemployed, in addition, the state monopolies and railways ran deficits as taxes and prices were kept relatively low. The government also ran substantial deficits which grew over the years, (see figure 1) it was financed by the government selling Treasury Bills to the Austrian section of the Austro-Hungarian bank, which led to the resulting rapid increase in the amount of 'high powered' money'. (See figure 2) High-powered money is where the magnitude of the monetary base is greatly expanded by the money multiplier, i.e., leverage.

Figure 1

Austrian Budgets 1919-1922 (in million paper crowns)

	Receipts	Expenditure	Deficits
1 Jan 1919-30 June 1919	1,339	4,043	2,704
1 July 1919-30 June 1920	6,295	16,873	10,578
1 July 1920-30 June 1921	29,483	70,601	41,118
1 July 1921-30 Dec 1922	209,763	347,533	137,770

Source: Pasvolsky (p 102)

The total notes in circulation grew at an enormous rate to fund these welfare benefits (see figure 2)

Figure 2

Total notes in circulation of Austrian Crowns (In thousands of Crowns)

1919

March 4,687,056

June 7,397,692

1920

January 13,266,878

June 16,971,344

1921

January 34,525,634

June 49,685,140

1922

January 227,015,925

June 549,915,678

1923

January 4,110,551,163

June 5,432,619,312

1924

January 6,735,109,000

June 7,774,958,000

(The peak of printing was in December 1925 with 8, 387,767,000 being printed)

Source: Young (Vol 2, p 292)

The expansion of central bank notes arose primarily from the policy of discounting Treasury Bills, but also from the central bank's practice of making loans and discounts to private agents at interest rates of between 6% and 9% per annum, whilst at the same time price rises between January 1921 – August 1922 averaged approximately 10,000%, (see Figure 3) this is serious hyperinflation territory and making loans at such meagre interest rates would only fuel the price rises, however for the person borrowing the money purchasing hard assets would become virtually free as they could buy the asset at one price, a year later the debt would not only be worthless relative to its original price, the interest rate would be totally irrelevant. Combining this with the depreciating currency (See Figure 4) led to the 'Flight of the Crown' with people attempting to hold foreign currencies or real assets.

In Vienna during this period of collapse, a phenomenon known as 'Mushroom Exchange Banks' sprang up on every street corner to enable people to exchange their Krone (Crowns) into Zurich Francs within minutes of receiving them, this was due to avoid the risk of loss during the time it would take to reach your usual bank, it was actually seen as prudent to order two beers at once, rather than one at a time as the depreciation that could occur in the time it took to drink the first one. (Keynes, 1944) The flight of the Crown had an obvious problem for the Austrian government as it needed to finance its deficit and this flight had the effect of diminishing the resources the government could command by printing currency, in other words, it was making its worthless money printing even more worthless, much quicker. To try and overcome this they established a system of exchange controls administered by an agency called Devisenzentrale, whose function was to increase the amount of Austrian Crown held by Austrians and make it illegal for Austrians to hold foreign currencies, however for a nation which once prided itself on its honesty and integrity, all bets were off as survival had become more important so it had no impact on the value of the currency. The Crown continued to depreciate until it abruptly stabilised in August 1922 at 77,300.00, dropping to 70,760.00 in July 1923 where it stayed until December 1924. This occurred despite the increase in the currency being printed and no currency reforms. The reason it stopped was due to the intervention of the council of the League of Nations which gave a binding commitment to the government of Austria to restructure the financial system of Austria, this commitment saw a return of confidence as it was seen that serious reform was underway.

The commitment given by the League was primarily backing the liabilities of the central bank with 100% of gold, foreign assets and commercial paper as notes and deposits, created through the open market operations in those assets, whereas before the central bank was backed by treasury bills, in other words not backed at all, it was fiat. The value of the crown stabilised due to the government agreeing to run a fiscal policy compatible with maintaining the convertibility of its liabilities to dollars, in conjunction with collecting appropriate levels of taxation. It was this that allowed the government to increase the liabilities sixfold and not create additional inflationary pressures because the crown would remain stable as long as the assets purchased by the bank were sufficiently valuable, in other words, it was being fiscally responsible which promoted both confidence and trust. All of this encouraged the Austrians to convert their hordes of foreign exchanges back into crowns; the one downside to all this was the substantial increase in the unemployment rate, (see figure 5) although unemployment did fluctuate over the years and it could be argued that the poor state of the economy was a factor, the stabilisation of the currency did add to the problem as it was not as freely available.

Figure 3

Austrian Retail Price Index 1921-1924 (January 1921=100)

1921- January 100

1921-June 150

1922-January 1,142

1922-June 3,431

1923-January 17,526

1923-June 20,482

1924-January 22,941

1924-June 24,267

Source: Young (Vol 2, p 293)

Figure 4

Exchange Rate, Austrian Crown per United States Dollar in the New York Market

<u>1919</u>

January 17.09

June 29.63

1920

January 271.43

June 145.00

1921

January 654.00

June 720.00

1922

January 7,375.00

June 18,900.00

1923

January 71,500.00

June 70,800.00

1924

January 70,760.00

June 70,760.00

Source: Young (Vol 2, p 294)

Figure 5
Number of Austrians Unemployed in Receipt of Relief (in thousands)
1922 1923 1924 1925 1926
January 17 117 98 154 208
April 42 153 107 176 202
July 33 93 64 118 151
October 38 79 78 119 148
Source: League of Nations (p 87)

The effect on the individual citizen's life is beautifully summed up in Adam Fergusson's book 'When Money Dies' where throughout he uses passages from an affluent middle-class lady's dairy called Anna Eisenmenger, she recalls having investments in 1914 which gave her a return of approximately 5,000 crowns per annum, this gave her a very comfortable lifestyle which included the hiring of servants. In October 1918 she went to the bank to cash in 20,000 for immediate use and was advised by the bank manager to buy Swiss francs, she declined as by then it was illegal and felt safe in the knowledge she had a large sum invested in government gilt-edged securities, by December she was informed that these securities were effectively worthless and that she should have bought the Swiss francs, with ruin laying before her, the dairy chronicles detail the hyperinflationary events where food if it could be found had become completely unaffordable, the desperation of people from the city roaming of the countryside in gangs looking for food as they believed it was being hoarded. She even describes the collapse of the crown on the international markets with the consensus being that it wasn't the collapse of the Crown but the strength of the dollar causing the massive disparity in the exchange rate and that it was the Jews and speculators causing the problem and when the stock market, which had now become her and millions of others only salvation (people had speculated on the stock exchange as there was no other options of where to put their money) finally collapsed in 1924 she writes

> "Panic has seized the stock exchange....my millions have dwindled to about a thousand....we belong to the new poor. The middle class has been reduced to proletariat.... I feel that my strength is deserting me. I cannot go on" (Fergusson, 1975).

In the space of ten short years, Frau Eisenmenger's ruin was complete, she would not be alone in this.

Often forgotten about was the plight of the Hungarian people and the hyperinflation which they endured. At the end of the war, Hungary experienced political and economic turmoil as the Hapsburg King Charles was replaced by the government of Prince Karolyi. In March 1919 the Karolyi was overthrown by the Bolsheviks led by Bela Kun. This regime only lasted four months as Romania invaded Hungary, occupied it for a few weeks then withdrew. This is where Admiral Horthy made his entrance, took power and imposed the 'White Terror' to replace the 'Red Terror'. The financial situation for Hungary was actually even more complicated than that of either Austria or Weimar Germany; at the end of the war the currency of Hungary consisted of the notes of the Austro-Hungarian bank, a provision of the peace treaty of both St Germain and Trianon was that the successor states of the Austrian-Hungarian empire were required to stamp the notes of the Austro-Hungarian bank that were held by their respective residents in the newly created countries, in effect recognising these stamped notes now as the debt of these newly formed states, unfortunately for Hungary to add to these notes and before it could enact the provision of Trianon, the Bolshevik regime issued new notes of its own. To Hungary's credit, these Bolshevik-issued notes were honoured by subsequent governments.

The Austro-Hungarian bank was liquidated in 1919 and replaced by a separate Austrian and Hungarian section. The functions of the Hungarian section were assumed in 1921 by a State Note Institute, under the control of the Ministry of Finance. In August 1921, the Note Institute issued its notes, the Hungarian Krone in exchange for the Hungarian stamped notes previously issued by the Austro-Hungarian bank, along with several other classes of notes including those that had been issued by the Bolshevik regime. As Austria owed war reparations, and had assets under control by the Reparations Commission, the amount owed and terms of payment left in the balance for years which caused instability and uncertainty, so Hungary also suffered under the same conditions. From 1919-1924 the government ran huge budget deficits (see figure 6) which were financed by borrowing from the Note Institute which was a major cause of a rapid increase in the note and deposit liabilities of the Institute. An additional cause of the increase of liabilities of the institute was the ever-increasing loans and discounts that it made to private agents at very low-interest rates. These private loans accounted for a much higher share of high-powered money than any of the hyperinflations experienced by the other four countries discussed.

Figure 6

Hungarian Budget Estimates 1920-24

Revenue Expenditures Deficits % of expenditure covered.

by the issue of paper money

1920-21 10,520 20,210 9,690 47.9

1921-22 20,296 26,764 6,468 24.1

1922-23 152,802 193,455 40,653 21.0

1923-24 2,168,140 3,307,099 138,959 43.1

Source: Pasvolsky (P299)

The Hungarian Krone depreciated rapidly between January 1921 and April 1924 on the Foreign Exchange market (see figure 7) whilst domestic prices rose rapidly in the same period, the price rises were on top of already hyperinflationary prices with the price index reaching 4,200 by July 1921. The advantage for the government was that the debt liabilities had decreased substantially, unfortunately for the person on the street this period of hyperinflation devasted their lives. The 'Flight from the Krone' seen in Austria was now taking place in Hungary with people now seeking assets and currencies denominated in more stable currencies. The response from the government was again the same as Austria's and the result was the same, people ignored it. The ignoring of the law in both Austria and Hungary has now become a major problem as running any country requires the obedience of the citizens of that state to follow the rules of law, when the mass of people, formally law-abiding, ignore the law, the collapse of that society is almost inevitable.

The League of Nations in conjunction with the War Reparations Committee having realised what chaos was ensuing, stepped in to provide help with financial reconstruction by both reducing and clarifying the terms of repayment and most importantly arranging for international loans that would help finance the government expenditure and commit the Hungarian government to establish a balanced budget as well as a new central bank to replace the Note Institute, which had specific legally backed instructions to refuse any government demand for unbacked credit such as loans or advances except on full receipt of gold or foreign bills, making it truly independent, it was also required to hold a percentage of gold reserves to be behind any of its liabilities. By 1924 the Hungarian National Bank was established taking over the assets and liabilities of the Note Institute along with the foreign exchange functions which had been handled by the Devisenzentrale. The Reparations Commission also gave up its claim to any of Hungary's resources so that these could be used to secure a reconstruction loan of 250 million Krones, which was approved in July 1924, the loan was secured on future tax receipts on custom duties, sugar taxes and revenues from the salt and tobacco monopolies. These actions provided confidence and trust in the government for economic activity to function once again.

Figure 7

Hungarian Price and Exchange Rate

Index of Prices Cent per Krone in New York

1921

July 4,200 0.3323

December 8,250 0.1512

1922

July 17,400 0.0760

December 33,400 0.0430

1923

July 286,000 0.0097

December 714,000 0.0052

1924

July 2,294,000 0.0012

December 2,346,600 0.0013

1925

March 2,117,800 0.0014

Source: League of Nations (p50)

When World War One started, the territory that was to become Poland was split between Russia, Germany and Austria-Hungary and the land was to be at the epicentre of many operations on the Eastern front. In 1916 the Central Powers attempted to gain the support of the Poles and declared a new state called the Kingdom of Poland would be created, in reality it was a puppet regime under the military, economic and political control of the German Reich Poland and had been devastated during World War One both from fighting and having its machinery and materials stripped by Germany. The new nation of Poland came into existence at the end of World War One, being formed from territories which had previously belonged to Russia, Germany, and Austro-Hungary. For Western Europe armistice day in 1918 symbolised peace, this was not the case for Poland as a costly war was being waged against Soviet Russia until 1920. At the time of the formation, it had been using a variety of currencies, including the Russian Rouble, German Mark, and the Krone of Austria-Hungary. In addition, it also issued the Polish Mark via the Polish State Loan Bank, which had been formed by Germany during the war.

After the war with Russia, the new government of Poland ran up huge deficits up to 1924 (see figure 8) which was financed by the government borrowing from the Polish State Loan Bank. From January 1922-December 1923 the outstanding notes of the Polish State Loan Bank increased by a factor of 523 (see figure 9) whilst over the same time period the price index increased by a factor of 2,402. (See figure 10) All the data shows that both rapid price increases and exchange depreciation (see figure 11) suddenly stopped First of January 1924, yet unlike the cases of both Austria and Hungary, this stabilization in Poland was achieved without foreign loans or interventions. Similarities can be seen in the substantial fiscal and monetary regime changes that were enacted, the dramatic move towards a balanced government budget and the establishment of an independent central bank that was prohibited from making additional unsecured loans to their respective governments all led to a fall in prices.

In 1924 the Bank of Poland was established and took over the role of the Polish State Loan Bank, with the eventual goal to restore the currency being convertible into gold. To achieve this the bank was required to hold at least 30% of its reserves to back the creation of notes, this 30% had to be made up of a combination of gold and foreign paper assets of stable currencies, in addition to the reserves the bank notes had to be secured by private bills of exchange and silver. Another stipulation was that a maximum of fifty million zlotys of credit were allowed by the government. (The gold zloty was created in January 1924 to replace the Polish Mark) The number of notes in circulation increased by a factor of 3.2 from January 1924, yet saw relative price stability this is attributed to the fact that the notes in circulation were effectively 100% backed by gold, foreign exchange and private paper, in essence, confidence was restored as the paper notes were now seen as 'sound money'.

Figure 8

Polish Receipts and Expenditures (in 000's zlotys)

1921 1922 1923 1924 1925

Receipts 345,311 530,428 426,000 1,703,000 1,981,884

Expenditures 880,852 879,313 1,119,800 1,629,000 1,981,593

Deficits 535,541 348,885 692,000

Surplus 74,000 251

Source Young (p193)

Figure 9

Balance Sheet of Bank of Poland 1918-1925

Notes in Circulation

<u>1918</u>

December 1,23.8

<u>1919</u>

June 1,784.6

December 5,318.3

<u>1920</u>

June 21,730.1

December 49,361.5

<u>1921</u>

June 102,697.3

December 229,537.6

<u>1922</u>

June 300,101.1

December 793,437.5

<u>1923</u>

June 3,566,649.1

December 125,371,955.3

<u>1924</u>

June 334,405,730.0

December 550,843,960.0

Source: Young (p348)

Figure 10

Polish Index Numbers of Wholesale Prices 1921-1925 (1914=100)

<u>1921</u>

June 35,392

December 57,042

<u>1922</u>

June 87,694

December 346,353

<u>1923</u>

June 1,881,410

December 142,300,700

1924

January 242,167,700

April 242,321,800

Source: Young (P349)

Figure 11

Polish Exchange Rate 1919-1925

Cents for Polish Mark Cents for Zloty

1919

July 6.88

December 1.29

1920

June 0.59

December 0.16

1921

June 0.082

December 0.0313

1922

June 0.0237

December 0.0057

1923

June 0.0013

December 0.0000234

1924

June 10.29

December 19.20

1925

June 19.19

Source: Young (p350)

The nation of Czechoslovakia was created on the 28th of October 1918 from several provinces of the former Austro-Hungarian Empire. The political union of the Czechs and Slovaks was made possible due to the ethnic groups having a shared language as well as cultural similarities and religious beliefs. The finance of the country was in the hands of Dr Alois Raisin who immediately after the union adopted conservative fiscal and monetary policies although not having escaped hyperinflation in the early years it managed to prevent its continuation and even saw deflation occurring between 1923 –24, (see figure 12) it managed to hold its debt expenditures to modest levels and after an initial bout of money printing between 1919- mid 1920, nor did it increase its money in circulation but decreased it, (see figure 13) and although it did lose half its value against the dollar between 1919-1924, (see figure 14) it still had a reasonably stable currency which allowed it to continue trading on the international markets.

Under Raisin Czechoslovakia showed from the outset that it was serious about achieving stability in its economy, even before the peace treaties required it to do so, it stamped the Austro-Hungarian notes in circulation within its borders with the Czechoslovakian stamp thereby recognising it as its own debt. A banking office in the ministry of finance took over the affairs of the old Austro-Hungarian bank and moved quickly to limit by statute the total government notes in circulation. A law passed on April 10th, 1919, strictly limited unbacked note circulation of the banking office to 7 billion Crowns, as the law was actually obeyed, it forced the government to finance its expenditures by either levying taxes or issuing debt which due to statutory restrictions on government note issue was interpreted as promises to tax in future. From 1920 onwards only modest deficits were run and tax-wise in 1925, it raised approximately eleven billion Crowns, with a progressive capital levy on taxes, whilst a popular tax at the time was an increment tax on the increased wealth individuals had obtained during the war. In essence, unlike the other four countries, the Czechoslovakian, government had acted swiftly and responsibly to restore confidence and trust in its economy, which meant its people were spared the horrors that many people like Frau Anna Eisenmenger in Austria endured.

Figure 12

Czechoslovakian Wholesale Price 1922-24

Wholesale Price Index

1922

June 1,471
December 999
1923
June 1,001
December 984
1924
June 981
December 1,024
Source: Young (Vol 2 p307)

Figure 13

Note Issue of Banking Office of Czechoslovakia 1919-24 (in thousands of Czech Crowns)

State Notes in Circulation

1919

July 161,106

December 4,723,303

1920

June 9,729,233

December 11,288,512

1921

June 11,167,515

December 12,129,573

1922

June 9,838,205

December 10,064,049

1923

June 9,375,991

December 9,598,903

1924

June 8,081,106

December 8,810,357

Source: Young (vol 2, p305-306)

Figure 14

Czechoslovakian Exchange Rates 1919-1924

Cents Per Crown

1919

July 5.525

December 1.900

1920

June 2.335

December 1.190

1921

June 1.420

December 1.249

1922
June 1.924
December 3.097
1923
June 2.993
December 2.925
1924
June 2.936
December 3.018

The move to Weimar, a modest-sized, central German city from Berlin in August 1919 was forced on the government because the capital city had become too violent and politically unstable for their safety to be guaranteed. In addition, the process of price rises that started five years earlier was becoming a problem long before the infamous period of hyperinflation of 1923. The German Revolution was initially born against the military for its failure in the war. The military was trying to cast blame for the failures on the army leadership onto someone else, it was intent on preserving the officer caste, it was here the legend, attributed to Ludendorff, of the *Dulchstos*s; the stab in the back of the army by corrupt politicians, treacherous and intellectuals, all under the influence of the Jews and Communists. The strategy worked which meant instead of the fledgling democracy ridding itself of the old autocratic military regime, it was saddled with an officer corps which continually incited right-wing discontent and disruption. (Ferguson, 1975) This military corps presence ensured political assassinations continued to occur in Weimar, with Matthias Erzberger being assassinated in 1921, due to him not being forgiven for his part in signing the Treaty of Versailles and Foreign Minister Walter Rathenau in 1922, due to his signing of the Treaty of Rapallo, the agreement signed on 16th of April 1922, between the German Republic and Soviet Russia where both parties renounced all territorial and financial claims against each other which led to friendly diplomatic relations being restored that was enjoyed until the outbreak of WW II was regarded as collaboration with the Communists and thus seen as treason by the right-wing military factions in Germany.

The hyperinflation which took place in Germany in 1923 is generally used as a blueprint to outline how futile wars and catastrophic mismanagement of an economy can utterly destroy, its citizens' wealth in several years. It is not in actual fact the worst ever bout of hyperinflation visited upon us, in fact, the numbers are almost amateurish compared to Zimbabwe between 2004-2009, and Yugoslavia 1992-1993 but the dubious honour of the worst by far goes to Hungary in 1946, who by the peak saw prices doubling every 14 hours. The reason Weimar is usually cited is because it was the first in modern times that showed the damage to a society that hyperinflation could inflict.

In Weimar, the fledgling democracy was struggling to deal with not only the internal instability of the country but the repatriation question as well, this came to a head when France after not having received the payments it was required by the Treaty of Versailles, which was needed to repay the Americans who were insistent on receiving their money, accused the Germans of deliberately defaulting, moved into the Ruhr valley in January 1923. After losing the coal and zinc resources in Upper Silesia, the iron ore of Lorraine and the potash of Alsace. In addition, Germany lost 14% of its cultivated land, 15% of its wheat crops and 18% of its potatoes. The invasion of the Ruhr was now going to account for the remaining 85% of Germany's remaining coal resources,80% of her steel and pig-iron production, 70% of her traffic in goods and minerals and annexed 10% of her population. (Ferguson, 1975) It was now becoming an intolerable situation for the Germans, the value of the Mark started to sink at an increasingly rapid rate as it became clear it had no means of producing anything, so the government ordered a policy of passive resistance, known as Ruhrkampf and started to make payments to striking workers financed by discounted treasury bills with the Reichsbank, as these loans were made at nominal rates of interest, far below the rate of inflation, they were in effect giving money away for free; the printing presses were getting red hot and the only thing that was going to happen was hyperinflation.

The French taking over the Ruhr had the effect of unifying the German people, they rallied in support of their fellow brothers in the Rhine, even the coal shortages which began in that winter were tolerated, a new wave of nationalism was being rekindled, with support from the army encouraging urban warfare which included, the blowing up of supply trains and shooting of French officers, the French (and Belgians) arrested, jailed and executed the perpetrators. To add to this heady, mix the newly former Soviet Union was sending agents, accompanied by money to destabilise the situation but discovered their political rhetoric found no favour with the Germans, so left in the March of 1923, to complicate matters further the French collaborated with the Communists in the region to undermine the German authorities. (Ferguson, 1975) This had now become a melting pot of violence, nationalism, and the start of hyperinflation. It was a massive 'recruiting sergeant' for right-wing parties such as the National Socialists and the Deutsch National Volkische Parei, with Adolf Hitler regularly appearing in these recruitment drives.

In addition to the Ruhr problem, the German government had two other issues to contend with, taxation and government spending. The government's method of assessing taxes in nominal terms along with the time lag in its collection meant the government was always behind the curve, leading to drastically reduced revenues as the government always appeared to constantly underestimate the rate at which price rises were happening; this rapid price rise added an incentive for the people to delay the payment of their taxes as each passing day eroded the value of the debt, another factor which also came into play was that it became more expensive to collect the tax than the value that was gained from the payment, in essence the government was losing money every time a tax payment was made. As a result of the explosion in public expenditure and the government's attempt to impose exchange controls, the inevitable 'flight from the German mark' occurred, as seen before dramatically devaluing the value of the Reichsmark (see Figure 16). In addition, there is an increase in price rises (figure 15) where between January 1922 and August 1923, wholesale prices rose by a factor of 25,723, but the Reichstag notes rose by a factor of 5,748. (Figure 17) In theory, prices should have slowed down, the problem now facing the government was one of confidence and velocity, the mindset of the German people was that it was best to get rid of their marks and instead hold foreign currency to conduct their transactions, the number of Marks in circulation (Figure 17) rendering them worthless.

Figure 15

German Wholesale Prices
Price Index
1914
January 96
June 99
December 125
1915
June 139
December 148
1916
June 152
December 151
1917
June 165
December 203
1918
June 209
December 245
1919
June 308
December 803
1920
June 1,380
December 1,440
1921
June 1,370
December 3,490
1922
June 7,030
December 147,480
1923
June 1,938,500
December 126,160,000,000,000
1924
June 115,900,000,000,000

July 115 (1)
December 131 (1)
Source: Young (p530)

1. Is Based on prices in Reichsmarks (1 Reichsmark = 1 trillion (10^{12})former marks)

Figure 16
German Exchange Rates 1920-24
Cents per Mark
1920
June 2.56
December 1.37
1921
June 1.44
December 0.53
1922
June 0.32
December 0.01
1923
June 0.001
December 0.000,000,000,022,700
1924
Jan 22.6
June 23.4
December 23.8
Source: Young (p532)
Figure 17
Notes in Circulation
1921
January 66,620,804
June 75,321,095
December 113,639,464
1922
June 115,375,766

December 1,280,094,831
1923
May 8,563,749,470
June 17,291[(2)]
July 43,595[(2)]
August 663,200[(2)]
September 28,228,815[(2)]
October 2,496,822,909[(2)]
15th November 92,844,720,743[(2)]
30th November 400,267,640,302[(2)]
December 496,507,424,772[(2)]
1924
January 483,675
June 1,097,309
December 1,941,440
[(2)]In Billions
Source: Young (p532).

Despite what was happening to the exchange rate and the hyperinflation that was starting the take hold, the Reichsbank commitment to money printing remained resolute, but were aware it couldn't continue forever to support the workers in the Ruhr to remain idle so February large amounts of foreign bills were being thrown on the market to stabilise the currency, this was made possible by the suspension of reparation payments whilst hostilities with France continued, and gold reserves were being used up yet still the printing presses to increase the number of marks, it was therefore only a matter of time before the banks capacity to support the mark on the international markets ran out. In March the government's attempt to raise money with treasury bonds went 75% unsubscribed, the game was up, and by the middle of the year, the hyperinflation already under way went stratospheric. The effect on the German people had drastic consequences.

Up until the invasion of the Ruhr, the German government's policy was to create as much employment as possible, correctly working out that having many idle, angry young men, mostly military-trained and battle-hardened, who had access to weapons was not conducive to creating a stable society. Now with the Ruhrkampf, unemployment arrived with a vengeance and the inflationary policy of money printing was pursued with vigour, with the unemployed in the Ruhr fully subsidised, additional wage claims around the country were impossible to refuse. Petty crime soared to an almost industrial scale; metal plaques which were on national monuments were now locked away and even the brass bell plates on the front doors of the British embassy were stolen. The crime wave was unstoppable, the police powerless to do anything about it, and foreigners became the main targets, especially the British Army of the Rhine, not because of any animosity but simply because foreigners had more 'robbable' items than anyone else. Most of Germany saw lead disappear virtually overnight from the roofs and petrol was syphoned from cars. Barter had emerged as a way of survival where a cinema seat could be purchased for a lump of coal, a bottle of paraffin for a shirt, which in turn could be bartered for a sack of potatoes to feed the family. There were stores where shoppers who used wheelbarrows to carry their marks in found thieves had stolen their barrows but tipped the paper currency out first. A customer would find a cup of coffee costing 5,000 marks when it was ordered would cost 8,000 by the time it had been drunk. Scarcity of food was now also becoming a problem, firstly by not having a stable currency to import enough food but also despite a bumper harvest in 1923, farmers refused to accept the paper currency for their produce. (Ferguson, 1975)

The social problems facing Germany now were becoming a real strain on the fabric of its society, a once proud, orderly race who diligently paid their taxes saw it now as their duty not to pay, harrowing stories emerged such as a Berlin retiree in his 60's who had 100,000 marks in his account which previously would have meant a comfortable life, drew it out, took one last tram ride around Berlin, then locked himself in his room and starved to death, another of a young 14-year-old girl who although near starvation and with only several thousand marks left purchased an opera ticket rather than a piece of bread, when asked why, she replied that she would still be hungry even if she purchased the bread but at least she had several hours of escapism to forget about her hunger. The decline of morality throughout the whole of society was there to see, women from all backgrounds sold their bodies in return for dollars, the Russian writer Ilya Ehrenburg who lived in Berlin throughout the period documented one wild night when they ended up in a respectable bourgeoise apartment which before the hyperinflationary period only the wealthy and elite would have lived in. The mother of the house part way through the party then paraded two naked teenagers in the hope that the men would exchange dollars in return for the pleasure of their bodies, the two teenagers were both her daughters; the humiliation of Germany was truly complete. (Taylor, 2013)

The President of the Reichsbank throughout the whole of the period before, during and after World War 1 was a man called Dr Rudolf Havenstein. He came from a family of government officials, and he was steeped in the civil service culture. In 1890 he worked for the Prussian Ministry of Finance, from 1900-1908 he was President of the Prussian State Bank and from 1908-1923 he was President of the Reichsbank. He oversaw the monumental money printing of marks (known as papier marks or 'paper marks') and believed the price rises were due to the strength of foreign currencies and the role of the Reichsbank was to continue to print sufficient marks to sustain the continuing higher price levels. Dr Havenstein firmly believed the money supply was absolutely unconnected to either the price levels or the exchange rates and saw it as his duty to supply to the limit the marks which were required by the Germans to purchase even the basic of goods and supply them, he did (see Figure 17) despite the ever-decreasing value they represented. By the time the Ruhr invasion took place, Havenstein was unstoppable, the marks were now becoming almost worthless the moment they left the printing presses, in addition to the increasing costs and the sheer logistics of transportation becoming a burden within itself. All this money printing was unsustainable, but they had now created a monster they couldn't control, Havenstein couldn't be sacked and call an end to the passive resistance in the Ruhr after all the additional sacrifices and the new nationalism it had created, would not only mean political death for anyone who tried it but physical death as well. The stresses led to the resignation of the Chancellor Dr Wilhelm Cuno and the appointment of Dr Gustav Stressman. It is difficult to conceive that Havenstein did not have an inkling that his policies were causing the problems he was professing to cure and when one of his key allies in his policy was a German Industrialist called

Hugo Stinnes, it is not difficult to belief that something more sinister than plain stupidity was at play.

Hugo Stinnes was a German Industrialist and politician who during the late era of the German Empire and the early part of Weimar was acclaimed as being amongst one of the most influential entrepreneurs in Europe. His family were prosperous merchants and Stinnes joined the family business, dabbling in retail and for a short period even working as a miner to learn and understand the coal business inside out. At 22 he founded his own trading company, Hugo Stinnes Ltd, and his business career was now well and truly under way. Initially dealing in coal and buying several pits along the way, he branched out into a variety of industries including purchasing 13 steamers, and now traded in iron ore, wood, and grain along the Mediterranean, the Black Sea, the North Sea and the Baltic. His imports included British coal from his depot in Newcastle to Rotterdam and Hamburg: these overseas contacts would serve him well in the hyperinflationary period of Weimar when he had access to foreign currency. (Taylor, 2013).

During the war, Stinnes lost many of his foreign interests due to sequestration, yet he just kept expanding within Germany, buying more coal, iron and steel businesses which were the vital ingredients for a nation on a war footing. By the end of the war and despite the defeat inflicted on the Germans, Stinnes had become a wealthy man; the hyperinflation that was created by Dr Havenstein and actively encouraged by Stinnes is straight from the economic model espoused by the 18th Century economist Richard Cantillon appropriately called the 'The Cantillon Effect' which states "He who was close to the king and wealthy will most likely benefit from the distribution choices" in other words the closer to the money printing you are the more you will benefit and Stinnes was exceptionally close to the 'King of the money printing' in Havenstein. Stinnes could borrow an unlimited amount at favourable rates due to the Reichsbanks policy of automatic loans to German Industry and then purchase physical assets, by the time it had come to pay the debt back it was worthless. He didn't become known as 'Inflation König' (translated into 'Inflation King') for nothing. Sadly, for Stinnes all was not to end well, once the confidence was restored to the currency in 1924 his overleveraged position was found wanting, he died in

1924 as a result of a gall bladder operation and his financial empire which had accumulated to around 4500 companies and 3000 manufacturing plants collapsed within a year of his death with only several companies still existing to this day, the largest being Hugo Stinnes Schiffahrt (a shipping company) and RWE the second largest energy supplier in Germany.

By the summer of 1923, it was clear that the mark was collapsing but two events one planned and one a quirk of fate allowed for the 'fever' of hyperinflation to break. The first and planned event was the appointment of Stresemann as Chancellor of Germany on the 13th of August. Stresemann was regarded as the most influential cabinet member in the Weimar's existence. His most notable achievement was to come several years later when as Minister of Foreign Affairs (13th August 1923- 3rd October 1929) he managed to achieve a reconciliation between France and Germany. Stresemann found himself in a more fortunate position than his predecessors and managed to take office just as international relations were thawing; the Ruhr occupation even in its heyday was not universally popular and was now losing popularity with its previous supporters in Paris. This was important as it started to give him some negotiating space, but more crucially the Americans who had previously been resolute in their payments from the allies and the French being one of the biggest borrowers, agreed to relax their terms and conditions on the proviso that France eased up on Germany. Stresemann also reshuffled the cabinet and in early October appointed Hans Luther as the Master of Finance, Luther eventually went onto become both the Chancellor of Germany (15th January 1925- 12th May 1926) and President of the Reichsbank. (7th March 1930- 17th March 1933) Luther worked alongside economist Karl Helfferich and Hjalmar Schacht, intending to implement Luther's predecessor Rudolf Hilferding's plan of the Rentenmark, which was implemented on the 15th of October 1923. Schacht had an unusual but interesting life, his first name was Horace Greeley, and being named after the famous journalist, Hjalmar was only added after the insistence of his Danish grandmother. In 1926 he joined the Nazi Party and became a supporter of Adolf Hitler, a choice he was later to bitterly regret. After serving under Adolf Hitler's government as President of the

Reichsbank between 1933-1939 and was lauded for being responsible for the 'economic miracle' that Germany saw after the collapse of the economy due to the wall street crash. He famously clashed with both Hitler and Goering leading to his sacking and in 1944 he was arrested by the Gestapo following the assassination attempt on Hitler for his alleged contact with the assassins. He was sent to the concentration camps in Ravensbruck and Flossenburg and eventually ended up in the infamous Dachau. He survived and was tried as a Nuremberg war criminal where he was fully acquitted. He died in Munich on the 3rd of June 1970.

The Rentenmark was based on a scheme started previously by the unusual alliance of Helfferich a prominent right winger, and Hilferding, a Marxist economist they addressed the cabinet in the summer of 1923 to propose a new standard called the rye mark, (Roggenmark) to be supported in conjunction with a wry bank, whereby the currency would be backed not by gold (as they had very little left) but by the countries reserves of rye. This may seem absurd now, but the cycle of hyperinflation had to be broken and the definition of a currency being backed by a commodity did have logic behind it. It also wasn't the only asset that backed the currency, other real assets were used based on loans such as butter, potatoes, flour, sugar, matches, bricks, coal, cubic meters of water and even kilowatt hours of electricity were used. The rye bank allowed farmers to release their harvests through debt securities, where the farmer could receive their payments in any of the other goods mentioned and many more, rather than the papiermark. (Deutche Bundesbank Eurosystem) Although it could not work as a long-term solution due to the number of potential goods that could be exchanged, its purpose was firstly to decouple the value of papiermark from the credibility of the Reich government, as the states deficits had now become so enormous that no-one had faith in the fiat currency any more, a currency linked to both the government and the Reichsbank which still unable to remove Havenstein as its President and so still printing trillions of marks worth of useless currency and secondly to get food to the populace, in this way the rye mark was an unmitigated success, it even had the effect of slowing the velocity of the currency as some faith was being resorted in the purchasing power of the rye mark. The people could start to see light at the end of the tunnel, and this provided some hope for the future.

The Rentenmark scheme was finally established on the 17th of October 1923; the head of the administrative council included the former Prussian finance minister, the deputy of the German National Peoples party and various representatives of the traditional elite including landowners, industrialists, and bankers. These elites were generally loathed, especially on the left as they were seen as having enriched themselves at the expense of the ordinary and middle-class Germans through the hyperinflationary process, yet they were a necessary evil if the international community was to have any real confidence that the scheme could work. The currency was to be issued on the 15th of November 1923 in strictly limited quantities so it could fulfil its function in squeezing hyperinflation out of the system, on the same day the old papiermark was to cease being printed. The previous five years had seen industry being effectively given printed money, now they had to 'cut their cloth' accordingly and act in a responsible, prudent manner as businesses should. It also acted as a constraint on government spending.

Despite the meticulous planning, the latter stages were fraught with problems and potential pitfalls that could have seen the scheme fail; the printing of the Rentenmark was slow going due to the printers now feeling a loss of income, went on strike. By November 10th approximately 78 million Rentenmarks had been printed, by the 15th 200 million had been created despite the strike, mainly due to white-collar workers taking over the responsibility of printing. Other problems included the grade of paper being low quality due to lack of supplies, which meant the currency was easy to counterfeit. The government also delayed the release but, in the end, decided for the morale of the people that having a new currency and equally importantly, keeping the confidence of the international community in the project. It took several days for the notes to reach the counter of the banks and the Germans were now going to have to get used to small denominations again, including pfennig coins as well as notes.

The other fortunate event for Stresemann was Havenstein who had been a thorn not only in his side, but the German government as well died of a heart attack on November 20th 1923, this led to his deputy Otto von Glasenapp, who was fully onboard for monetary reform, replacing him as Chancellor. Schacht who in his capacity as the Currency Commissioner and by default the true master of Germany's money now moved quickly and 'unbacked' issuances of emergency money whether they had been created by individual states such as Bavaria or self-printed currencies issued by large private companies such as the German railways, estimated at 114.7 quadrillion papiermarks (a quadrillion is a thousand trillion) were now not to be accepted after 24th November (Taylor, 2013). A remarkable amount had been achieved by Stresemann, but he would not see the success he deserved as Chancellor as he lost a vote of no confidence, accused of partisanship for sending the Reichswehr against Socialist Saxony and Thuringia but not nationalist Bavaria to quell civil disorder, the left feared the dictatorial direction of his government.

Despite the setback of Stresemann's resignation, the fate of the German currency was now in the hands of Dr Schacht and the administrative committee; what everyone was looking for and desperately needed was the restoration of confidence in the currency by both the German people and the international community. Schacht played it cool, in the coming weeks he did nothing except telephone every German and foreign establishment that had anything to do with finance, these included banks, ministries of finance, industrialists, investors and many more. In doing all this he was trying to create that most precious of commodities that is so hard-earned but so easily lost, trust.

The end of hyperinflation in the Weimar republic is generally regarded as an overnight success, whilst it was ended within a couple of months from the introduction of the Rentenmark, an amazing achievement, those two months between the introduction and success were still fraught with the possibility of failure; journalists were still reporting that Germany could run out of money and then need to start the printing presses again, the government held out and by the end of January the currency was regarded as stable.

It worked, and the hyperinflation fell within several months, yet this was not the end, Germany was going to have to get used to being fiscally responsible again no matter how difficult the experience or how high unemployment was going to rise, another threat to the programme was the right-wing parties that had used hyperinflation as a recruiting sergeant and had no interest in seeing the end to all the hyperinflation the German people were facing, they actually relished all the strife caused by soaring price rises. The left wasn't happy either as the formation of the committee was seen as a coup by the old guard elites to seize back their old power and the hard-earned rights of the unions for things such as the eight-hour day would be repealed, on this and many issues their fears were founded as by December the non-socialist government abandoned most of the gains the workers had achieved, although it is to be noted those achievements weren't always to the benefit of the society as a whole.

A tough winter lay ahead in 1924 with high unemployment being exacerbated by mass redundancies in the civil service and railways, the Germans had gone through a lot since the start of 1914 and could begin to see hope. By early 1924 Germany was finally being allowed to discuss the restructuring of the Versailles Treaty reparations and the American Dawes Plan allowed for flexible loans. The Germans had finally come through the hyperinflation and could now start to make plans. The next few years were quite prosperous for the country which was even known as 'The Golden Twenties' all seemed calm, and order appeared to be restored, but beneath this veneer were many fault lines, the most important one being most people, especially the middle classes had lost everything, from properties to the money they had so entrusted in the government in war bonds, so when the next downturn came just five years later because of the Wall Street Crash, the people were neither prepared financially nor willing to accept what the government at Weimar was telling them; by 1933 the Weimar Republic was over and the fear of the German Left, from the time of the Revolution, that a dictator from the right would come to power had now come to pass when President Paul von Hindenburg appointed Herr Adolf Hitler as Chancellor on January 30th 1933.

As a footnote it is interesting to observe that the reason the United States demanded payment for its war loans in 1921 was due to the much-forgotten depression of 1921; (unlike the crash of 1929 which many people are familiar with, known as the Wall Street crash, occurring primarily due to wild speculation and massive overleveraging on the American stock market, and lasted approximately ten years was deflationary and only ended with the Second World War) When World War One broke out. Demand for American products soared with combatant nations running huge trade deficits and importing more than they exported, to pay for these goods they sent gold. As this gold flowed inwards America could expand its monetary base with Economist Hugh Rockoff estimating that the money supply doubled in the four years the war was being fought. This rapid expansion of the money supply saw more dollars in the economy increasing demand for goods and services, however, the supply was severely restricted as much of the goods being produced were military, and consumer price inflation rose from 2% in 1915 to 20.4% in 1918. Once the war had ended there was a reversal in the gold flows, this now posed a challenge for the Federal Reserve to maintain convertibility with the number of dollars printed. (Phelan, 2021) In addition, returning troops were now flooding the jobs market in an economy which was shrinking in addition Europe was also slowly but surely requiring less grain as they started to return to producing for themselves, meaning American farmers who had overleveraged found themselves in financial constraints. All these factors meant that the money which it was owed by countries France, simply could not be ignored, yet once the depression had finished, America could relax the financial obligations it was owed. (Murphy, 2009)

The 1920-21 Depression was short-lived, and the policies enacted by the government, which seem counter-intuitive to modern-day Keynesian economic theory which sanctions the increase of public spending, lowering interest rates and printing currency, appeared to work but this was over within 18 months. The economic situation in 192O was particularly grim, by the end of the year unemployment had climbed from 4% to 12% and GDP had fallen by an eyewatering 17%, the President at the time Warren G Harding was under tremendous pressure to fiscally stimulate the economy, however, he did the opposite, he cut the government budget in half between 192O and 1922 and further laissez-faire polices were enacted with tax rates being slashed for all income groups (Woods, 2009). By one estimate output fell by 8.7% compared with the great recession of 2007-2009 where it fell

4.3%, approximately half. In addition, the Federal Reserve's index of industrial production fell by 31.6% compared with 16.9% in 2007-2009. Another issue that had to be dealt with was during the war the fact that as America was on the gold standard it proved advantageous as gold poured in, now the war had ended the reverse was happening and gold started to flow outwards, this meant that there was not enough gold to support the number of paper dollars that had been printed; the newly formed Federal reserve had to react to this outflow of gold by not only stopping it leaving but to also attract the gold back into the country, in addition, it had to reduce the number of dollars in the economy which could be converted into gold. To do this it had to raise interest rates, deflation was inevitable, and they knew it. On February 3rd, 1919, the Federal Reserve of New York raised its rates which it loaned to banks against its commercial paper from 4% to 4.75%. In January 1920 the rate was hiked to 6% and in June to 7%. The crash came and as the easy money had financed the boom dried up, it became clear that now borrowing expensive money was going to smother it. (Grant, 2014) the Governor of the Federal Reserve, Benjamin Strong was fully aware of the implications saying,

"I believe that this period will be accompanied by a considerable degree of unemployment, but not for very long and after a year or two of discomfort, embarrassment, some losses, some disorders caused by unemployment, we will emerge with an almost invincible banking position ... and with prices more nearly at competitive levels with other nations."

Strong had called it, as output slumped unemployment surged and calls for public spending increased, Harding held firm, consumer prices which had been 15.6% in 1920, fell into a deflation of 10.5% in 1921, yet whilst lower prices meant reduced incomes for some and many businesses couldn't survive, these lower prices meant reduced costs for others and as consumer confidence started to grow, by the summer of 1921 producers and consumers began to buy again. In addition to this, the raising of interest rates now started to attract gold from overseas, with the bullion stock going from $400 million to $3 billion, by May 1921, 80% of the volume of Federal Reserve notes was supported by gold, this now could lead to interest rates falling to further support the economy; The roaring twenties had begun in earnest. (Phelan, 2021).

9. THE WALL STREET CRASH OF 1929

"I do not think it is an exaggeration to say history is largely a history of inflation, usually inflations engineered by governments for the gain of governments" F. A. Hayek.

Although none of these cases below are discussed in any detail, they do need to be recognised as we are now seeing hyperinflation happening on a more frequent basis; the former Yugoslavia between 1992 and 1994 with inflation peaking at a monthly rate of 313 million per cent in January 1994, daily inflation was 62% and the hourly rate of 2.03% is higher than most economies annual rate, whilst Zimbabwe's hyperinflation began in 2007, eventually becoming impossible to calculate as the government gave up producing statistics, however, it is estimated that the peak month of inflation was 79.6 Billion per cent of 89.7 sextillions per cent a year-on-year by mid-November 2008, whilst the newest hyperinflationary kids on the block Venezuela saw their problems start in 2014 with the annual rate has been 69%, reaching 2 million per cent by 2018. By 2012 with the help of loans from the IMF, the hyperinflationary pressure had eased, however, there are signs of it accelerating again with annual inflation by October 2022 reaching 155%.

It may have become apparent now that inflation and hyperinflation do not happen in isolation and the pressures can be built up over decades. With this in mind, it would be appropriate to bring us up to 2023 by describing what happened once Germany had left its Weimar hyperinflationary period behind and started to enter its golden era for the rest of the 1920s and try and peer into the crystal ball to see what the future may. Unfortunately for Germany, the lifestyle was built on a false premise, it seemed like they were now living the dream yet, in reality, it turned into another horror movie not just for Germany but the rest of the world. What happened to Germany was not isolated but affected the whole world; it was the Wall Street Crash of 1929. The Wall Street crash was the worst market crash of all time where share prices fell by 89% (Atherton, 2009) Before the collapse a boom of epic proportions was precipitated due to several factors both internal and international, it was these factors which ultimately led to the rise of the National Socialist Workers Party, more usually referred to as the Nazi Party.

The internal problems were created by the international dealings which occurred after the First World War. To prop up the British government after they went onto the gold standard at a price that was too high for it to be sustainable and thus prevent the gold from leaving the UK, the governor of the Bank of England Sir Montague Norman, convinced the newly elected New York Fed Chairman Benjamin Strong to create inflation in America, which he did by lowering interest rates and this led to an economic boom. Unfortunately for America, the Secretary of State of the Treasury Andrew Mellon had not only resolved the 1920-21 crash but by 1924 oversaw an economy flush with cash generated from the inflow of gold from Europe, which was now paying its war debts, meaning the system was exceptionally liquid. By having the interest rates lower in America than Britain it meant the dollar being lower than sterling, making American exports cheaper and imports more expensive. In addition, a protectionist policy was adopted which meant overseas customers found it harder to sell to America, yet at the same time America was loaning money to the rest of the world from coffee plantations in Brazil to the Ruhr factories in Germany, along with selling foreign bonds which allowed the rest of the world to join in the Wall Street frenzy, (Stockman, 2014) thus should something go wrong the contagion would spread across the planet.

The ultra-low interest rates caused credit growth to explode, however, this did not go into the building of new car assembly plants or steel works, it went into the speculation frenzy of Wall Street. By 1929 1,548,707 customers had accounts with the 29 stock exchanges in America, with a population of 12 million meant nearly 30 million households had an active association with the stock markets, one million of these could be called speculators, with 600,000 trading on margin calls, that is borrowed money they either didn't or couldn't produce the funds should the value of the shares fall below the value that had been paid, thus requiring additional payment to the broker to make up the difference. (Johnson, 2000) Margin debt on Wall Street by 1929 stood at 12% of GDP, which is the equivalent of $3 trillion, compared to January 1923 where it stands at $641 billion. (Finra Statistics)

All this leverage and debt was unsustainable, both in America and the rest of the world, in 1929 the inevitable happened and by June the economy had ceased to expand, by September 3rd, the bull market effectively came to an end, and the market had peaked. On Monday 9th October, the ticker tape could not keep up with the pace of shares being sold. Marginal calls had been sent out the Saturday before by telegram and by the end of the week the realization was beginning to dawn on the speculators that the game was up, and they could lose everything they owned. On October 12th shares saw a vertical dip, everyone was selling, no one was buying, and the speculators were being sold out to as they failed to respond to their margin calls. The fateful day known as 'Black Tuesday' was October 19th when quality stocks that were sound financially were being sold to raise desperately needed liquidity, by October 24th eleven well-known investors had committed suicide. The immediate panic subsided by November 13th and although the index had fallen from 452 to 224, a truly severe correction, (Johnson, 2000) in context the index in December 1928 had been 245, only 21 points higher, this was what it was, a correction.

The difference this time as opposed to the crash of 1920-1921 was the duration of the 1929 crash. The fundamental difference between the two was the first crash was allowed to correct itself, whilst in the 1929 crash both the government and the Federal Reserve interfered, by allowing the conditions to occur with the secret deal arranged between Montague and Strong, whilst in 1929, the President, Herbert Hoover created a type of 'New Deal' in the form of the Farm Price-Support Programme, along with keeping wage rates up, expanding public works and government deficits, lending money to failing businesses in order to try and keep them afloat, In effect, Hoover pioneered the prototype of the Keynesian model, (Rothbard, 2009) which F.D. Roosevelt continued and expanded. All this interference meant the normal corrective functions which eliminate all the distortions which had entered the system couldn't work, leading to a prolonged period of decline so by July 1932, the Index which had fallen sharply to 224 in 1929 fell to 58. Unemployment rose from 3.2% to 26.7% by 1934, (Johnson, 2000) with the pattern being repeated all over the world. The policy of

Benjamin Strong to loan foreign countries money with the sole purpose of buying American goods, in conjunction with tariffs they placed, meant overseas countries could no longer afford to pay back their loans, and thus with no ability to borrow more, could not continue to purchase American goods. It is this collapse in trade that was the final nail in the coffin for the German people and brought the National Socialist Workers Party, or the Nazi Party led by Adolf Hitler, to power, the combination of the defeat and harsh Versailles Treaty, Weimar Germany's Hyperinflation and this final collapse in trade was just too much for the German people to take.

Britain had officially come off the gold standard in 1931 following the Great Depression, precipitated by the Wall Street Crash, The United States followed suit in 1933. One of Franklin Delano Roosevelt, the newly elected President Acts was to declare a 'National Emergency' as Americans were withdrawing their gold and currency from the beleaguered banking system, he ordered all banks to close between March 6-9 in order to prevent hoarding and exporting. The next steps he took with the belief it would prevent a bank run and even more gold withdrawals was on April 5th 1933 it was made illegal for US citizens to own gold, making it punishable by up to ten years in prison, paying double the value of the gold being hidden or a $10,000 fine. All gold was to be handed over to the Federal Reserve via the banks in exchange for paper currency; Americans had by May 1st, 1933, to comply. The Federal Reserve in return redeemed an ounce of troy gold for $20.67. On January 30, 1934, once all the gold had been collected the official gold price was raised to $35.00 per troy ounce, (Mariotti, 2017) making the government a 69% profit from its citizens at a stroke. The law prohibiting individuals from owning gold was finally rescinded by President Gerald Ford only on December 31st, 1974.

By 1944 it was apparent that Germany was going to lose the war, that all the nations involved were broke, that Britain was going to lose its international status in the financial world and that the United States which faced a massive debt overhang just like it did after World War 1 was going to take over Britain's role and become the financial creditor nation to the rest of the world. All the main currencies were wrecked, along with their economies, the advantage America had was the huge stockpile of gold which served it well in the move to make the dollar the international reserve currency, taking the role of the British pound. From July 1st to July 22nd, 1944, the world's elites' representing 44 governments including the Soviet Union, met at the Mount Washington Hotel in Bretton Woods, New Hampshire, where they drafted an article of agreement that was finally ratified in December 1945. The agreements drawn up included a project for the International Bank for Reconstruction and Development, (IBRD) its role being to make long-term capital loans to states which required foreign aid, this institution along with the International Development Association (IDA) which offers concession loans and grants to the world's poorest developing countries is now collectively known as the World Bank, sharing the same leadership and staff; in addition, the International Monetary Fund (IMF) was set up to finance short term imbalances in international payments to try and create stability in the foreign exchange rates, along with the General Agreement on Tariffs and Trade (GATT) later to become the World Trade Organization (WTO)

The Bretton Woods agreement rather than imposing a gold standard on all nations, implemented a gold exchange standard, much to the benefit of the United States. An international gold exchange standard is where gold or a currency is convertible at a fixed price and is then used as a medium of international payments. Under such a system both countries' exchange rates are fixed, so if the exchange rate was to rise or fall above the fixed rate then gold would have to be shipped from one country to another until parity was restored. The fixed rates at Bretton Woods were for gold to be fixed at $35 per troy ounce, with $1 being equal to £2.80, 4.20 German marks, 625 Italian lire and ¥360, this would mean that any nation who for example held £98 in sterling could convert it to $35 and purchase 1oz of gold from America. This new position meant the dollar was now the new world reserve currency. The caveat with this was the convertibility back to gold could only take place by foreign governments, not American citizens. In essence, the United States would peg dollars to gold, whilst other countries would peg their currency to the dollar, thus effectively putting everyone on the gold standard. The problem with this system of the Bretton Woods agreement is it does not refer to the Balance of Payments problems that countries created, almost assuming they were acts of God, that these things happened like earthquakes and natural floods, it was dealing with the symptoms rather than the causes and the treatment of the problem was the setting up of institutions such as the IMF and World Bank to lend additional money would only exacerbate the problem. By centralizing the system, it ensured that if one country devalued, it would see its currency fall in value in the international markets, however if this is done with the cooperation of everyone else, the country can avoid all the penalties normally required such as raising interest rates to return it to the strength required for the parity it had agreed. The plan was therefore always destined to fail as under it the creditor nations the United States and Britain would pledge themselves to buy the currency of net debtor nations to keep the currency value at parity, if countries devalued, the United States would be on the hook to keep purchasing the currency to maintain the fixed paper-to-gold ratio. By doing this you now cannot find the true value of the currency, just like a stock share which is essentially worthless but still sells for £100 and can maintain that price as long as the buyer still has the resources to continue purchasing, the problem arises when the resource of the purchaser runs out or they throw in the towel. For the US the solution to continue purchasing was not to sell its gold reserve to purchase foreign currencies but to print more dollars. (Rockwell. Jr, 2010).

Bretton Woods under President Dwight D Eisenhower, who served between 1953-1961 remained in operation with no real problems as he continued the New Deal programmes and expanded agencies, all fuelled by unprecedented economic growth and prosperity, due to an almost devastated Europe. However, in his farewell address to the nation, he expressed his concerns over the dangers of the massive military spending, in particular deficit spending, along with government contracts to private military manufacturers, which he called "The military-industrial complex". As a former five-star general of the army and supreme commander of the allied expeditionary force in Europe the Americans would have been wise to heed his words, sadly they were not and the impact of ignoring him is reverberating around the world to this day.

Following the election and then the assassination of John F Kennedy, Lyndon B Johnson became the next US President, he followed a path known as 'Guns and Butter' which not only saw a massive increase in public spending to support the welfare programme but also a huge increase in defence spending which Eisenhower warned against. The deployment of troops in Vietnam grew from 16,000 in November 1963 when Kennedy was assassinated to a peak of 537,000 troops by 1968. The problem Johnson faced which Eisenhower didn't was Europe by now was getting back on its feet and was eating into the US economy, so much so that between 1950 and 1969 as Germany and Japan recovered, the US share of World economic output dropped from 35% to 27%, these numbers would have a massive impact on the US economy, it would mean for America that if it was to carry on spending the way it was it had only one solution, debase the dollar and print. By 1971 Richard Nixon had become President and it only took him until the summer of that year to make an announcement which affects the whole world to this day. Earlier that year France had sent a warship to collect gold in return for dollars, this wasn't the first time they had done this, also by 1971 they weren't the only country demanding gold for dollars, pressure was being put on the dollar.

In 1958 President Charles De Gaulle ordered the Banque de France to increase the rate at which it converted new dollar reserves into bullion; In 1965 he sent the French Navy across the Atlantic to pick up $15O million worth of gold. On Sunday 15th of 1971, as the most popular TV series of the time Bonanza started, it was interrupted by President Nixon sitting at his desk in the White House and began his sombre announcement, that he was 'temporarily' suspending the convertibility of dollars into gold, and blaming speculators for the woes of the dollar and the instability in the international markets, where in reality the US gold reserves were facing enormous pressure due to Balance of Payments concerns, the Vietnam war debt and the Great Society programmes; so much so that between 1958-1971 the US gold reserves fell from 20,000 tonnes to 8,000 tonnes, at the rate this convertibility was happening America would have been soon out of gold. Nixon with that announcement ended the 25-year Bretton Woods era of fixed currencies and convertibility of the dollar for gold and the 'temporary' suspension has lasted to this day. In addition, he announced a 10% tax on imported goods to the US along with price controls, as well as quadrupling its grain prices. All these measures were obviously going to cause prices to rise, the Americans were in a dilemma.

With America now not only being off the gold standard and so technically if not actually defaulting on its debts by not honouring its promise to pay gold for dollars, but it also has government spending continuing unabated, as well as imposing trade barriers and price controls, Washington became worried that demand for the US 'paper' dollar or to give it its proper term 'fiat dollar' would subside. To combat this, they pulled off a masterstroke which was probably the most brilliant/economic coup in modern history, between 1973/74 they convinced Saudi Arabia to enter into a deal known as the 'petrodollar system'. The deal ensured that Saudi Arabia priced all sales of oil in dollars, in other words, you could only buy the oil in dollars, this would mean if you had sterling/yen or any other currency, you would have to go onto the international market and buy dollars to pay Saudi Arabia, in return the Americans were to provide the Saudi's, with weapons and military support along with bases to protect the oil fields. The clever part of the deal which was kept quiet for over 40 years was that some of the dollar profits the Saudis were to be re-invested in US Treasury Securities, Henry Kissinger called this the 'petrodollar recycling'. By 1975 the Americans made a similar deal with all the OPEC. (Organization of the Petroleum Exporting Countries) Richard Nixon wasn't nicknamed 'Tricky Dickie' for nothing.

For my two cents worth and to try to understand what the future may hold after delving into the past, I need to make a disclaimer known as a black swan event. A black swan event was initially proposed by Karl Popper using it to describe scientific reasoning, for thousands of years Europeans had only ever seen white swans so the assumption was only white swans existed, however with the exploration of Australasia and the discovery that black swans existed, his point being that no matter how many and how long an observation is made there is always a possibility in the future new evidence may refute what you know and believe. (Plato made the same point two thousand years earlier when he argued regarding science, we only know what we know at this moment in time and any future discoveries could change what we have previously taken as a fact) Nassim Taleb (2010) took this explanation of science and applied it to modern economics and politics and it is the central point of his book 'The Black Swan' is concerned with the "blindness concerning randomness" in other words it is an outlier that lies outside the what we could regularly expect might happen as nothing from the past can convince us that the possibility may occur. It is with this caveat that I make my predictions for the future of Western nations.

Several significant modern geopolitical historical events occurred which I will try and link together. All the events have been condensed but I believe the information is sufficient to try and predict the outcome that awaits America and by default the Western world. One event was to influence the 1970s and throw the perceived economic orthodoxy since the mid-1930s in turmoil and that was stagflation. Stagflation is characterized by rising prices accompanied by rising unemployment, in essence, the economy is stagnant, but prices keep rising. According to Keynesian theory which had been the prevailing economic model then practiced in the Western world, this couldn't happen. The belief was that demand deficiency causes recession and therefore stimulating the demand side by creating employment would cure the recession, at the same time prices would not rise as more goods were being supplied due to the unemployed now being employed and beginning to produce goods and providing services. He also argues the stimulus should be short-term to release what he called 'the animal spirit' and once the economy was moving again government surpluses should be saved until required for the next downturn. What caused the stagflation to occur? It was the 4th Arab Israeli war, (often known as the Yom Kippur War, the Ramadan War or the October War) in which America supported Israel both financially and militarily, as retribution oil which had been relatively cheap for the West, the Saudi's researched how much extra they could squeeze out of the price of a barrel of oil found the West would and could pay four times what they were paying, so the prices went up. It is this supply shock that threw out the Keynesian economic model, in modern society oil and its by-products are essential. To get a sense of perspective from both the US and the UK; In the US at the beginning of the decade inflation stood at 6%, by 1974 it had an annual average of 12.34% and by 1980 it was 12.52%. In the UK Inflation stood at approximately 5%, by 1975 it had peaked in August at 26.87% giving a yearly average of 24.11% and only decreasing slightly by 1980, where in May it peaked at 21.91% with the annual average being

18.07%. (Inflation Tool, 2023) The figures were better for the United States for the main reason that the dollar was still the reserve currency due to its petrodollar status. At the same time, unemployment had risen in the US from 3.5% in 1969 to 7.2% in 1974 and peaking at 10.8% in 1982. (Amadeo, 2022) Unemployment in the UK rose from approximately 3.7% in 1974, reaching 11.8% by 1984.

Both nations saw inflation fall off after the 1980s due to the adoption of the monetarist policies of Milton Friedman. Friedman looked at what had happened under the Keynesian philosophy and came up with his own model which he called monetarism. Monetarism suggested there was a natural rate of unemployment in any given society and if the government spend money to stimulate the economy it would succeed in lowering unemployment in the short run, but the inflationary aspect of price rises would eventually lead to the unemployment level being returned to its natural level but this time with the added burden of higher inflationary prices, and the cycle would continue every time governments kept trying to stimulate the economy, unemployment would fall in the short term, inflationary price rises would compound the original price rise leading to even higher prices and unemployment would yet again revert to its natural state. To solve the inflationary problem, he argued you had to reduce the money supply to squeeze inflation, doing this by raising interest rates above the level of inflation, this in the short term would lead to even more unemployment but once you had shifted the inflationary price pressures, unemployment would fall back down to its natural rate. Both the British and American governments followed this policy. In America, the Fed chair under Paul Volker with the blessing of newly elected President Ronald Reagan, interest rates at one point went up to 20%. (Volker was elected as the Fed chairman in 1979, the last year of President Jimmy Carter which is when he started to raise interest rates much to the horror of President Carter when he saw the short-term effect on unemployment, Regan after being elected in 1980, continued to let him do his work.) This theory has appeared to work however its fundamental flaw is it doesn't consider the velocity of money; Friedman saw velocity as fundamentally stable to make his model work, unfortunately as we have seen in the example of Weimar, if the conditions are right and psychologically people fear for the value of the currency, they are holding is rapidly losing its value, velocity can play a significant role in price inflation.

Another key event occurred in the 1990s which shaped the events of the world in 2023 and was the collapse of the Iron Curtain and the end of communism in Russia. The process had effectively begun in 1989-90 with the Communists' abandoning one-party rule in Eastern Europe, in late 1991 the Soviet Union collapsed entirely, and 15 new independent nations were borne from the ashes, including Russia. This new Russia after decades of suppression under communism where the state effectively took care of everything left the people bewildered, confused, and frightened and a state that was weak and open to corruption. Under the leadership of Mikhail Gorbachev who ruled between 1985-1991 and then Boris Yeltsin from 1991-1999 emerged the all-powerful new oligarchs who as a set of well-connected, smart, ambitious people grabbed the previously state-owned assets, corporations, and financial institutes, in particular oil, gas and finance. In addition to this corruption, Russia experienced a period of hyperinflation, by 1990 price inflation was 19%, and by the end of 1991 it was 200%, Gorbachev financed the budget deficits with the old favourite of money printing. Gorbachev by now was losing power and influence, and this is when Yeltsin took the reins, however, the hyperinflationary period was here to stay for a while, and by 1992 it had peaked at 2,318%. This hyperinflation meant the Russians had to bear even more social misery with a huge drop in living standards and a huge increase in poverty which continued for decades, life expectancy for a male by the time Vladimir Putin took office in 1999 was a mere 56, and alcoholism and the breakdown of the family was rampant. Russia was a nation that appeared to be in terminal decline, and the West looked poised to capitalise on it.

The final event we can look at is the rise of China and the events that have shaped the Chinese psyche towards the West. In 1839 the first of the two Opium Wars was fought; it was the result of China trying to suppress the illegal opium trade which had led to both a serious economic and social crisis as addiction had become widespread in the country. The Chinese had been introduced to opium as far back as the 7th Century, by the early 18th Century it had become such a problem the government unsuccessfully tried to prohibit the sale and smoking of it, with the primary source having become British traders, exporting it mainly from India. The British discovered the value of opium as there was a huge demand for Chinese goods such as silk, porcelain and tea. Sadly, for the West, there was no appetite in China for Western goods, after a while gold was haemorrhaging from the coffers so they tried to pay with opium instead. In 1839 the Chinese government made a concerted effort to suppress the trade, leading to antagonism and tension which spilled over when drunken British soldiers killed a Chinese villager, the British government subsequently refused to hand over the sailors to be tried by the Chinese legal system. Hostilities broke out later that year with the British eventually succeeding, leading to the Treaty of Nanjing where the Chinese paid the British $21 million, ceded the territory of Hong Kong and British merchants who had previously only been able to reside and trade in 1 port (Canton) now were permitted five 'treaty ports' enabling even more opium to be imported. A second war took place in 1856 after the Canton police boarded the British registered ship 'Arrow' and charged its crew with smuggling. This led to the second war and saw the French join in. The Chinese subsequently lost that war in 1860 and ceded the Southern portion of the Kowloon Peninsula adjacent to Hong Kong.

These two wars led to what has become known in China as the 'century of shame.' (Sometimes known as the 'century of humiliation) The British and Chinese saw the war through different lenses, Britain called it a 'trade war' arguing that China had violated the rules of trade at the time, whilst conveniently downplaying the misery that the drugs played on Chinese society. The merchants were backed by the might of the British Empire's military, forcing legal drug trafficking, armed force was deployed against a sovereign nation's right to prohibit the sale of opium, it then heaped further insult and shame on the Chinese by making their government compensate the British merchants for their loses whilst allowing the door to be opened for them to flood China with opium. The two wars ran heavy and deep in China as they then allowed over the next century to be opened to rounds of endless humiliation by many Western imperialist countries who took advantage of existing conflicts between various groups and minorities, sending in troops to occupy Chinese lands, grabbing Chinese, and effectively blocking Chinese progress. In addition, the subsequent rise of Japan also led it to join the ranks of nations that bullied China.

This all changed in 1949 when Mao Tse-tung under the communist umbrella started to assert the independence of China which included industrialisation on a grand and rapid scale, just like Stalin this was to cost many lives (it is estimated between 80-100 million people died through his various programmes and diktats) but what cannot be argued is it did free China to start on a road to independence from western exploitation. When Chairman Mao died in 1976, he was succeeded by various leaders of the communist party but the most influential figure behind the scenes from the late 70's until his death in 1977 was Deng Xiaoping. He abandoned many of the orthodox communist doctrines and attempted to incorporate elements of free enterprise into the capitalist system, along with many reforms moving China away from the disastrous excesses of Mao's cultural revolution. Under his leadership, China acquired a rapidly growing economy, rising living standards, expansion of cultural and personal freedoms and growing ties to the world economy. Despite all the reforms he did leave a mildly authoritarian government that remained true to the ideology of the Chinese Communist Party's (CCP) one-party rule, even though it did rely on the free-market mechanisms to transform China.

Xi Jinping is the present leader of the People's Republic of China, he was born into the Communist Party upper echelons with his father serving as Deputy Prime Minister under Mao. His father unfortunately fell to the fate of many under Mao and was forced along with his family to work as agricultural labourers in a commune, when he fell out of favour under the cultural revolution. Despite this Xi joined the communist party in 1974 where he had a reputation for prudence and following the party line, his career was boosted when in early 2007 a pension fraud scandal embroiled the upper leadership of Shanghai. In 2012 he was elected as party secretary where he quickly consolidated power in an anti-corruption campaign, which saw the removal of thousands of both high- and low-level officials, emphasising the rule of law with the judiciary being seen as a means of developing "Socialism with Chinese characteristics." Xi has also been particularly assertive of his country's territorial sovereignty claiming nearly half of all the South China Seas and also Taiwan. His other main project is the 'One Belt, one Road' initiative for joint trade, infrastructure and development projects with East Asian, Central Asian and European countries.

10. MY TWO CENTS WORTH

"The first panacea of a mismanaged nation is inflation of the currency: The second is war. Both bring a temporary prosperity; both bring a permanent ruin, but both are the refuge of political and economic opportunists" Ernest Hemingway.

Three key areas we need to look at before we can then tie it in with the links to Saudi Arabia, the Middle East, Russia and China are: - a) banking, the financial system, interest rates and debt. b) The end of the Soviet Union. c) War and the start of de-dollarization.

a) BANKING, THE FINANCIAL SYSTEM, INTEREST RATES AND DEBT

"It's a big club, and you ain't in it" George Carlin.

Although the commercial banking system since the 1990s had some hiccups, with the notable failures of the Bank of Credit and Commerce (BCCI in 1991 and the highly leveraged hedge fund Long Term Capital Management (LTCM, in 1998 which needed a group of fourteen banks brokered by the Federal Reserve Bank of New York, the seeds were sown for the disaster that was to follow in the next century. What the banking and financial systems learnt from these bailouts was moral hazard, they could act irresponsibly and get away with it, the central bank and by default the taxpayers were on the hook for all the malpractices and the inevitable debt, which was a consequence of reckless casino-style gambling. In 2008 came what at the time was the largest bailout of the whole banking system with the banking financial crisis. The crisis can be traced back to a former bond trader and former vice-chair of the Saloman brothers, Lewis Ranieri. In 1977 the commercial banks were feeling the pinch where they had to fund short-term, high-interest demand deposits, (because of the price inflationary effects from the coming of the gold standard) with longer-term, low-interest mortgages that had been previously agreed. As a result, banks were reluctant to hold give and hold any mortgages. Ranieri devised a clever product which was 5- and 10-year bonds based on 30-year mortgages, which came to be called Mortgage-Backed Securities. (MBS) This helped Ranieri attract a large number of investors, whilst simultaneously taking the mortgages and the risk off the bank's books and additionally providing increased liquidity to issue new mortgages as the initial ones were packaged and bundled up and sold off in tranches (Slices). The bank could then record the sale as an asset on its balance sheet and lose nothing if the homeowner defaults at any time. The MBS was in essence turning the banks into an intermediary between the investment industry (hedge and pension funds) and the homeowner, with the bank handling the loans, then selling them off as an MBS at a discount in the form of a collateralized bond.

All this works well if everyone does what they are supposed to do; banks need to keep reasonably high standards when granting mortgages, the homeowner needs to ensure they can pay the mortgage on time and the credit ratings agencies that review the MBS should be performing due diligence. The problem arose in the early 2000s when the banks effectively ran out of good quality customers to package the MBSs around, what they did was go to customers who were described as subprime. The sub-prime customers had a history of defaults and non-payments, what the banks did was put in an introductory discounted interest rate loan to these subprime customers for approximately two years, after which the rate would double and in some cases triple, doing this to people who had a history of defaulting was only going to end one way, but in that time period the loan was off the banks books and onto a pension or hedge funds balance sheet. An additional consequence was house prices started to accelerate sharply, existing homeowners who had paid off most or even all their mortgages were now sitting on potentially newly found equity in their house prices so were able to take loans against it, which they did with a great deal of enthusiasm; the money supply is now going into overdrive and the market was being severely distorted. The problems really started when the interest rates on the sub-prime mortgage lenders went up after the initial two-year discount offer ran out, they found that the loan was unaffordable and simply handed the keys back in and walked away. This had two effects, firstly house prices started to fall as the supply of housing stock for sale increased and secondly, the funds that were holding the MBS and the even riskier Collateralized Debt Obligations (CDOs) which not only included mortgages in their 'bundles,' but car and credit card loans, were not getting paid, they were effectively holding a product which was not only becoming worthless, they didn't even know what they were holding in these 'bundles.'

The banking system was in meltdown in what was to become known as the Global Financial Crisis, (GFC) governments around the world stepped in and by 2009 introduced a programme known as Quantitative Easing, (QE) Which is a process involving the injection of vast sums of liquidity into the market. QE was first introduced by the Bank of Japan between March 2001 and March 2008, when interest rates had already fallen into negative territory in 1999 and they used QE to fight the deflationary effects that were causing economic problems. The principle of QE is that governments purchase long-term government bonds, MBS and other assets via the central bank to provide liquidity to the system. By purchasing a premeditated quantity of bonds and other financial assets on the financial markets, from private financial institutions, the action increases the excess reserves on the bank's books, the purpose being to inject liquidity into the banking system and allow them via a 'trickle-down theory' to allow banks to lend currency to stimulate both businesses and consumer spending. What happened was the banks lent huge amounts to the financial institutions to indulge in share buybacks, mergers and acquisitions, etc leading to price inflation in asset classes such as stocks and shares, along with the lending on housing again. The cost to the UK's debt saw £200 billion spent on QE in November 2009, with several QE programmes since despite it being classed as a 'temporary, emergency measure' seeing that deficit of the QE purchases in the UK economy by 2020 rise to £895 Billion, in the US that figure was an eyewatering $4.3 Trillion. The banks, in this time period, saw bankers earning record bonuses; moral hazard it would seem has never been so profitable.

Another side effect of all this injection of cash into the system via QE was it gave companies who should for whatever reason, be it bad product, bad management, etc go out of business, stay afloat by constantly borrowing and reborrowing to either fund day to day activities or share buybacks giving the impression of it being healthy, the problem with this is it not only ties up labour making it unproductive, it doesn't allow new companies which could be more dynamic and innovative a foothold into the market place. These companies are known as 'zombie companies. The definition of a zombie is unable to stand on its own two feet and needs either bailouts or kept afloat by lenient creditors or needing to borrow at ultra-low interest rates. It also refers to a company which is only capable of paying the interest on its loans, but not the capital; the problem these companies face is if interest rates rise, they go out of business.

Economist Hyman Minsky foresaw all these problems in his 'financial instability hypothesis' which he developed in the 1970's. In it he states that the economy creates its own bubbles and then crashes, arguing that stable economies create their own destruction through a cycle which goes through three stages which he dubbed: hedge, speculative and Ponzi. During the hedge stage lenders and borrowers are both cautious because of the losses incurred in the previous recession. Borrowers become wary of taking on debt and lenders make prudent, cautious loans, in this stage debt is reasonable. The speculative stage sees both borrowers and lenders become more confident in taking greater amounts of debt and the economy appears to boom, lenders now reduce the criteria for people and businesses to obtain credit and asset prices would only continue to go up. During this stage, they can cover the interest payment on the loans but find it increasingly difficult to pay back the principal. The Ponzi stage dubbed 'The Minsky Moment' by Paul McCulley of PIMCO occurs when the insiders take their profits, leaving everyone else to panic, thus ensuring a crash, where most borrowers and lenders are wiped out. The cycle then continues again.

Once all the government spending around the world on the Covid crisis has been added into the spending, we can see it has led to the present day where the world economy is distorted and disfigured beyond recognition, what appears to be free trade capitalism is cronyism, where governments feel obliged to bail out the failings of an elite parasitical few at the expense of the majority. Official statistics show all world debt (that's debt owed by governments businesses and individuals stands at an eyewatering $3OO trillion, yet this is not the full picture, this does not take into account unfunded government obligations such as pensions, healthcare, etc, but the real stinger is over the counter derivatives, these are personal deals done between two parties that are not recorded on the official stock exchange. Derivatives are complex instruments, and they cover many different types of contracts, they are like a side bet where the value of the derivative comes from an underlying asset, MBSs and CLOs (Collateral Loan Obligations are the same as CDOs except changing the name from debt to loan, the banking industry does weave a tangled web, but one must give credit for persistence) are derivatives but so is something like the dollar. An example would be a side bet on what the dollar will do in the future, someone will bet it will go up and someone bets it will go down, however, it doesn't stop there as other people will have side bets on the Side bets and they just keep going, with no regulations to stop this going on *ad infinitum*, it then becomes an unregulated market full of casino gamblers who know they can carry on, using other people's money, in the full confidence that if anything goes wrong the government will bail them out. What makes these derivative trades even worse is that traders then leverage up the deal increasing the risk even more, it is also pertinent to note that these trades are not illegal. Because of the over-the-counter trades, there is no clear figure as to the amount of debt there is, however, estimates range from between $1.5 to $3.5 Quadrillion. (a quadrillion is a thousand trillion) these sums are eyewatering and with a global GDP estimated at $80 Trillion (and even that number will fall should a crisis occur) the debt to GDP ratio is at the lowest estimate of 500%, should the respected economists Carmen Reinhart and Kenneth Rogoff (2O11) be anywhere near correct where they go back 800 years of debt and estimate once you go past the 90% debt to GDP every $1 spent brings in a return of less than the $1 spent, in other words, every dollar spend actually reduces productivity. As a disclaimer it was discovered that their calculations had omitted some crucial data which both economists agreed with, but still maintained it didn't affect the overall assertion, since 2013 when the error was discovered, we have seen many countries go over 100% debt to GDP and a real concern has been the lack of productivity to offset the fall in living standards many in the West have had since the 2000s.

b/ THE END OF THE SOVIET UNION AND THE FALL AND RISE OF RUSSIA

"The people pretended to work, and the government pretended to pay us" Unknown quote about the Soviet economy.

Mikhail Gorbachev was elected as President of the Soviet Union on March 11th 198S, who although a committed communist, had seen the need for reform both politically and economically, he called this political reform *Perestroika*. In 1989 his commitment to non-intervention in the affairs of foreign states led to two key events; the first was the conclusion of the Soviet-Afghan War, and the second was the wave of mostly peaceful revolutions against the communist governments in Eastern Europe. The elections in March 1989 to the new parliament saw an important step in the breaking of the communist party of the Soviet Union (CPSU) monopoly on power so instead of solidifying Gorbachev's support base, voters became drawn to the more radical Boris Yeltsin. In June 1991 Yeltsin was elected as the first President of the Russian Federation and despite a *coup d'état* against Gorbachev to prevent the break-up of the Soviet Union on August 19th, 1991, two days later the coup was defeated and on December 2Sth 1991, Gorbachev announced he was resigning as President of the Soviet Union, one day later the Union was officially dissolved with the red empire falling apart and broken into fifteen independent states, amongst them was Ukraine.

By 1993 there was a massive economic dislocation occurring as the Soviet style of socialist economics was replaced by a market economy, which after 70 years of communism, left the people by and large essentially reliant on the state for everything from housing to work, the creation of this market economy was a strange, alien and frighting concept. Yeltsin embarked on a privatisation campaign with the help of American advisors and global creditors, in particular the IMF, Russia was a good bet as it has more abundant raw materials including oil, gas, rare minerals, gold, etc than any other country in the world, America it would seem wanted a piece of the action. They instigated what was known as 'The Shock Therapy Programme' which was instigated almost from day one of Yeltsin's election, meant the lifting of price controls as the Soviet economy collapsed this policy unleashed hyperinflation which by the end of 1992 price inflation had reached 2,318 per cent. At the forefront of Yeltsin's economic reform was Russian economist Anatoly Chubais, he was tasked with transforming a nation whose whole economy was based on state-controlled industries into private enterprises. Privatisation was to occur in two stages, the first wave started in October 1992, which had a degree of being open and fair where all Russians were issued with vouchers or 'privatisation checks' of state companies which could be sold or traded. This is where the opportunists stepped in and were to become known as the oligarchs. These oligarchs were a bunch of people who either came up from nothing or former government insiders They scoured the country purchasing hundreds of thousands of shares worth 10,000 Roubles or approximately $40 or less. With the average Russian struggling with hyperinflation, many were eager to sell, eventually leading to these oligarchs' owning companies which just a few short years earlier were state-owned.

With 70% of the state industries sold by 1994, the remaining 30%, which were the biggest companies the second phase came into play. This was a much shadier form of privatisation where Chubais planned to sell the remaining state-owned companies in a 'loan for shares' scheme. By 1995 Yeltsin was unpopular, hyperinflation was peaking, the government had no funds, a decline of law and order with mafia-style killings on the streets of Moscow, in addition to all this Yeltsin was a notorious drunk. The 'loans for shares' scheme relied on the now very wealthy oligarchs lending the government billions of dollars, in exchange for shares in Russia's most valuable state enterprises such as oil and gas. When as was expected the government defaulted on paying the interest on the loans back, the oligarchs would then own Russia's most profitable corporations, and the government in return would keep the billions of dollars and then pay its bills. Yeltsin was now very unpopular; the oligarchs who had gained tremendous wealth and power and so had vested interests in keeping Yeltsin in power started to invest some of their wealth in the media which they predominantly owned into a campaign to get him re-elected. In 1996 they succeeded, but by the late 1990s Yeltsin's health was failing him, so both Yeltsin and the oligarchs set about finding a new successor, both had different reasons, the oligarchs wanted someone they could control to keep their positions of power and wealth, whilst Yeltsin wanted someone that wouldn't arrest him and throw him in jail on corruption charges. They realised the way to a natural successor was whoever was Prime Minister at the time, as once Yeltsin stepped down as President, the PM would automatically become acting President, this would then give that person a natural advantage during election time. In 1999 both Yeltsin and the oligarchs agreed on an obscure, former KGB officer called

Vladimir Putin to become the next PM. He was seen as a nobody, someone who was known for his loyalty but easily controlled. This appointment worked for Yeltsin, but for the oligarchs, it was a fatal mistake.

In the summer of 2000, 21 of the richest oligarchs entered the Kremlin, they would have been happy with this meeting, six months previously they had engineered the new President's success and were fully expecting him to pay homage to them, it didn't quite go according to plan. Instead, Putin offered them a deal, stay out of his way and bend to his authority and they could keep their billion-dollar corporations, their private jets, mansions and super yachts. The smart oligarchs quickly learnt to move aside and keep a low profile, those that weren't as smart ended up being thrown into a Siberian prison, forced into exile or die in suspicious circumstances. The old oligarchs were effectively no more influential in Russian politics, in their place Putin appointed people whom he knew and trusted from the military or security services, along with a few trusted friends who became known as the 'siloviki', roughly translated means 'men of force' or 'strongmen'. Like Putin, these 'siloviki' reviled the reforms under Gorbachev and Yeltsin, where Russia had lost its empire and saw a host of liberal and pro-western intellectuals take over the effective running of the government and the economy. The West and America in particular, have seen their influence on Russia via the old oligarchs eradicated. Under Putin Russia was going in a different direction, a nation which had lost all its sense of self, with rampant alcoholism, crime, and the breakdown of the family all being reversed and, in its place, came a strong government, a rise in the values of the church in particular Orthodox Christianity, nationalism and patriotism, with a belief in the nation's history and its place in the world.

After the fall of the Soviet Union, agreements were made between Russia and the West that NATO would not expand as James Baker the Secretary of State for America at the time said "not one inch" towards Russian territory, as part of the independence deal for Ukraine, they had to agree to get rid of their nuclear arsenal. By the time Putin came into office, the West had reneged on the deal and NATO expanded ever Eastward with countries such as Poland and Lithuania albeit two small counties Estonia and Latvia, which are significant particularly significant as they border Russia. The Russian psyche about invasion needs to be understood, the land mass of Eastern

Europe is soaked in blood from invasion and counter-invasion. Russia just in the last two hundred years was invaded by Napoleon, they fought the Ottoman Empire in the 18th Century, finally defeating them and claiming more land, but in particular the strategically important Crimea with its access to the Black Sea. In the last century alone, they faced the Austro-Hungary empire in the First World War and the Nazis in World War Two. In the Second World War the Russians lost a staggering 27 million men defending its country and is known in Russia as the Great Patriotic War, and is celebrated on the 9th of May with every citizen taking to the streets carrying a picture of a loved one who fought in that and subsequent wars, the defence of their borders needless to say means a lot to the Russians.

Between 2-4 April 2008, at the NATO summit in Bucharest, Croatia and Albania were invited to join the alliance. Georgia and Ukraine had hoped to join the NATO Membership Action Plan and although initially not successful it was agreed they would both eventually become NATO members. In the Russian eyes, this was like a red rag to a bull and the famous comment by Russian foreign minister Sergey Lavrov "Niet means No" refers to Russia saying that this is a line in the sand they would not countenance the West crossing and would take action to stop this happening. Putin stated at the same conference that Georgia joining NATO would be seen as a direct threat to the security of Russia. On August 7th Russia invaded Georgia, it lasted only 5 days when Russia called for a ceasefire on August 12th. It was an extremely short but bloody conflict for a brief period, but it sent a message to the West that Russia was ready to reassert itself. The Russians performed very poorly in the war against the American-trained Georgians, this was seen in Washington as Russia was still weak, the Russians realised they got lucky that they came up against a small military nation; they would have to step up their game if they were to be taken as a serious military threat in the future.

To understand the present conflict between Russia and Ukraine we need to have a brief look at the land mass that was to become known as Ukraine and its bloody history. The first recorded empire occupying the area was the Vikings from Sweden around the 900s AD; since then, the area has been overrun by the Mongol Empire in the 13th and 14th Century, the Ottoman

Empire from the 14th Century, interspersed with the Polish Lithuanian empire in the 16th and 17th Century, the Russian empire in the 18th Century, and its recent history, included domination by the Soviet empire and Nazi Germany. As can be seen, it is a nation forged in conflict. By 1654 the Ukrainian territory was a small area and asked for support from the Russian Empire in its conflict with the Polish Empire. Russia agreed and expanded the Ukrainian territory under various Tsars between 1694 and 1917, the area was to incorporate many towns and cities, including Kyiv. In 1922 Lenin added East Ukraine, which was effectively West Russia, including the four Ukrainian Oblasts (regions or provinces) of Luhansk, Donetsk, Zaporizhzhia, Kherson and Odessa. Stalin went even further and added Western areas which had previously belonged to Poland, the main city being Lviv. In 1954 Nikita Khrushchev, in celebration of the 300th anniversary of Russia's support of the Ukraine, gifted the region of the Crimea.

After the NATO summit in Bucharest and the short war against Georgia, Russia became increasingly wary of the West and America in particular. The main lever it had was it was exporting cheap oil and gas to Western Europe, particularly benefiting the European Union (EU) economic powerhouse, Germany. Russia it would appear was wise to have such concerns about the influence America was trying to exert on it, the regime changes Washington had been engineering around the world and in particular the Middle East, was now targeting them. In November 2013, democratically elected President Viktor Yanukovych was ready to sign a deal with the EU for approximately $7 billion, but he turned it down at the last minute after the EU demanded reforms to make Ukraine more financially accountable, the Ukraine then as now is regarded as one of the most corrupt countries in the world. Russia stepped in and offered the money with no strings attached to it. This sparked mass protests, backed by the US government and the EU, both of which wished to extend their influence on Eastern Europe; the Russians threw their support behind Yanukovych. In February 2014 anti-government protests toppled the government and Yanukovych fled the country. Russia now fearful of ever-increasing NATO expansion on its borders invaded and annexed Crimea in March 2014, because of its vital importance as a military seaport; it was effective as it saw it as taking its gift from Khruschev back. In April 2014 pro-Russian separatists, backed by Russia, seized territories in the eastern regions. The people of these Eastern regions from the Sea of Azov to Odessa see themselves as essentially Russian, they predominantly speak Russian and adopt Russian customs, which is why to this day they generally do all they can to aid Russia. Due to these acts, the West imposed sanctions on Russia, which included targeting both individual supporters of Putin (the siloviki) and companies and corporations (owned by the siloviki) with the seizure of assets, and lending money to certain businesses and banks. This was done in the hope that the Russian economy would falter and the siloviki would turn on Putin and instigate regime change in Russia itself.

Since 2014 the Ukrainian government has fought Russian-backed separatists for control over the heavily industrialised regions of Donetsk and Luhansk. (Also known as the Donbas) The intensity of the fighting between 2014 and February 2022 differed from month to month, but it is estimated that the Ukrainian military killed approximately 14,000 people. From March 2021 till February 2022, the Russians embarked on a military build-up, leading to the invasion of Ukraine on February 24th, 2022, which the Russians called a Special Military Operation; (SMO) which was initially intended to deal in the Donbas region. The Ukraine's in the time between 2014 and 2022, were trained, armed, and funded by the West, not necessarily a shrewd move considering Ukraine's reputation for corruption, who had in that time turned international arms smuggling into an art form. Despite fluctuating fortunes for both countries throughout 2022, it would appear by April 2023 that the Russians were in the ascendency and despite a lot of rhetoric from both the Ukrainian and American governments this war will not end well for them and de-facto also for the West and NATO.

11. WAR, END OF HEGEMONY AND DE-DOLLARIZATION

"The dollar is our currency but it's your problem" John Connally Governor of Texas at the G10 meeting in Rome in 1971. (He was also famous for being in the car with John F Kennedy when he was assassinated in 1963)

a) IRAQ

To understand the process of de-dollarization we need to look at the wars America has embroiled itself since the inception of the petrodollar, in particular the Middle East this region and although it doesn't have the importance that it had in the 1980s with new countries such as Russia, the United States China, Canada, Venezuela, Norway, Nigeria, Brazil and Algeria, adding to the world's oil production, yet Saudi Arabia, along with Iran, United Arab Emirates, Kuwait, Iraq and Syria, still hold considerable influence on the oil market.

To understand the backdrop of the events unfolding in the Middle East today, we must go back to 1979, when the Iranian regime of Shah Pahlavi was overthrown in the Iranian Revolution led by Ayatollah Ruhollah Khomeini. Initially, Saddam Hussein welcomed the change as he despised the Shah, however, when the Ayatollah began to call for a Shi'a revolution in Iraq to overthrow Saddam's secular/Sunni regime his attitude changed and began to call for a new Battle of Qadisiyyah. (a reference to the 7th Century AD battle where the Muslim Arabs defeated the Persians) Khomeini retaliated calling the Ba'athist party of Saddam a "puppet of Satan". In Iraq Shi'as began to respond to the Ayatollah's call for regime change, Saddam cracked down on these uprisings hard, eventually leading to Iraq's invasion of Iran on September 22, 1980. After eight years of Invasion and counter-invasion, in 1988 a peace deal was begrudgingly signed between the two countries which effectively left both countries geopolitically with the status quo from before the start of the war, the only difference was an estimated 500,000-1,000,000 million Iranians lost their lives, whilst around 300,000 Iraqis lost theirs. (Szcepanski, 2023)

Following this conflict, despite Iraq having received an abundance of political, logistical, and even financial support from many countries including the United States, United Kingdom, France, Italy and even the Soviet Union; Iraq found itself heavily in debt, its economy crippled and owing Kuwait $14 billion, a huge sum for the time which it was unable to repay. In addition, its attempt to raise the price of oil through OPEC became impossible as soon as it reduced output Kuwait increased theirs. It is in this cauldron that Saddam accused Kuwait of stealing Iraqi oil by using 'slant drilling' and invaded Kuwait in 1990. This time the US supported Kuwait and this led to its first Gulf War on Iraq which became known as Desert Storm. Along with the support of Saudi Arabia which permitted the Americans to be based in the Kingdom, and its immense firepower and military capability, ably supported by many other countries, the war lasted approximately seven months.

Saddam was not toppled and continued to rule Iraq, seething at what he saw as American betrayal and realising he couldn't defeat the Americans militarily but saw an opportunity to hit them where it would hurt most; the economy, with this in November 2000, Saddam announced he no longer wanted to deal "in the currency of the enemy" the US dollar but in Euro's instead. It was a move that would have hurt Iraq financially as well as the Euro had fallen in value at the time to about 1Euro= 0.82 cents, thus reducing the interest earnings and reparation payments Iraq was making for the Gulf War. Regime change became inevitable as the United States sought to re establish its power in the region. It got the opportunity when in 2002 the new President George W Bush argued that the US was vulnerable after the September 11th attack in 2001, alleging that Saddam Hussein had continued the possession of Weapons of Mass Destruction (WMD) along with its support of terrorist groups.

On September 11th, 2001, 19 members of Al-Qaeda, a group which was granted sanctuary by the Taliban-controlled Afghanistan, hijacked four commercial airlines in the United States. Two of the planes were flown into the World Trade Centre in New York, one was flown into the Pentagon and the fourth crashed into a field in Pennsylvania. On October 7th 2001, the Taliban refused to hand over Al-Qaeda leader Osama bin Laden; within two weeks the US-led forces overthrew the Taliban but by 2003-2008 the Taliban were able to regroup in their strongholds of the South and East of Afghanistan due to the US attention being diverted from Afghanistan to the new war in Iraq. By 2009 despite the continued drain of resources in Iraq, US troops peaked at 100,000. On May 2nd, 2011, bin Laden was killed by US special forces in Pakistan. In June Obama announced the withdrawal of US forces from Afghanistan. In 2O2O the Taliban and the Trump administration agree that all US forces will be withdrawn by May 1st, 2021. In April 2021, the newly elected President Joe Biden accelerated the withdrawal but put the deadline back to September 11, 2021, marking the 20th anniversary of the 9/11 attacks. In the meantime, Taliban forces made lighting advances and on August 15 2O21 entered the capital city of Kabul with no resistance; the speed of the advance saw the Americans both unprepared and incapable of stopping this advance, meaning many of its citizens and vulnerable Afghans who supported them are unable to be evacuated through Kabul airport. On August 30th all US troops left Afghanistan with at least 100 US citizens and manyvulnerable Afghans who worked for the US government. The scene of the chaotic withdrawal is seen throughout the world, evoking images of the fall of Saigon which ended in humiliating defeat for the Americans in 1975.

In March 2003 Iraq was once again invaded by the US, the UK and a contingent of several smaller countries, by April a quick victory saw the collapse of the Ba'athist Party and the country erupting into violence and looting. The occupying forces were now dealing with having to restore law and order and prevent an all-out civil war. In May 2OO3 the head of the coalition Provincial Authority, Paul Bremer disbanded the Iraqi army and intelligence services along with barring the long-ruling Baath Party from being involved in the formation process of a new government. This decision alienated hundreds of thousands of trained men, creating a security and governance vacuum, which destabilised the country for many years to come. In the same year, it was eventually admitted that Iraq had no WMD, and the invasion was essentially predicated on a lie.

By the mid-2000s the transition from US to Iraqi rule saw the death of tens of thousands of Iraqis, the launch of an al-Qaeda-led uprising, the outbreak of a sectarian civil war and the eventual rise of ISIS. When the last of the US troops finally left in 2011, the security void that was left behind led to ISIS strengthening its grip on much of the region and declaring a Caliphate. Although largely defeated in 2017, again via a US-funded military campaign, the region is inherently unstable. This is the legacy two decades after the invasion was meant to usher in the dawn of a new liberal democratic era of peace in the Middle East.

b) LIBYA

"From barbarism to civilization requires a century; from civilization to barbarism needs but a day" Will Durant 'The Reformation-The Story of Civilization'.

The US who by now with the collapse of the Soviet Union had all-but acquired hegemony in the world and with the Hawks (Neo-Cons) in the White House now in the ascendency, hubris and ego started taking over. When another Arab leader Muammar al-Gaddafi challenged the dollars position on oil payment, it was never going to end well. Before 2011 Libya had achieved economic independence, with its water, its own food, its own oil, its own money, and its own state-owned bank. In addition, educational and medical treatment was free, having a home was a human right, and the country boasted the largest irrigation system in the world, bringing water from the desert to the cities and coastal areas. Qaddafi had turned Libya from one of the poorest countries in Africa to one of the richest. Gaddafi took Saddam Hussain's plan one stage further and not just attempted to sell his oil in another currency, but attempted along with other African nations, a pan-African gold standard, in other words, an independent 'hard currency'. It attempted to do this as the government held 143 tons of gold and a similar amount of silver, this was intended to be used as the basis for a pan-African currency, based on the Libyan golden Dinar. In 2011 President Sarkozy of France even called the Libyan leader a threat to the financial security of the world, in reality he probably meant the Western world. What Gaddafi was doing was trying to enable Africa to secure financial independence from the West and in particular America. The US responded to the challenge on the dollar, by leading a US-NATO intervention on humanitarian grounds after reports of mass atrocities, they proceeded to bomb the irrigation system, wreak havoc on the country, find and kill Gaddafi and leave the country now with a real human rights disaster, with killings, kidnappings, thousands of detainees (including children) languishing in prison with no proper judicial review and now becoming the transit and destination country for men and women from sub-Saharan Africa and Asia, for the purpose of forced labour and commercial sexual exploitation. The damage that the military intervention inflicted was intended to disrupt any attempt at independence and self-reliance within Africa.

12. PERSONAL OPINION

I always have the wise words of J. K. Galbraith in the back of my mind when trying to assess what may be happening in the future, "economic forecasting exists to make astrologers look professional" However it is abundantly clear that there are moves by large sections of the globe to de-dollarize. If this happens it will be catastrophic for not only America but the West as a whole, who have been riding on their economic and military tailcoats. Since globalization, Southeast Asian countries and in particular China have been the engine that produces the goods that the West readily buys, unfortunately for the West they have been buying these products in fiat currencies and backed by American military power; this will all come to an end if Saudia Arabia ends the petrodollar and de-dollarization occurs.

When the Russians invaded the Donbas in East Ukraine in February 2022, the Americans and their allies froze $300 billion of their overseas assets, in essence stealing it; the rather embarrassing part of all this is that after seizing $100 billion the US and EU recently stated that they couldn't locate where the other $200 billion as they don't know where it is; it truly inspires and fills you with confidence in the leadership of the West! By the invasion of 2022, the Russians got cut off from using the SWIFT payment system, this is an international system that is used to make international payments, if you can't use this a country and its citizens in theory cannot trade internationally; not only did Russia circumnavigate this, it left the rest of the non-western world looking on thinking if they can do this to Russia, what happens if we do something they don't like? So, what has happened? Firstly, many of these non-Western countries, in particular China, India and Saudi Arabia have been buying an extraordinary amount of gold, this are two reasons behind it, especially for China; there would be no way Saudi Arabia would move from the dollar to the Yuan without it having the backing of gold, this effectively makes the Yuan real money and not a fiat currency anymore. It is also highly plausible that the non-Western countries are going to use all the gold purchased to create a gold-backed currency, this could be the Yuan as the main currency or a newly formed BRICS currency, or alternatively a new currency could be made up from a basket of commodities which would include a basket of commodities such as oil and gas. BRICS is an independent organisation which aims to promote political, cultural and economic cooperation among its members, the five members being Brazil, Russia, India, China and South Africa. The BRICS was originally formed in 2012 but is now starting to become a big deal on the world stage. It is now powering ahead and as of March 2023 now provides 31.5% of global GDP, whilst the G7 (Canada, France, Germany, Italy, Japan, United Kingdom and the United States) provide 30.7% with an additional nineteen nations applying to join' nations such as Saudia Arabia, Iran, United Arab Emirates, Turkey, Indonesia, Mexico and Argentina amongst them, will only see the BRICS nations increase their share of GDP. Here is the real point in the comparison of the BRICS and G7 nations, the BRICS have the commodities whilst the F7 control the finances; the G7 cannot grow their commodities but the BRICS can create a new currency and an alternative financial system, especially as it is being linked to commodities such as gold and oil. In addition to BRICS challenging the West on the production front, it also has the BRICS bank (New Development Bank) which funds projects in developing countries that the IMF and World Bank don't. It is based in Shanghai and the ex-President of Brazil Dilma Rousseff is to become its President. Once the bank is fully developed, the developing nations will have a choice to either borrow from the Western IMF or World Bank, which rarely funds infrastructure projects but instead, US military bases or corrupt leaders and government officials, or borrow from the development bank to build up its nation's infrastructure which it can then use as a springboard to increase its GDP and purchase goods from China and other BRICS nations, with the Belt and Road Initiative (BRI) being an integral part of the nations development, in reality unless you are a corrupt nation, with corrupt leaders, the choice would appear to be simple.

The first stage of the end of the petrodollar would be to allow nations to purchase oil in currencies other than the dollar, it has just started happening, however unlike Libya and Iraq who tried to go it alone, there is a much more coordinated global campaign, in early 2023 Saudi Arabia just agreed to let China buy its oil in Yuan, In addition, Brazil and China have agreed to trade in their respective currencies, the Real and Yuan, even Myanmar and Iran have started to trade using the barter system where Tea will be exchanged for oil, countries like Russia, Malaysia, Brazil and Saudi Arabia are amongst 18 countries who have agreed to trade in Indian Rupees.

What probably is the most important event for many decades happened in March 2023, it has gone under the radar of Western media but is going to be seen as of major importance at the end of American hegemony is a deal which was originally started by Russia and finally finished off by China, and that is the rapprochement between Saudi Arabia and Iran, this is a huge event as the conflict between the two nations was the lever America used to maintain military dominance in the Middle East; it also now makes Beijing look like the go-to place to solve world problems and not America. In rapid succession, Saudi Arabia is looking at rapprochement with Syria. In addition, Syria and Turkey had a meeting in Moscow to sort their differences out, after 30 years of American involvement in the Middle East which has caused millions of deaths, it would appear that these nations would rather deal with China who would prefer business and trade being the order of the day and not war. To see how concerned and reliant America and American citizens are reliant on the dollar as the world's reserve currency, we need to look no further than the quote by White House spokesperson Karine Jean-Pierre on the April 2O23.

"We are deeply concerned about the transition of Brazil and China to national currencies when conducting mutual settlements. This is a violation of the right of our citizens who rely on a stable dollar exchange rate on the world market. America will not allow other countries to dictate terms to it in mutual trade. We want to warn that the violation of the rights of ordinary Americans will not remain without consequences for these countries".

It seems Brazil and China didn't get the memo that they owe Americans a living.

The final nail in the coffin of the dollar is the war between Russia and Ukraine, this war is a de facto war with NATO and by default the Americans, the US were looking for regime change in Russia by making life difficult for the ordinary Russian via economic sanctions, this has not happened, in fact the Russian economy after an initial blip when the war started has not only stabilized but looks like it will grow in 2023, an amazing feat for a nation on a war footing. India and China have taken up the slack of purchasing cheap Russian oil and gas which was previously being sold to

Europe, in fact, what has been happening in India and China are amongst several countries who are buying more oil and gas than they need from Russia and selling the surplus with an additional fee to Europe, in essence, Europe is still buying Russian oil and gas only paying more for it and travelling halfway around the globe to get it. After blowing up the Nord Stream 2 pipeline, and depriving Germany of the much-required cheap energy it needs to sustain its manufacturing base, the Americans very kindly sold them LNG (Liquified Natural Gas) but at a much higher premium than the Russians had previously been purchasing from the Russians, this has meant many industries in Germany have closed down and there are no signs this trend is stopping.

The real problem that America will face with regard the Russian-Ukrainian conflict is they back the dollar with military power, in essence, they use fear as a tool to keep the rest of the world in place, they have at least 800 military bases around the world and probably many more in secret locations. Should Russia win the war in Ukraine, which in all probability it will, the media portrayal in the West of Russia as being weak, ineffectual and ready to overthrow Putin at the drop of a hat can be seen as the false narrative that it is, the world watching on would have less fear of American military power as they had just recently seen the withdrawal of Afghanistan being shambolic, which is being followed quickly by the defeat of Russia; Nation states around the world would be emboldened to not trade with the dollar.

Here is the prediction that could alter the world balance of power for the 21st Century, Once the petrodollars are no longer widely used, the reliance on the dollar as the world currency will diminish like sterling after World War Two will be replaced. The Russians and Chinese have been working on an alternative payment system to SWIFT, the Russians have developed the System for Transfer of Financial Messaging, (SPFS) at present due to sanctions it is mainly for internal use, however as power shifts, this will surely change; in addition, they have developed a MIR card which is an alternative to Visa and Mastercard. The Chinese have also developed the Cross-Border Interbank Payment System, (CIPS) this is already a system that is internationalizing. In addition, the BRICS nation along with the new countries joining are looking to form an alternative currency to the dollar, they will be ably supported by other organisations such as the Shanghai Cooperation Organisation (SCO) but unlike it is a fiat currency, it will be one backed by gold and other commodities such as oil and gas, in other words, real money that the trading nations involved will have trust in. With less demand for dollars around the world these dollars will start flooding back into America; compound this with the potential of China, Saudia Arabia and many more countries starting to sell their US treasury bills, this will not only crash the bond market, but it will also force interest rates up on new bonds as countries will be selling not buying. The argument that they cannot dump all their bond holdings as they would end up destroying the value of what bonds they have left is a valid one, however, if China intends to destroy American hegemony this firstly may be a price worth paying, but also the rationale could be with a new world reserve that they have a major influence in are the bonds effectively worthless anyway.

If the dumping of dollars and treasuries does happen, several factors are going to hit the West almost together to create the perfect storm and collapse its economies. One is price inflation in America, Europe and the UK would rise at an alarming rate, firstly because there are more dollars, Euros and Sterling floating around the economy and secondly since globalization, most of the manufacturing base has been destroyed and shipped to Southeast Asia, so the goods the West have been buying which in reality has cost nothing, (as all they have done is simply printed the money) would end, just like the Opium Wars when China insisted on gold for their products as they didn't want anything produced by the West, they will insist on commodities not dollars, Euro or Sterling to trade. This time however the Chinese are better prepared to withstand any attempt at any equivalent of opium exports to their country. If anything, the moral decline is the West's problem, in fact, China have been exporting vast quantities of the chemical ingredients which make fentanyl to Mexico, with the open borders the drug is flooding America, latest estimates it is costing the American population about 100,000 predominantly young lives a year; this is a problem that is going to get much worse, and China have no incentive to stop selling to Mexico, as it was mentioned earlier that the Chinese have long memories. The other effect of price inflation will be the increase in the cost of oil which will be imposed on the West, although America is relatively self-sufficient in oil, Europe is most certainly not. Britain could be if it chose to frack but at this moment in time appears along with the rest of Europe to have an unshaken belief that it will become self-sufficient via green energy, let's hope they are right soon, otherwise, we could be for some very cold harsh winters in the years ahead; an example of what may be to come is OPEC+ have agreed in April 2023 to reduce the supply of oil by 1 million barrels per day, reduced supply means higher prices; they can read the room and see the slowdown in the economy of the West so by reducing supply the increase in the price of oil will offset the slowing sales.

The final thing that would happen should China dump its holdings in US treasuries is the collapse of derivatives, zombie companies, pension funds, the banking system, and the property market both commercial and retail. These markets are so interlinked that when one goes the others would surely follow. The West has been the architect of its own folly, it exported many jobs to Asia, and continually reduced interest rates meaning the price discovery mechanism was no longer applicable; businesses, governments and individuals borrowed too much, for too long, too cheaply, they produced nothing and printed to buy overseas goods, we had become an economy based on consumerism and credit and now the party is finally finishing and the hangover awaits, once the dollar, euro and sterling starts to get 'dumped' the currencies will fall, this means although exporting would be cheaper, we literally make nothing worth of note to export, (for example 80% of the British economy is made up of the service sector) yet imports will become increasingly more expensive, interest rates will have to rise to attract buyers putting added pressure on prices. The argument being made that we are heading for a stagflationary period similar to the 1970s, unfortunately, it is going to be much worse, the debt to GDP in the 1970's was approx. 50%, now it is running double at around 100 per cent and rising; as it passes the 90% point getting a return on any additional spending as calculated by Carmen Reinhart and Kenneth Rogoff means for every pound we are spending we receive less than a pound this then actually makes the problem worse, this will also apply to all Western nations who have debt to GDP above 100%. Even worse the debt also doesn't factor in any of the unfunded liabilities such as pensions, health care for the increasingly elderly population and the real canary in the coal mine the quadrillions of debts around the world in derivatives. What is likely to happen here is a new phenomenon I would like to call crash-split/flation, this is where economies will crash for the reasons mentioned above, however, inflation will split into two components; any goods that require paying for as you shop such as food, fuel, petrol, heating bills, etc will rise sharply in price, other goods that usually require credit to purchase such as cars, or items that need loans such as houses will fall sharply as interest rates will have risen to compensate the falling currency. There will have to be a fundamental transition back into manufacturing/production for a goods-based economy. We will also have to start to pay our own way in the world and start amassing commodities which the rest of the world may find useful or desire, gold would be a good start.

Another crippling factor to enter the equation is as price inflation starts to take hold, the government have only several tools available to control it, they could on fiscal policy either raise taxes, reduce government spending or a combination of the two, or on the monetary side reduce the printing of money or allow interest rates to rise. Any of these measures are used to reduce the problem of too much money chasing too few goods. The interest rate rise is the tool being used by default as the bond market where the government go and sells bonds to raise money to fund its spending, once the purchasers of these bonds (pension funds, hedge funds, etc) start to get concerned about the ability of governments to pay back its debt they will then insist on higher interest rates to reflect the risk that is being taken on for lending the money, (this naturally leads into a vicious feedback loop where the higher the debt that has to be paid back due to increase interest rates, the less likely the debt will be paid). The effect of the bond market insisting on requiring higher interest rates feeds into the mainstream with higher interest on mortgages, business loans, etc. If the government refuse to pay the high-interest rates it can do yield curve control (as Japan has been doing) whereby they monetize the debt (effectively the central bank prints money to buy the government debt at the lower interest rate) However, the effect of this would be even higher inflation.

Higher interest rates are going to be particularly perilous for homeowners who have borrowed large amounts on low-interest rates and although many have locked in rates between two to five years, as is the standard time period in the UK, in general, these deals are coming to end, many homeowners later into 2023 and 2024 will be finding their monthly payments rising to eyewatering amounts, this should have the effect of lowering the prices of homes in the UK as banks will be forced to lend less money for mortgages as potential new buyers would have to reassess their affordability. In the US it is different as they can take 30-year loans so can ride out the storm, however, this poses a problem for the housing market as anyone on a 30-year loan deal will be essentially trapped in their house, unable to move for fear of losing their low-interest deal. It also leaves the banks in a dilemma, as houses are seen as an asset on the bank's books, they have used this as leverage to lend more money out, if house prices fall, they are then overleveraged and the books don't look so rosy, in addition, more mortgage defaults which will rise compound this problem. The US banks would have additional problems even if they could convince themselves that as people don't move the value of the house would remain the same making their leverage appear fine, new borrowers would be in short supply due to affordability issues and as the banks are in the business of lending, no borrowers mean reduced profits. Another problem for the US banks is as they are receiving low premiums on the 30-year deals they will be having to pay savers higher interest rates, for example, if they are receiving 2.5% from a $100,000 30-year fixed loan but are now having to pay 3.5% in interest to someone with $100,000 in savings, they are losing money each and every month.

Another serious problem with the interest rates rising is 'zombie companies' companies which at virtually zero interest rates can only generate enough capital to pay the interest on the loan and not the capital it has borrowed are going to find themselves in serious trouble if this happens, we will see mass layoffs occurring.

All fiat currencies end this always due to greed, stupidity, attempting to hold onto power both internally and internationally and the most destructive of reasons, to fund wars. Western nations now find themselves in a bind, facing rising interest rates which means all debts from government, businesses, and individual citizens face paying more when they have to roll their debts on; debts which were unaffordable at low rates are going to be impossible to pay back so they have a choice, keep raising interest rates to defeat inflation but in the meantime destroy anyone or any business that has to rely on loans to keep functioning by forcing bankruptcy or default, which will lead to a 1930's style deflation only much worse as there is much more debt that has to be written off. The rising interest rates would also have a profound effect on the banking system, as most of their leverage is based on two main items, the government bonds they hold which will fall in value once interest rates rise and the value of high house prices which would again fall thus leaving their reserve value underwater and in turn have less ability to lend via fractional reserve banking; yet the real problem with the banking system and the low-interest rate climate is that due to the system of fractional reserve banking the banks have been the real culprits in expanding the money supply by lending ever increasing amounts which has led to the creation of household and business debts that the world is facing, whilst government QE programmes have been responsible for creating the Sovereign debt problem. Both QE and the money lending by banks via fractional reserve banking have combined responsibility for the rise in prices for items such as housing, stocks and shares, art, etc, effectively causing a 'bubble of everything'. The serious problem begins when this lending slows and goes into reverse, the decline in the value of these assets is inevitable. Another problem faced over the years by the lowering of interest rates again leads into the moral hazard conundrum, which this time is not the making the bankers and financial institutions' fault, legally hedge and pension funds are required by law to keep a percentage of their portfolio as government bonds, this is done to provide some protection for the investor, unfortunately as the rates were lowered to such a level that the returns were getting so small it effectively forced these institutions into taking greater and greater risks to offset the reduced returns from the lower yields of these government bonds. The increased investment risks were undertaken to achieve the investment returns hedge funds required to make reasonable dividend payments to their clients or for pension funds to meet their contractual obligations to pay their clients their pensions.

The alternative would be to go back to the QE programmes and/or direct currency printing leading to even higher inflation than we have now, or even the possibility of hyperinflation. The only real solution however would be to return to sound money, which is what is happening with the

BRICS nations, and that is a currency backed by a commodity, it would be a painful transition and a lot of people would suffer financially, if not ruined in the short term but stability would eventually ensue, the two alternatives of raising interest rates or QE without a return to sound money would mean a prolonged, contraction of the economy which could take decades to play out. The BRICS nations are well on course for creating a new currency that is backed by at least one commodity- gold; we would do well to see what they are doing and follow their lead, the world is changing and changing fast and if we are not careful then being left way behind is not just a possibility but an almost foregone conclusion.

Price inflation emerges to non-economists like a bolt from the blue, the underlying effects of inflation begin very quietly and under the radar to most people for potentially decades, it only grabs the attention once it has begun to compound on itself, just like the compounding of interest rates once payments are missed and starts to affect the everyday lives of everyday citizens living standards. Looking back over the millennia of various nations and mismanagement /debasement of economies should be used as a warning sign for future events, empires come, and empires go and the message is always once we hit prolonged periods of price inflation and/ or hyperinflation territory it is generally too late; it is like a warning light flashing on a car, the warning light is not the problem, it is letting you know that under the bonnet is where the real issue is and any driver who has ignored a warning light that says your running low on oil for too long and kept driving without taking the necessary measures to rectify the problem can testify, the engine will eventually blow up. The problem the West has is that the only courses of action it has is left unpalatable, it can reduce public spending, which would be very unpopular, and raise interest rates but it would have to be at least 1% above the inflation rate, otherwise, it would be still financially sensible to keep borrowing as the inflation would mean base rates would be negative in real terms for example if price inflation was at 10% and interest rates were 5% that is essentially the interest rates being negative by 5%, i.e you would be borrowing at 5% to buy something worth 10% hence the negative 5%; in the UK in April 2023 interest rates would need to be about 11.5% as inflation by CPI is approx. 10.5%, if it were to be measured the old way as RPI, the interest rates would need to be near 15%, whichever figure we use is way above what households and businesses could sustain, let alone governments as all are already overloaded with debt, the government could default but would then find it difficult to borrow at least short term on the bond market, and so having to raise interest rates anyway, individuals and businesses could also default but this affects lenders both financially but also it reduces the pool that they can lend to. The final age-old solution is going to war; there is already a NATO proxy war in Ukraine with Russia, and it appears America is already looking to add to this process with its rhetoric regarding China and Taiwan, hopefully we can find alternative solutions to this course of action, but past episodes cannot fill anyone with too much optimism.

Governments once they have run up unsustainable debts from borrowing and printing their fiat currencies leading to price inflation have effectively four ways of clearing those debts and make no mistake those debts will have to be brought down eventually because if they don't either lenders will start demanding increasingly higher interest rates on the bonds government issue making the debt load even more unsustainable or even worse stop lending. The first option is governments have to drastically reduce their public spending programmes, the second way is to increase taxes, and the third way is to offer a 'haircut' which means they admit they cannot pay the full debt and offer a percentage of what is owed say 50%, throwing in the threat of a full default if this offer isn't accepted and finally use price inflation as a way of avoiding their responsibilities of having to pay their debts and obligations by eroding the debt that they have created. Whatever path or combination of paths are chosen it almost certainly means a lot more difficult and darker times are ahead of us.

One other crucial point to note is that price inflation does have the ability to cause a huge amount of inequality in society and understanding this would go a long way toward eradicating it. It is summed up perfectly by an 18th century economist and financier Richard Cantillon and has become known as 'The Cantillon effect'. Cantillon was of Irish descent but spent most of his life in France, where he made a fortune as a banker and in particular profiting from the Mississippi scheme but met an unfortunate demise when a cook he had dismissed came back, murdered and robbed him then set fire to his house. However, his one surviving piece of work 'Essai sur la Nature du Commerce en General' (Essay on the Nature of Trade in General) explained how a change in relative prices came about due to a change in the money supply but it was the uneven expansion in the money supply that was the crucial point. It is this uneven expansion that has benefitted both investors and owners over the workers. (wage-earner) The theory states the beneficiaries of the new currency are the people nearest to the ones who create it, in essence in Cantillon's time were to be the people nearest the 'king'. In modern society the beneficiaries of fiat currency are the ones nearest the Central Banks which print the currency; these will initially be the Investment banks, then moves on to the central banks, followed by the large corporations, then government contractors and finally the workers in society. The original beneficiaries of the currency can purchase assets such as properties, stocks and shares before the price gets pushed up, by the time the workers in the society get to see any of the extra currency printing, prices have already risen, and their purchasing power has been greatly reduced; to sum up price inflation in a nutshell it is this reduction in the purchasing power that hurts people and why savers are ultimately destroyed. It is no accident that since the 21st Century inequality has started to grow and is increasing at an ever-rapid rate, the ultra-wealthy have increased their net worth whilst the rest of society is gradually falling further behind due to the Cantillon effect.

We started this book with a quote from the Roman senator Cicero, so it seems apt to finish with his truly wise words "The only thing we learn from history is we learn nothing from history".

THE END.

REFERENCES

Adshead, Samuel. (2004). T'ang China: The Rise of the East in World History. Basingstoke, U.K.: Palgrave Macmillan. Ascher, William.

Amadeo, Kimbely. (2022) *Historical US Unemployment Rate by Year,* thebalancemoney.com December 6th, 2022.

Atherton, Mark. (2009) *The Beginners Guide to Stock Markets,* Times Online May 8th, 2009.

Balfour, Michael. (1968) *West Germany,* Publisher Ernest Renn, P53, London.

Bannister Judith. (1987) *Chins Changing Population,* Stanford, California: Stanford University Press.

Bardo, Michael, D & White, Eugene, N. (1990) *British and French Finances During the Napoleonic Wars,* National Bureau of Economic Research, Working Paper 3517, November 1990.

Barraclough, Geoffrey. (2022) *Holy Roman Empire,* Encyclopedia Britannica 21st September 2022.

Barth, Jonathan. (2021) *The Currency of Empire; Money and Power in 17th Century America,* Cornell University Press.

Bayer-Xambeu, Marie-Theres, Ghislain Deleplace and Lucian Gillard. (1994) *Private Money and Public Currencies: The 16th Century Challenge,* Armonk, NY: M.E. Sharpe, 1994.

Benn Charles (2002) *China's Golden Age: Everyday Life in the Tang Dynasty,* Oxford University Press.

Bernholtz, Peter & Kugler, Peter. (2007) *16th Century: Empirical Results from a Structural Vectorautoregression Model,* WWZ Working Paper, No 12/ 07, University of Basel, Centre for Business Economics (WWZ) Basel.

Bessel, Richard. *Germany After the First World War,* Oxford 1993.

Bisgaard, Lars (2014) *Monastic Culture: The Long Thirteenth Century,* University Press of Southern Denmark.

Blomquist, Thomas W. (1990) *Some Observations on Early Foreign Exchange Banking, Based Upon New Evidence From 13th Century Lucca,* Journal of Economic History 19(2) P353-75.

Boissoneault, Lorraine. (2017) *Bismark Tried to End Socialism's Grip in Germany by Offering Government Healthcare,* Smithsonianmag.com July 14th, 2017.

Bowsky, William, M. (1970) *The Finance of the Commune of Sienna, 1287-1355,* Oxford.

Bradbury, A.J. (1977) *Before the Black Death,* Economic History Review, P393-410.

Braudel, Fernand. (1984) *Civilization and Capitalism 15th –18th Century,* Volume 3, The Prospect of the World, New York, p76-80.

Braudel, Fernand. (1982) *The Wheels of Commerce,* New York: Harper and Row, 1982.

Broadberry Stephen. (2013) *Accounting for the Great Divergence. Economic History Working Paper No 184/13, London School of Economics*

Bruner, R. F., & Miller, S. C. (2020). *The First Modern Financial Crises: The South Sea and Mississippi Bubbles in Historical Perspective. Journal of Applied Corporate Finance, 32(4), 17–33.* doi:10.1111/jacf.12429

Bruun Christer (1991) *The water Supply of Ancient Rome: A study of Roman Imperial Administration,* The Finnish Society of Sciences and Letters, Helsinki

Cagen, Phillip (1956) *The Monetary Dynamics of Hyperinflation, In, M., Ed., Studies in the Quantity Theory of Money, University of Chicago Press, Chicago*

Callu J.P. (1975). "Approches numismatiques de l'histoire du IIIe siècle (238 à 311) » in Aufstieg und Niedergang der romischen Welt (Vol.II.2): Edited by H.Temporini. Berlin: Walter de Gruyter & Co., pp.594-613.

Carcopino, Jerome (1943) *'Daily Life in Ancient Rome: The People and the City at the Height of the Empire,'* Routledge, 1943

Cartwright, Mark (2019) *Yuan Dynasty,* World History Encyclopaedia, 29th October 2019. Web 26th May 2022.

Ch'en, Jerome. 1965. Sung Bronzes: An Economic Analysis. Bulletin of the School of Oriental and African Studies, University of London 28, no. 3: 613–26.

Clayre, Alasdair. (1985). *The Heart of the Dragon*. Boston: Houghton Mifflin Co.

Deng, Kent G. 2013. Demystifying Growth and Development in North Song China, 960–1127. Economic History Working Paper no. 178. London: London School of Economics and Political Science.

Deutsche Bundesbank Eurosystem, *When Gold and Silver Go on Holiday, Rye Money and Rye Loans During the Weimar Republic.*

de Roover, Raymond Adrien. (1949) *Gresham and Foreign Exchange,* Cambridge: Harvard University Press, P166.

Duncan-Jones. (2015) *The Impact of the Antonine Plague,* Cambridge University Press, Cambridge University.

Ebrey, Patricia Buckley. (1996) *The Cambridge Illustrated History of China,* Vol 1 Cambridge: Cambridge University Press.

Ebrey, Patricia Buckley, and Anne Walthall. 2013. East Asia: A Cultural, Social, and Political History. Boston: Cengage Learning.

Economist. (1977) *The Dutch Disease, 26th November 1977, p 82-83.*

Eichengreen, Barry (2019) *Globalizing Capital: A History of the International Monetary System,* 3rd Edition, Princeton University Press.

Einzig, Paul. (1951) *Primitive Money in its Ethnological, Historical and Economic Aspects,* Eyre and Spottiswoode, University of California, (Digitized 3rd October 2008)

Favier, Jean (1998) *Gold and Spices: The Rise of Commerce in the Middle Ages,* New York: Holmes and Mercier P133.

Feldman, Gerald, D. (1992) *Army, Industry and Labour in Germany 1914-1918,* Providence RI and Oxford.

Ferguson, Adam. (1975) *When Money Dies: The Nightmare of the Weimar Hyper-Inflation,* Old Street Publishing.

Ferguson, Niall. (1999) *The Pity of War 1914-1918,* London 1999-Indices of Industrial Production.

Ferguson, Niall (1998) *The Pity of War: Explaining World War One,* Publisher Allen Lane.

Fischer, David Hackett. (1996) *The Great Wave: Price Revolutions and the Rhythm of History, Oxford University Press.*

Fisher, Douglas. (1989) *The Price Revolution: A Monetary Interpretation,* The Journal of Economic History, Vol 49, No 4 (Dec 1989) Published by Cambridge University Press.

Fouriezos, Nick. *(2019) To Avoid Trump's Sanctions, Countries Turn to Stone Age Bartering, Jan 9th 2019.*

Frehen, Rik. Goetzmann, William, N and Rowenhurst K, Geart (2013) *New Evidence on the Financial Bubbles,* Journal of Financial Economics 108, No 3 P585-607.

Gaettens, Richard. (2010) *History of Inflation from Old Ages to Present, The Vellon Inflation in Castille,* P52-73.

Galbraith, John, Kenneth. (1952) *A Short History of Financial Euphoria,* 1993, New York, Penguin Books.

Garber, Peter M. (2000) *Famous First Bubbles: The Fundamentals of Early Manias,* Cambridge MIT Press.

Gernet, Jaques. (1962) *Daily life in China on the eve of the Mongol Invasion 1250-1276,* Stanford California, Stanford University Press.

Gill, N.S. (2020) "*The First and Second Triumvirates of Rome.*" ThoughtCo, Aug. 27, 2020, thoughtco.com/first-and-second-triumvirates-of-rome-117560.

Gill, N.S. (2021) "The Dynasties of Ancient China." ThoughtCo, Jul. 29, 2021, thoughtco.com/the-dynasties-of-ancient-china-117659.

Goetzmann, William N and Koll, Elisabeth. (2005) *The Origins of Paper Money in China. In the Origins of Value: The Financial Innovations That Created Modern Capital Markets,* edited by William N Goetzmann and K Geert Rouwenhurst P91-104. Oxford. Oxford University Press.

Golas, Peter J. (1980). Rural China in the Song. Journal of Asian Studies 39, no. 2: 291–325

Goldgar, Anne. (2007) *Tulipmania: Money, Honour and Knowledge in the Dutch Golden Age,* Chicago, University of Chicago.

Goldweijk, Kees Klien, Beusen Arthur, Van Drecht, Gerard, De Vos Martine (2011) *Global Ecology and Biogeography,* Volume 20 Issue 1, P73-86, Jan 2011 **https://doi.org/10.1111/j.1466-8238.2010.00587.x**

Goodson, Stephen Mittford. (2014) *A History of Central Banking and the Enslavement of Mankind,* Black House Publishing.

Grant, James. (2014) *The Forgotten Depression: 1921: The Crash That Cured Itself,* Published Simon & Schuster.

Haffner, Sebastian. (1980) *The Rise and Fall of Prussia,* Publisher Littlehampton Book Services Ltd.

Hall, Richard. C. (2000) *The Balkans War 1912-1913: Prelude to the First World War, (1st* Edition) Routledge, London.

Hartwell, Robert M. 1962. A Revolution in the Chinese Iron and Coal Industries during the Northern Sung, 960–1127. Journal of Asian Studies 21, no. 2: 153–62.

Hartwell, Robert (1967) A Cycle of Economic Change in Imperial China: Coal and Iron in Northeast China, 750–1350. Journal of the Economic and Social History of the Orient/Journal de l'Histoire Economique et Sociale de l'Orient 10, no. 1: 102–59.

Hamilton, E, J (1952) *Prices as a Factor in Business Growth,* Journal of Economic History 12, Fall 1952, P325-349.

Hawtrey, R.G. (1918) *The Collapse of the French Assignat,* The Economic Journal Volume 28, No11 (September 1918) PP 300-314, Published Cambridge University Press.

Hazlitt, Henry. (1971) *Poor Relief in Ancient Rome,* FEE, Foundation for Economic Education, http://fee.org/freeman/detail/poor-relief-in-ancient-rome

Henriques, H.S.A (1902) *The Jews and the English Law IV,* The Jewish Quarterly Review, Vol 14, No4, July 1902, P653-697.

Herlihy, David (1976) *The Medieval Marriage Market, M*edieval and Renaissance Studies 6 P3-27.

Hirzel, Thomas, and Nanny Kim. 2008. Monies, Markets, and Finance in China and East Asia. Volume 1 in Metals, Monies, and Markets in Early Modern Societies: East Asian and Global Perspectives. Berlin: Lit Verlag Munster.

Homer, Sidney and Sylla, Richard (1996) *A History of Interest Rates,* 3rd edition (Revised) Rutgers University Press, New Brunswick, New York.

Horn, Jeff. Rosenbrad, Leonard & Smith, Merritt. (2010) *Reconceptualizing the Industrial Revolution,* Cambridge MA, London MIT Press,

Hubble, Nickolai (2018) *How the Euro Dies,* Published in ||UK by Southbank Investment Research.

Humpage, Owen.F. (2015) *Paper Money and Inflation in Colonial America,* www.clevelandfed.org[1]

Hutt W,H. (1977) The Theory of Idle Resources: A Study in Definition, Liberty Fund, Indiana USA.

Hunt, Edwin S. (1994) *The Medieval Super-Companies, A Study of the Peruzzi Company of Florence,* Cambridge: Cambridge University Press, P64.

Inflation Tool. (2023) www.inflationtool.com

Irsigler, F.J. (1980) *On the Seventh Day They Created Inflation,* Wynberg, Cape, South Africa

Joffe-Walt, Chana. (2010) *How Fake Money Saved Brazil,* www.nrp.org[2], October 4 2010.

Johnson, Paul. (2000) *Paul Johnson on Murray Rothbard,* Mises Daily, May 15th 2000.

Johnson, Roger T. (1977) *Historical Beginnings... The Federal Reserve* The Federal Reserve of Boston.

Jones, Sarah Ress & Watson, Sethina. (2013) *Christian and Jews in Angevin England: The York Massacre of 1190, Narrative and context,* Publisher Boydell and Brewer, York Medieval Press http://www.jstor.org/stable/10.7722/j.ctt2jbm1c

Jonke, Neitzel. (2008) *Weltkrieg Und Revolution in 1914-1918-19,* Berlin.

Keynes, J.M. (1944) *Monetary Reform,* New York, Harcourt, Brace and Co, p 51.

Kemmerer, Edwin Walter. (1935) *Money the Principles of Money and Their Exemplification in Outstanding Chapters of Monetary History,* Macmillan, New York.

1. http://www.clevelandfed.org
2. http://www.nrp.org

Kennedy, Paul. (1989) *The Rise and Fall of the Great Powers,* Publisher Fontana, P271, London.

Kershaw, Ian. (1973) *The Great Famine and Agricultural Crisis in England 1315-1322,* Past and Present, Volume 59, Issue 1, May 1973 P3-50.

Kohn, Meir. (99-01) *Finance Before the Industrial Revolution: An Introduction,* Department of Economics, Dartmouth College, Hanover NH 03755, Working Paper 99-01.

Kohn, Meir. (99-02) *Medieval and Early Modern Coinage and its Problems,* Department of Economics, Dartmouth College, Hanover NH 03755, Working Paper 99-02.

Kohn Meir. (99-05) *Merchant Banking in the Medieval and Early Modern Economy,* Department of Economics, Dartmouth College, Hanover NH 03755

Latham, Andrew. (2021) *Justinian's Plague and the Birth of the Medieval World* https://www.medievalists.net/2020/11/justinian-plague-medieval-world/

League of Nations. (1926) *The Financial Reconstruction of Austria,* General Survey and Principle Documents, Geneva.

Levasseur. E. (1894) The Assignat: *A Study in the Finances of the French Revolution, Journey of a Political Economy,* Volume 2, No 2, (March 1894) University of Chicago Press.

Lopez, Robert, S. (1976) *The Commercial Revolution of the Middle Ages 950-1350,* Cambridge: Cambridge University Press.

Mackay, Charles. (1852) *Extraordinary Popular Delusions and the Madness of Crowds,* Wordsworth Edition, New edition 1995.

Macleod, Alisdair. (2018) *John Law and the Mississippi Bubble- 300 years later.* Mises Wire, https://mises.org/wire/john-law-and-mississippi-bubble-300-years-later

Macrotrends (2022) *World GDP Per Capita, https://www.macrotrends.net/countries/WLD/world/gdp-per-capita*

Mariotti, Steve. (2017) *When Owning Gold was Illegal in America: And Why it Could Happen Again. HuffPost December 6th 2017.*

Mark, J. J. (2019) *Battle of Actium, World History Encyclopaedia.* Retrieved from https://www.worldhistory.org/Battle_of_Actium/

Marks, Sally. (1978) *The Myths of Repatriation,* Central European History 11(3) P231-255.

Mate, Mavis. (2008) *High Prices in Early Fourteenth Century England: Causes and Consequences,* The Economic History Review 28 P1-16 February 2008.

McEvedy, Colin & Jones, Richard. (1978) *Atlas of World Population History,* New York, P24-25.

Mishkin, Frederic S.[3] (2007). *The Economics of Money, Banking, and Financial Markets* (Alternate ed.). Boston: Addison Wesley. p. 8.

Miyakuwa, Hisayuki. (1955) *An Outline of the Naito Hypothesis and its effects on Japanese studies of China,* Far Eastern Quarterly, No.4 P533-522

Mundell, Robert, A The Birth of Coinage[4], Discussion Paper #:0102-08, Department of Economics, Columbia University[5], February 2002.

Murphy, Antoin E (1997) *John Law: Economist, Theorist and Policy-Maker,* Clarendon Press, Oxford.

Murphy, Robert, P. (2009) *The Depression You Never Heard of:1920-1921.* Article Wednesday November 18th 2009, www.fee.org

Narron, James & Skeie, David. (2014) *Crisis Chronicles: The Mississippi Bubble of 1720 and the European Debt Crisis. https://libertystreeteconomics.newyorkfed.org/2014/01/crisis-chronicles-the-mississippi-bubble-of-1720-and-the-european-debt-crisis/*

Nourse, Mary Augusta. (1942) *Short History of the Chinese,* New York: New Home Library.

O'Sullivan, Arthur[6]; Steven M. Sheffrin (2003). Economics: Principles in action[7]. Upper Saddle River, New Jersey 07458: Prentice Hall. p. 246.

---

3. https://en.wikipedia.org/wiki/Frederic_Mishkin

4. http://academiccommons.columbia.edu/download/fedora_content/download/ac:114139/CONTENT/econ_0102_08.pdf

5. https://en.wikipedia.org/wiki/Columbia_University

6. *https://en.wikipedia.org/wiki/Arthur_O%27Sullivan_(economist)*

7. *https://www.savvas.com/index.cfm?locator=PSZu4y&PMDbSiteId=2781&PMDbSolutionId=6724&PMDbSubSolutionId=&PMDbCategoryId=815&PMDbSubCategoryId=24843&PMDbSubjectAreaId=&PMDbProgramId=5657*

Outram, Dorinda. (2006) *Panorama of the Enlightenment,* Getty Publications.

Parker, G (1970) *Spain, Her Enemies and the Revolt of the Netherlands 1559-1640.*

Parkin M. (1987). "Inflation." In the New Palgrave. A Dictionary of Economics. London: The Macmillan Press Ltd. Vol. 2. pp.832-7.

Parshall, Gerald. (1992) *The Great Panic of 1992,* US New World Report 113.17

Pasvolsky, L. (1928) *Economic Nationalism of the Danubian States,* New York, Macmillan.

Patterson, C, C. (1972) *Silver Stocks and Losses in Ancient and Medieval Times,* economic history review, second series 25, 2 p205-235.

Peden, Joseph, R (2017) *Inflation and the Fall of the Roman Empire* https://mises.org/library/inflation-and-fall-roman-empire 10/19/2017

Phelan, John. (1921) *The Depression of 1920-1921: Why Historians-And Economists Often Overlook It,* Article www.fee.org[8] Thursday July 15th 1921

Postan, Michael Moissey. (1973) *The Medieval Economy and Society: An Economic History of Britain, 1100-1500,* University of California press p252-276.

Prasad, Eswar, S. (2017) *Gaining Currency; The Rise of the Renminbi,* Oxford University Press.

Prodromidis, P.I. (2009) *Economic Environment, Policies and Inflation in the Roman Empire up to Diocletian's Price Edict,* The Journal of European Economic History, Rome Vol 38, Issue 3

Quinn, S. & W, Roberts. (2006) *An Economic Explanation of the Early Bank of Amsterdam, Debasement, Bills of Exchange and the Emergence of the First Central Bank,* FRB Atlanta Working Paper2006-13 Federal Reserve Bank of Atalanta.

Radford, R.A. (1945) *The Economic Organisation of a POW Camp,* Economica, Vol 12.

Ra'anan, Uri. (1991) *State and Nation in Multi-Ethnic Societies: The Breakup of Multinational States,* Manchester University Press, p106.

8. http://www.fee.org

Reed, Lawrence. W. (2023) *Winstons Churchill's Gold Standard Folly,* Article www.fee.org[9] June 1st 2023.

Reinhart, Carmen, M. & Rogoff, Kenneth, S. (2O11 *This Time is Different, Eight Centuries of Financial Folly.* Publisher Princeton University Press.

Rockwell Jr, Llewellyn, H. (2010) *Hazlitt's Battle with Bretton Woods,* www.mises.org[10], Mises daily Articles, 06/18/2010.

Rotschild, K. (1946) *Austria's Economic Development Between the Two Wars,* Publisher, Muller.

Rowan, Lily. (Year Unknown) *During the Panic of 1893, JP Morgan Used $60 million in Bonds to Bail Out the United States Government,* History Daily

Rothbard, Murray. (2009) *Reliving the Crash of '29,* Mises Daily Articles, first published in 'Inquiry' November 12th 1979.

Sargant, Thomas, J. (1982) Inflation: *Causes and Effects, The End of Four Big Inflations, University of Chicago Press, p41-98.*

Scheidel, Walter (2007) *Roman Population Size: The Logic of Debate* July 2007, Princeton/Stanford Working Papers in Classics, https://www.princeton.edu/~pswpc/pdfs/scheidel/070706.pdf

Schiller, R.J. (2000) *Irrational Exuberance,* Princeton University Press, Princeton NJ

Schlichter, Detlev S. 2011. Paper Money Collapse: The Folly of Elastic Money and the Coming Monetary Breakdown. Hoboken, N.J.: Wiley.

Schulz, Piotr, O. (2001) *Eunuchs and Castrati, a Cultural History,* Markus Weiner Publishers, Princeton.

Smitha, Frank, E. (2015) *Stagnation and Decline in Spain, http://www.fsmitha.com/h3/h25spain.html*

Snell, Melissa. (2021) *The Early, High and Middle Ages,* ThoughtCo, Feb 18th 2021.

Spufford, Peter. (1988) *Money and it's Uses in Medieval Europe,* Cambridge: Cambridge University Press.

9. http://www.fee.org

10. http://www.mises.org

St Onge, Peter. (2017) *How Paper Money led to the Mongol Conquest: Money and Collapse of Song China,* The Independent Review 22(2) P223-43

Stael. Germaine de. (1818) *Considerations of the Principles of the French Revolution,* London Published Baldwin, Craddock and Joy.

Starr, C.G. (1982). The Roman Empire: 27 B.C. - A.D. 476. New York: Oxford University Press

Steinberg, Jonathan. (2012) *Bismark: A Life,* Publisher, Oxford University Press, Oxford

Stockman, David. (2014) *How the Artificial boom of 1914-1929 Caused the Depression,* 18th March 2014.

Strouse, Jean. (2014) *Morgan: American Financier,* Random House Trade.

Szczepanski, Kallie. (2021) *What Was the Umayyad Caliphate?* ThoughtCo September 24th 2021.

Szczepanski, Kallie. (2019) *The Iran-Iraq War, 1980 to 1988.* ThoughtCo, November 18th 2019, www.thoughtco.com[11]

Taleb, Nassim Nicholas. (2010) *The Black Swan: The Impact of the Highly Improbable,* Publisher Penguin Group.

Tapon, Francis. (2012) *The Hidden Europe: What Eastern Europeans Can Teach Us,* Thomson Press, India, p221.

Taylor, Frederick. (2013) *The Downfall of Money,* Bloomsbury Publishing.

Titow, J.Z.(2010) *Winchester Yields: A Study in Medieval Agricultural Productivity,* Cambridge University Press, Revised Edition.

Thayer, Theodore. (1953) *The Land Bank System in the American Colonies,* The Journal of American History, Volume 13, No 2 PP145-159.

Theobold, Ulrich (2000) *An Encyclopaedia on Chinese History, Literature and Art,* www.chinaknowledge.de[12]

Thompson, Earl A. "The Tulipmania: Fact or Artifact?" *Public Choice* 130, no. 1/2 (2007): 99–114. http://www.jstor.org/stable/27698044.

Tucker, Spencer, C & Wood, Laura, M. (1996) *The European Powers in the First World war: An Encyclopedia,* Garland Publishers p698

11. http://www.thoughtco.com

12. http://www.chinaknowledge.de

Twitchett, Denis and Smith, Paul Jakov. (2009) *The Sung Dynasty and its Precursors 907-1279,* Part 1, Cambridge University Press, pp 414-419.

Usher, Abbot Payson. (!934) *The Origins of Banking: The Primitive Banks of Deposit 1200-1600,* Economic History Review 4, 1934.

Van der Veen, A. Maurits. (2012) *The Dutch Tulip Mania: The Social Foundations of a Financial Bubble,* Department of Government, College of William and Mary, October 2012.

Van Der Wee, Herman (1993) *The Low Countries in the Early Modern World,* Aldershot: Variorum, 1993.

Von Glahn, Richard. 2005. The Origins of Paper Money in China. In the Origins of Value: The Financial Innovations That Created Modern Capital Markets, edited by William N. Goetzmann and K. Geert Rouwenhorst, 65–90. Oxford: Oxford University Press.

Wagner, Donald B. 2001. The Administration of the Iron Industry in Eleventh-Century China. Journal of the Economic and Social History of the Orient 44, no. 2: 175–97.

Wang, Chi. 1997. Some Historical Reflections on Chinese Economic Reforms: From Wang Mang to Deng Xiaoping, 9 A.D. to the Present. In Assessment of China into the 21st Century, edited by A. M. Canyon, 23–34. New York: Nova Science.

Weber, Max, (1927) *General Economic History, Glencoe, Illinois, The Free Press.*

Wernham, RB. (1968) *The Counter-Reformation and Price Revolution, 1559-1610,* Cambridge, Cambridge University Press.

White. Eugene, Nelson. (1995) *The French Revolution and the Politics of Government Finance 1770-1815,* The Journal of Economic History Volume 55, No 2, (June 1995) PP 227-255, Published by Cambridge University Press.

Williams, Jonathan. (1997) *Money: A History,* Palgrave Macmillan.

Wilson, Peter, H. (2017) *The Holy Roman Empire: A Thousand Years of Europe's History,* Publisher Penguins Books 1st Edition.

World Bank (2021) https://data.worldbank.org/indicator/SI.POV.GINI?locations=GB

Woods, Thomas, E, Jr. (2009) *The Forgotten Depression of 1920,* Mises Daily Articles, 11/27/2009

Wright, Tim (2007) *An Economic Cycle in Imperial China? Revisiting Robert Hartwell on Iron and Coal,* Journal of the Economic and Social History of the Orient 50, No 4: 398-423.

Young, J.P. (1925) *European Currency and Finance,* Volume's 1 and 2 (Commission for Gold and Silver Inquiry, United States Senate, Serial 9) Washington, Government Printing Office.

Zeigler, Phillip. (1969) *The Black Death,* Sutton Publishing Ltd, New edition 2003.

Don't miss out!

Visit the website below and you can sign up to receive emails whenever Pawlo Lawriw publishes a new book. There's no charge and no obligation.

https://books2read.com/r/B-A-YSJBB-JQJQC

BOOKS 2 READ

Connecting independent readers to independent writers.

About the Author

Born in the industrial Northern town of Huddersfield West Yorkshire to a Ukrainian father and an Italian mother, the formative years of life were at times gritty and hard but honest and fair. Most of my adult life was spent in various employments ranging from being in the Military Police (a stint which included serving in the First Gulf War) to becoming a croupier and working around the world including on cruise ships around the Caribbean and various 'joints' in South Africa. I undertook my first writing project, this book on hyperinflation after returning to education in my late 50's and studied for a BA in Economics, which I completed in 2021. As part of my dissertation, I combined two subject areas I have always had an interest in, history and money. Starting the research thinking it would be primarily about modern history I very quickly discovered that a modern problem, inflation is firmly rooted in the past. I became so engrossed and fascinated in the subject I promised myself if I had any spare time I would try and author a short book on the subject. A year later and with no real time on my hands as I was working with children with emotional and behavioural problems, I decided to undertake the writing of this book anyway, in truth not expecting to finish it, but somehow with lots of encouragement from the kids I was working with it became a mission, so here we are, my first attempt at a book. I have tried to add interesting and unusual episodes of history to keep the readers interest such as how the eunuchs became a powerful force in the ancient Chinese dynasties and contributed to these dynasties' downfalls and also kept data to a minimum, too much data, in my opinion, is a bug bear and probably has contributed more than most things to bad decisions being made by modern governments around the world; all this can be related to Goodhart's Law, which is an adage from British economist Charles Goodhart in 1975 when discussing the problems of the British economy, where he sums it up perfectly stating 'When a measure becomes a target, it ceases to be a good measure.' On this subject of data and the overuse of it, I think the most perfect quote to encapsulate this can be attributed to the British economist Ronald Coarse who said about the subject "If you torture the data long enough and hard enough, you'll eventually get it to confess to anything".

www.ingramcontent.com/pod-product-compliance
Ingram Content Group UK Ltd.
Pitfield, Milton Keynes, MK11 3LW, UK
UKHW021135090426
469753UK00006B/44